Honest, hard-hitting, unflinching—this boo[...] topic of death but does so with creativity, w[...] my friend Clay Jones for his insights, compassion, and wit. But most ~~[...] tantly, you'll walk away grasping the only truth that can ultimately save you.

—Lee Strobel, bestselling author of *The Case for Christ* and *The Case for Faith*

Immortal is exactly what I have come to expect from Clay Jones—insightful, well-researched, and convicting. This book is a game-changer for how Christians can think about the inevitability of death with both hope and biblical clarity. If every Christian would read this book and take its message to heart, it would transform how we relate to our nonbelieving friends and neighbors.

—Sean McDowell, PhD, Biola University professor, speaker, and author

You should be dying to read this book. Actually, you're dying regardless. That's why *Immortal* could be one of the most important books you'll ever read. After revealing the fascinating but ultimately futile ways modern people are trying to secure their immortality, Clay Jones brilliantly shows us what eternity will be like and how we can secure the glorious future that awaits us. But *Immortal* isn't a book just about the eternity— it will help you live more fully right now. Highly recommended!

—Frank Turek, DMin, coauthor of *I Don't Have Enough Faith to Be an Atheist*

This is an extraordinarily insightful book that I couldn't put down. No matter what you believe happens after you die, this book will convict you that death is truly staring you in the face every day, and if you don't confront that reality, you're living in denial. But it will also convict you that if you confront death in Christ, there is nothing to fear—a perspective Christians often lose but desperately need. *I love this book!*

—Natasha Crain, speaker and author of *Keeping Your Kids on God's Side* and *Talking with Your Kids About God*

If you are a Christian leader and you want to see those in your care get truly serious about their own faith and about spreading the gospel, Clay Jones has provided the perfect tool—*Immortal*. In this utterly convincing and engaging study, Jones pulls back the black curtain to reveal all the ways we attempt to suppress and avoid thinking about something that is more certain than birth and taxes— *death*. Clear thinking about death inevitably leads to clear thinking about sin and our desperate need for the Savior. Jones takes us down that path and leads us to the joy that comes from knowing that we have eternal life through the resurrected

Son of God. Do everyone you know a great favor and get one of these books into their hands. It is accessible, transformative, and a source of immense hope.

—Craig Hazen, PhD, professor and director of Christian
Apologetics, Biola University, and author of *Fearless Prayer*

Immortal is a deeply insightful treatment of a phenomenon many people haven't recognized: the immortality project. I believe Christian readers will find Jones's book to be tremendously helpful, not only for self-examination and cultural understanding but also for thoughtful engagement with nonbelievers who are seeking meaning and purpose through such projects.

—Melissa Cain Travis, PhD, Houston Baptist University,
author of *Science and the Mind of the Maker*

In *Immortal*, Clay Jones examines our cultural interest in eternity and offers a reason why every Christian ought to celebrate the hope we have in the promises of God.

—J. Warner Wallace, *Dateline*-featured cold-case detective, author of *Cold-Case
Christianity* and *God's Crime Scene* and creator of the Case Makers Academy for Kids

Thank God for Clay Jones's declaration and affirmation of what God says about death and immortality. Very few people have the voice and clarity that Clay brings on a subject that can bring the greatest anxiety or the greatest peace. We get to choose! I am so excited that you have this book in your possession. Drink deep at this well of wisdom and insight and sense and feel your fear of death swallowed by truth and faith.

—Kenny Luck, leadership pastor, founder of Every
Man Ministries, and author of *Dangerous Good*

With both an insightful mind and a compassionate heart, Clay Jones speaks with a prophetic voice against the idols of our time and the spirit of the age. This is a fascinating, powerful book about our deep longing for immortality, the fear of death, and misguided human attempts to overcome death or to trivialize its sting. This book repeatedly points us to the good news of the gospel—that Jesus Christ is able to rescue us from the kingdom of darkness and death and that he has graciously provided a sure way to everlasting life with the redeemed in God's unfading, glorious presence.

—Paul Copan, Pledger Family Chair of Philosophy and Ethics, Palm Beach
Atlantic University and author of *A Little Book for New Philosophers*

IMMORTAL

CLAY JONES

HARVEST HOUSE PUBLISHERS
EUGENE, OREGON

Cover design by Bryce Williamson

Cover photo © Danler/gettyimages

Immortal
Copyright © 2020 by Clay Jones
Published by Harvest House Publishers
Eugene, Oregon 97408
www.harvesthousepublishers.com

ISBN 978-0-7369-7827-9 (pbk.)
ISBN 978-0-7369-7828-6 (eBook)

Library of Congress Cataloging-in-Publication Data

Names: Jones, Clay, author.
Title: Immortal / Clay Jones.
Description: Eugene : Harvest House Publishers, 2019.
Identifiers: LCCN 2019020311 (print) | LCCN 2019980210 (ebook) | ISBN 9780736978279 (pbk.) | ISBN 9780736978286 (ebook)
Subjects: LCSH: Death--Religious aspects--Christianity. | Immortality. | Future life--Christianity.
Classification: LCC BT825 .J658 2019 (print) | LCC BT825 (ebook) | DDC 236/.22--dc23
LC record available at https://lccn.loc.gov/2019020311
LC ebook record available at https://lccn.loc.gov/2019980210

Printed in the United States of America

20 21 22 23 24 25 26 27 28 / BP-AR / 10 9 8 7 6 5 4 3 2 1

Thanks Be to God Who Gives Us Victory over Death
Through the Lord Jesus Christ!
Thank You!

I thank God for all your love and support, Jean E.
I look forward to enjoying forever with you!

CONTENTS

Detachment
Live in the Present
Individual Existence Is Unreal
Our Particles Go On
The Misery of the Mortality-Mitigation Mind-Set

Denial, Distraction, and Dissipation
Sexual Addiction
Meaninglessness
Anxiety
Depression
Psychosis
Drugs
Suicide
Anarchy
Debris
Death
Eternal Punishment

There Is a God
Reliable Primary Sources
Jesus Died of Roman Crucifixion
Jesus Was Buried, but Later His Tomb Was Found Empty
Jesus's Disciples Proclaimed That Jesus Was Raised
Jesus's Disciples Were Willing to Suffer and Die for This Belief

The Reason You Might Wish to Stay Alive
Staring Down Death

Resurrected
Perfected
Resplendent
Renowned
Conclusion

PREFACE

This book is about the fear of death, about how humans outside of Christ—and all too often, even those in Christ—try to manage that fear, and about how you, dear Christian, can be free of the fear of death because you enjoy the abundant, glorious eternity that awaits all who trust in Jesus. I think you'll find this discussion about how people deal with death insightful, even fascinating, as you discover how the fear of death explains much of what we do and most of our culture. In fact, it explains most of every culture on earth. The last three chapters will focus on the reason for and the wonder of the Christian's hope—the glory of eternal life in Jesus—and how we may enjoy that hope. No one has to fear death, and this book will help you conquer your own fear, give you greater joy and peace, and will help you glory in—revel in—what God has planned for your supremely joyous eternity.

Audience

I have written this book for the Christian—the reflective layperson, pastor, counselor, professor, and apologist. I've written it for the Christian so I don't have to spend much time arguing for what the Christian already regards as true. If I didn't do that, this would be a much longer book.

Style

Those who are already familiar with my teaching know I can be direct, even blunt (but hopefully, always loving). I'll continue that in this book. I'm also a kidder, and I came by that the old-fashioned way: my father, brother, and I kidded each other a lot (*mostly* good-naturedly). At the publisher's request, there is no coarse language in the book. Instead, I replaced offensive words with other words in brackets or eliminated them with ellipses. As I did in *Why Does God Allow Evil?*, I'm going to continue capitalizing divine pronouns. Also, if I quote an author several times in the same paragraph but all the quotes are from the same page, then only the last occasion in that paragraph will have an endnote so I can avoid having to use even more endnotes than already exist.

Scope

Except for discussing some aspects of Eastern religions, I'm not going to talk about how adherents of other religions cope with death, since the failures of those projects are answered by showing those religions to be false through typical apologetic argument. Rather, this book will do two things. First, it examines secular attempts to overcome the fear of death and how these secular attempts fail. Second, it presents the evidence for, and the nature of, the hope for eternal life for those who trust in Jesus and explains how to enjoy that hope.

Structure

The introduction will discuss how I came to this study, will define key terms, and will explain how this knowledge helps the Christian. Then in chapter 1, I will examine the desperation of the human condition and how all people, save those with a robust view of eternal life in Jesus, are terrified by their deaths. Chapter 2 reviews how people seek literal immortality—namely, many people today are literally striving to live forever through healthful living, transhumanism, and cryonics. Chapter 3 reviews how people seek symbolic immortality by creating a name for themselves, creating a legacy, having children, being politically active, or doing something (really anything) that will cause future generations to remember them. Chapter 4 reviews how atheists strive to make themselves feel good, or at least okay, about their deaths. Chapter 5 explains the ultimate failure of all secular attempts to eliminate the fear of death and how this fear leads to denial, distraction, depression, drugs, mental illness, suicide, and societal collapse. In chapter 6, I change direction by arguing the evidence for the resurrection of Jesus, which is the basis for the Christian hope of eternal life. Chapter 7 presents steps for how Christians can revel in their hope of eternal life secured by Jesus's resurrection. Chapter 8 concludes by explaining the wonder of the Christian's hope—their eternal glorification.

INTRODUCTION

When I was in grade school, my parents worried that I was going to die. That's because I was sick a lot. Once I had rheumatic fever, and over the years there was often a vaporizer in my bedroom, but most of all, my heart didn't sound right. I was four or five years old when I first heard a doctor say I had a "heart murmur." At swimming lessons, the instructor would put his hand on my chest to feel my pulse and report back to my mother. My mom and dad regularly would do the same. On one occasion, the instructor told my mom my heart was "beating like a trip-hammer." I didn't know what that was, but the meaning was unmistakable: something was wrong with my heart. During the entirety of the third grade, I was forbidden to run, which meant I had to sit and watch my friends play. My parents often looked worried. I remember the doctor's office where I got a physical so my parents could take out a life insurance policy on me. That was significant even in my eight-year-old mind. Eventually the doctors told my parents I could run again, but that didn't stop their worry.

Then when I was 15, a 16-year-old friend of mine got cancer. I was a Christian by this time, and I prayed for him regularly, but a year later, he died. That's when the horror hit me. I'd find a lump and fear it was the beginning of the end. My doctor assured me it was just a swollen gland, but then there'd be another lump, or something odd, and the fears would start anew. Most parents would do everything possible to shield their child from experiencing all this, but I thank God I went through it! During that time, I was also growing in Christ, and I learned that to be happy, I had to trust in Jesus. As I increasingly understood the glory that awaits us in heaven forever, I found that the fear of death diminished until the fear of being dead no longer troubled me.

Let me bring you now to the present day. I'm not a morning person—I've often kidded, "I'd wake up to see the sunrise if it didn't come so early in the morning"—but recently I woke early in my dark bedroom, and while staring at the ceiling and thinking about death, it occurred to me that the thought of my death didn't bother me. As I thought further about it, I realized that the thought of my death didn't bother me at all. It didn't bother me any more than thinking that I needed to turn on the sprinklers. I was comforted that it didn't bother me, but I know the thought of death frightens people. In fact, although many won't admit it, death frightens everyone unless they have a robust view of the glorious eternal life that is available in Jesus. That doesn't mean I don't have a healthy fear of suffering—suffering is suffering, after all. I tell my classes, "You can believe this or not," but I no longer fear my being dead. Neither do you have to fear your death. The kingdom of God is truly the pearl of great price and the treasure in the field. And now I see death as a graduation. An upgrade. As Paul puts it in Philippians 1:21, "To die is gain." You too can enjoy that!

While completing the research for my last book, *Why Does God Allow Evil?*, I came upon *A Brief History of Thought* by Parisian philosopher Luc Ferry. Ferry writes that the human "knows that he will die, and that his near ones, those he loves, will also die. Consequently he cannot prevent himself from thinking about this state of affairs, which is disturbing and absurd, almost unimaginable."[1] That people fear death isn't news to me, but I am surprised that Ferry says, "The quest for a salvation without God is at the heart of every great philosophical system, and that is its essential and ultimate objective."[2] Even though I majored in philosophy, I had never heard anything like that, and I wondered if Ferry is right. So I started reading what the famous philosophers had to say about death, and sure enough, he is. Much of philosophy is about how to conquer the fear of death. For now, I'll give just one example. In his *Phaedo*, Plato (428/427–348/347 BCE), arguably the most famous and influential philosopher of all time, tells about the last hours before the death of his teacher Socrates (ca. 470–399 BCE). Plato writes that Socrates said, "Truly then…those who practice philosophy aright are cultivating dying, and for them, least of all men, does being dead hold any terror."[3] Later in the *Phaedo*, Socrates said, "Practicing philosophy in the right way" is "in fact, training to die easily."[4] Later I'll give more examples of philosophers who say that the fear of death drives philosophy.

I knew nonbelievers feared hell, but I didn't realize the extent to which they feared death. This led me to hunt for how people handle death without Jesus. I read (and watched) what the new and old atheists thought about how to feel good, or at least feel okay, about death. I then read what secular psychologists, anthropologists, sociologists, and self-help gurus said about how to feel good about death. Fascinating! There's a tremendous amount written about how people try to transcend their deaths—to in some way deny that they are going to die. In fact, as you'll see, many social scientists now argue that the fear of death drives *all* of culture—all of it. These social scientists say *there wouldn't be any cultural advancement whatsoever* if people weren't afraid of death. I don't go that far—people are more complex than that—but certainly much of what people do on earth is to somehow deny or transcend their deaths.

Christians shouldn't be surprised that non-Christians fear death because Hebrews 2:14-15 (NIV) tells us Jesus died for us so "that by his death he might break the power of him who holds the power of death—that is, the devil—and free those who *all their lives* were held in slavery by their fear of death." Let me emphasize this: the Bible tells us that "all their lives," people are "held in slavery by their fear of death"! Thankfully, freedom from the fear of death is available through Jesus—only through Jesus—who gives eternal life to those who trust Him. Since Scripture is plain about this, we should then expect that nonbelievers would devise strategies and philosophical systems to attempt to free themselves from their fear of death. As I understood all these strategies, a lot of human behavior made more sense to me. I hope you will find it as fascinating as I have.

Also fascinating and encouraging was something I never expected: many secularists agree, some in the most glowing terms, that Christianity offers the best possible answer to death. Philosopher Stephen Cave writes that reconciling our mortality with our desire to live forever is something "Christianity achieved spectacularly well, with enormous consequences for the development of Western civilization."[5] As Sam Harris tells an atheist conference in Australia, "There's no other story you can tell somebody who has just lost her daughter to cancer, say, to make her feel good. You know it is consoling to believe that the daughter was just taken up with Jesus and everyone is going to be reunited in a few short years. There's no replacement for that."[6] Of course, Harris goes on to reject the truth of Christianity, but he agrees that if Christianity were true, then it does answer our deepest need.

Although Christians are inheritors of true, glorious, literal immortality, often they take little comfort in it. Why? There are three main reasons. First, many Christians don't know the amazing evidence for the resurrection of Jesus. If we don't have confidence that Jesus was raised from the dead, then how can we have confidence that we will likewise be raised? Second, and related to the first, the overwhelming majority of Christians are hedging their bets and investing themselves in various secular immortality projects and the recognition that these projects are doomed to fail saddens them. Finally, few Christians have a robust view of the glory that awaits them forever. That's why this book concludes with a presentation of what the Scripture teaches about the eternal glory. As we study the futility of secular attempts to transcend death, please keep in mind, dear Christian, that we are going to live forever!

Definition of Terms

Heaven. By "heaven," I mean our future eternal state of supreme enjoyment of the Creator, each other, and His creation. For the purpose of this book, I'm not taking a position on whether we'll be in the new heavens or on the new earth, whether heaven will be on earth, or whether "new heavens and new earth" is a merism for all things, and so on.

Immortality project. Immortality projects are attempts to, in some way, live forever. There are two types of immortality projects: literal (examined in chapter 2) and symbolic (examined in chapter 3).

Secularists would classify Christianity as just another immortality project, but as I will argue in chapter 6, Jesus really was raised from the dead, so when I use "immortality project," I'm not referring to Christianity. It is important to note, however, that many—maybe most—Christians also employ secular immortality projects to give them a sense of transcending their deaths without God.

Mortality mitigating project. By "mortality mitigating project," I mean the naturalist's attempt to make death into something that isn't so bad. I differentiate this from "immortality projects" because many atheists reject the idea that one can be immortal. Chapter 4 examines mortality mitigating projects and their ultimate failure.

Materialism. Materialism is the belief that nothing exists beyond matter. The universe is solely made up of material stuff. Therefore, the materialist believes you don't have a soul because a soul is nonmaterial. Like naturalists, materialists reject belief in God because God isn't material stuff (Christians believe "God is spirit"; John 4:24).

Metaphysics. Metaphysics is the study of the real, fundamental nature of things. Therefore, a metaphysician examines whether there is a God, because if there is a God who created the universe, then nothing could be more fundamental to the universe than that.

Naturalism. Naturalism is the belief that nature is all there is. Naturalists therefore believe there is no God and nothing caused the universe. Astronomer Carl Sagan (1934–96) famously writes for the opening sentence of his book *Cosmos*, "The cosmos is all that is or ever was or ever will be."[7] We apologists like to point out that this statement has nothing whatsoever to do with science—it's a philosophical statement.

How This Knowledge Helps Us

I found this study helpful in the following ways. First, understanding immortality projects identifies and explains the allegiance to today's false gods. This understanding then explains much of why secularists behave as they do and why non-Christians—and too often Christians—cling to these false gods: these immortality projects, these counterfeit gods or idols, are an ersatz salvation from death. This perspective provides a different way of thinking about an age-old problem and will allow Christians to better identify these false gods.

Second, understanding the futility of secular immortality projects and mortality mitigation projects encourages non-Christians and Christians to abandon these projects and turn to the only One who can give them eternal life.

Third—and this surprised me—understanding how non-Christians fear death gave me a greater compassion for the lost. I never dreamed that understanding the lost's futile attempts to obtain self-worth and immortality without God would increase my compassion for them, but that's what happened. Non-Christians aren't *just* sinful; they're desperate—desperate to escape their impending demise. Let's help them understand the wonder of the eternal life available in Jesus!

Fourth, understanding how the fear of death drives us aids in the development of a correct psychology and anthropology. Many psychologists and anthropologists are now convinced that the fear of death explains why humans do what they do. Also, depression abounds, as do psychoses and schizophrenias, and *many* secular psychologists argue that psychosis and schizophrenia occur precisely because a person is afraid of death. We'll talk about that in chapter 6.

Fifth, understanding how people cope with their fear of death explains *much* about what motivates human evil—namely, murder, mass shootings, and genocide. Also, Christians who put any confidence in their failed attempts to obtain a sense of immortality without God will always hurt others.

Sixth, understanding what motivates lost family members, friends, coworkers, and everyone else helps us better know how to help them.

Seventh, and most importantly, this book will help you, dear Christian, pursue the glorious immortality available through Jesus so you can be comforted by and revel in your possession of eternal life. There is no greater problem for Christians than being consumed by a this-worldly salvation instead of having a robust, unremitting, joyous appreciation of the supreme happiness that awaits them in heaven forever. This is the focus of the last three chapters of this book.

1

The Human Condition

Humans fear death. But it's even worse than that. Hebrews 2:15 tells us that "all their lives," the lost are "held in slavery by their fear of death." That's clear, right? Christian philosopher and mathematician Blaise Pascal (1623–62) sums up the human condition in his *Pensées*: "Let us imagine a number of men in chains, and all condemned to death where some are killed each day in the sight of others, and those who remain see their own fate in that of their fellows, and wait their turn, looking at each other sorrowfully and without hope. It is an image of the condition of men."[1] Thankfully, Pascal was a sincere Christian. After he died, a servant found this message sewed into Pascal's favorite jacket: "'Righteous Father, the world has not known You, but I have known You...' Joy, joy, joy, tears of joy...'This is eternal life, that they know you, the one and true God, and the one whom you have sent, Jesus Christ.'"[2] Pascal indeed found the cure for the human condition: it's in Jesus!

The oldest-known fiction, *The Epic of Gilgamesh* (ca. 2100 BCE), is about King Gilgamesh, who was on a fevered quest to find eternal life: "How can I rest, how can I be at peace? Despair is in my heart...I am afraid of death."[3] About this fear of death, Stanford emeritus professor of psychiatry Irvin D. Yalom, in his book *Staring at the Sun: Overcoming the Terror of Death*, writes, "Gilgamesh speaks for all of us. As he feared death, so do we all—each and every man, woman, and child. For some of us the fear of death manifests only indirectly, either as generalized unrest or masqueraded as another psychological symptom; other individuals experience an explicit and conscious stream of anxiety about death; and for some of us the fear of death erupts into terror that negates all happiness and fulfillment."[4]

Psychology professors Sheldon Solomon, Jeff Greenberg, and Tom Pyszczynski write that if humans had an "ongoing awareness of their vulnerability and mortality," they would be "twitching blobs of biological protoplasm completely perfused with anxiety and unable to effectively respond to the demands of their immediate surroundings."[5] Similarly, sociologist and philosopher Zygmunt Bauman (1925–2017) writes, "There is hardly a thought more offensive than that of death; or, rather, the inevitability of dying; of the transience of our being in the world."[6] Bauman continues, "The horror of death is the horror of the void" and is "bound to remain, *traumatic*."[7]

When I was an undergrad in the mid-1970s, I heard often of the work of psychiatrist Elisabeth Kübler-Ross (1926–2004). In 1969, she wrote the groundbreaking, now famous, *On Death and Dying: What the Dying Have to Teach Doctors, Nurses, Clergy and Their Own Families*. There Kübler-Ross explains what she calls "the five stages of death and dying": denial, anger, bargaining, depression, and acceptance. She says that if they live long enough, all terminally ill patients will sooner or later experience each of these stages of grief, ultimately accepting that one day they will die.

It interested me to learn that people came to acceptance about their deaths. I thought that meant the terminally ill became okay with their dying. I concluded this because Kübler-Ross writes that the terminally ill "will reach a stage during which he is neither depressed nor angry about his 'fate.'" But she explains that "acceptance should not be mistaken for a happy stage. It is almost void of feelings."[8] Wait, "void of feelings"? As in numb? When not referring to the physical body, numb means "unable to think, *feel*, or react normally because of something that shocks or upsets you: indifferent."[9] That's not good!

In her 1969 book, Kübler-Ross calls the belief in life after death a form of denial—specifically, "religious denial."[10] But after hearing patients talk about their "near death experiences," Don Lattin in

SFGate reports, Kübler-Ross began "making headlines with the claim that she had 'hard data' proving the existence of life after death." She even opened her own Shangri-la called "Shanti Nilaya," in which participants joined séances and then entered dark rooms to have sex with "afterlife entities" (or at least someone who talked like an afterlife entity—in the heat of passion, it might be hard to tell).[11] Lattin continues, "Suddenly, the woman who told America to look death squarely in the face was saying, 'Death does not exist.'" Wow. The psychiatrist who became famous for teaching the world about accepting death concluded that death does not exist. After Kübler-Ross had several strokes, Lattin reports that she "doesn't miss a beat when asked which of the five stages of death she finds herself in at the moment. 'Anger.'"[12] It is documented that at the end of her life, she accepted that she would die, but that was because she claimed to "know beyond a shadow of a doubt that there is no death the way we understood it. The body dies, but not the soul."[13] Thus the famous instructor of how humans should handle death decided that she herself would never die.

The late Harvard philosopher William James (1842–1910) puts it well: "Back of everything is the great spectre of universal death, the all-encompassing blackness."[14] James continues, "The fact that we *can* die, that we *can* be ill at all, is what perplexes us; the fact that we now, for a moment live and are well is irrelevant to that perplexity." Even when everything in our lives is going well, James says that for most of us, "a little irritable weakness...will bring the worm at the core of all our usual springs of delight into full view, and turn us into melancholy metaphysicians."[15] Metaphysicians indeed! Because of the specter of death, James also turned to séances and other occult experiences in a scientific search for life after death, but all he succeeded in was damaging his reputation while becoming a ghost hunter.[16] However, James was right that the thought of death drives us to think about the big picture. It forces us to ask the important questions. The specter of death compels *everyone* to seek some salvation—thankfully in Jesus, that salvation comes! As Paul puts it in Romans 2:7, "To those who by patience in well-doing seek for glory and honor and immortality, he will give eternal life."

Denial of the Fear of Death

Even though many psychologists, anthropologists, philosophers, and, most importantly, Scripture tell us that humans fear death, if you ask people if they fear their own deaths, most will say no. When I've told people that I'm writing about how humans respond to the fear of death, some announce, "I don't fear death!" I've concluded that these people are somewhat honest because most people don't think about their deaths. In fact, they don't think about their deaths at all. Of course, they will acknowledge in the abstract that one day they will die, but then they go happily back to *not* thinking about their deaths. But when they find a lump, have a chest pain, or receive a positive result on a blood test, their fear of death towers in front of them and won't leave the room.

Solomon, Greenberg, and Pyszczynski document how facing death influences people. In 1987, they began "conducting studies in which one (experimental) group of participants was reminded of their mortality, and another (control) group was not."[17] They "reminded" the experimental group of death to see how the participants would respond in various situations. For example, they tested court judges to see how they changed their sentencing when asked to "jot down, as specifically as you can, what you think will happen to you as you physically die, and when you are physically dead." All the judges were given a fictitious case of a prostitute. Those judges who didn't consider their own deaths before their judgment imposed an average bond of $50, which was typical at that time. But those who did consider their deaths imposed an average punitive bond of $455! In another study, those reminded of death "tripled the monetary reward people recommended for someone who reported a dangerous criminal to the police."[18] As of the publication of their book in 2015, Solomon, Greenberg, and Pyszczynski report that "more than five hundred studies and counting" reveal how people are affected by the "terror" of "the knowledge of the inevitability of death."[19]

How the Fear of Death Drives Human Behavior

But whether we admit our fear or deny it, the fear of death drives us. As Elisabeth Kübler-Ross and grieving expert David Kessler put it, "It all boils down to the fear of death, arguably the cause of most of our unhappiness. We unknowingly harm our loved ones out of fear; we hold ourselves back personally and professionally for the same reason. Since every fear has its roots in the fear of death, learning how to relax about the fear surrounding death will allow us to face everything with greater ease."[20]

As I mentioned in the introduction, social scientists increasingly conclude that the fear of death drives *all* human behavior. In 1973, cultural anthropologist Ernest Becker (1924–74) published his seminal and Pulitzer Prize–winning book *The Denial of Death*. In it, Becker writes that "the idea of death, the fear of it, haunts the human animal like nothing else: it is *the mainspring of human activity*—activity designed largely to avoid the fatality of death, to overcome it by denying in some way that it is the final destiny of man."[21] Later Becker says, "*All* culture, *all* man's creative life-ways, are in some basic part of them a fabricated protest against natural reality, a denial of the truth of the human condition, and an attempt to forget the pathetic creature that man is."[22] Similarly, philosopher Stephen Cave writes in *Immortality: The Quest to Live Forever and How It Drives Civilization*, "I aim to show how we, like all living things, are driven to pursue life without end; but also how we, alone of living things, have in the process created spectacular civilizations, with stunning artworks, rich religious traditions and the material and intellectual achievements of science." "*All of this*," writes Cave, is because people are following "paths that promise immortality."[23] Zygmunt Bauman states, "There would probably be *no* culture were humans unaware of their mortality."[24]

Similarly, Solomon, Greenberg, and Pyszczynski declare in *The Worm at the Core*, "The awareness that we humans will die has a profound and pervasive effect on our thoughts, feelings, and behaviors in almost every domain of life—whether we are conscious of it or not."[25] They continue,

> The terror of death has guided the development of art, religion, language, economics, and science. It raised the pyramids in Egypt and razed the Twin Towers in

Manhattan. It contributes to conflicts around the globe. At a more personal level, recognition of our mortality leads us to love fancy cars, tan ourselves to an unhealthy crisp, max out our credit cards, drive like lunatics, itch for a fight with a perceived enemy, and crave fame, however ephemeral, even if we have to drink yak urine on *Survivor* to get it.[26]

Then they add, "The fear of death is one of the primary driving forces of human action."[27]

This striving to cope with the meaning of life and mortality is what Ecclesiastics is all about. As Duane A. Garrett writes, "Ecclesiastes could be accurately described as a report on the failed quest for eternal life."[28] In the next three chapters, I will examine the contortions and circumlocutions, the suppressions and succumbings that occur as people attempt to cope with their deaths without hope in Jesus. Chapter 2 will examine literal immortality projects—how many strive to literally live forever. Chapter 3 will examine symbolic immortality projects—how most of us strive to accomplish things that will survive our physical deaths. Then in chapter 4, I will examine mortality mitigating projects—how naturalists attempt to philosophize death into something that is either good or at least not so bad.

2

Literal Immortality Projects

One way to deny death is to strive to live literally forever, and today many people engross themselves in literal immortality projects. I suspect, however, that if you asked people if they were trying to live forever, few would admit it because it would be embarrassing if it didn't work out. But down deep, many hope that if we keep our bodies healthy enough through proper diet and exercise, and if we live long enough, medical science will one day do what it was always supposed to do: find a cure to *everything* that might kill us, and then we can coast to immortality! Thus many obsess over exercise, eating enough healthy foods, and avoiding unhealthy foods. If medical science is delayed in curing everything that might kill us, then we might employ some stopgap measures—like being cryonically preserved (aka frozen stiff)—until science no longer disappoints.

Healthful Living and Medical Science

The Ancient Striving

Seeking to physically live forever is nothing new. The first emperor of China, Qin Shi Huang (259–210 BCE), builder of China's Great Wall, "had everything," as Jonathan Clements put it, "yet was plagued by signs of his own mortality."[1] In fact, the first emperor refused to believe it: "As he entered his forties, his mid-life crisis manifested itself in extreme ambition. He had already done the impossible by conquering the world, so how hard would it be to conquer death?"[2] To conquer death, he sent thousands of young boys and girls in search of the elixir of eternal life, and he himself traveled long distances by sea and climbed mountains in the search.[3] He also ordered his scholars to solve the problem, and when he realized the scholars were stalling, unable to present him with a life everlasting elixir, he had 460 of them buried alive.[4] The emperor was not to be trifled with. Some even suspect that one of his attempted elixirs was mercury based and probably killed him.[5]

In 1645, philosopher René Descartes (1596–1650) told an English nobleman, "The preservation of health has always been the principal end of my studies." Descartes devoted himself to the medical prolongation of his life. His friends were shocked when he died of pneumonia at only age 54.[6]

Sadness over Being Born Too Soon

On seeing the first ascent of the Montgolfier brothers' hot air balloon from the Tuileries Palace in 1783, the octogenarian Maréchale de Villeroy, a noblewoman of the ancien régime, fell on her knees and sobbed, "Yes it is decided, now it is certain. They will eventually find the secret of eternal life but I will already be dead!"[7] Even Benjamin Franklin rued that he was born too early. In 1780, Franklin wrote to Joseph Priestley,

> The rapid Progress true Science now makes, occasions my Regretting sometimes that I was born so soon. It is impossible to imagine the Height to which may be carried in a 1000 Years the Power of Man over Matter...All Diseases may by sure means be prevented or cured, not excepting even that of Old Age, and our Lives lengthened at pleasure even beyond the antediluvian Standard.[8]

Born Soon Enough?

Today, however, many people happily believe that they weren't born too soon to escape death. They hope that medical advancements, like stem cell research and nanobots, will give them a much longer, if not immortal, life. As the first Facebook president, Sean Parker, boasts, "Because I'm a billionaire, I'm going to have access to better health-care...I'm going to be like 160 and I'm going to be part of this, like, class of immortal overlords."[9] Similarly, 45-year-old Bulletproof Coffee founder and biohacker advocate, David Asprey, claims to have spent $1 million on a quest to live to 180. To accomplish this, he has bone marrow extracted from his hips and then has the stem cells filtered out and injected into every joint in his body, his spinal cord, and his cerebral fluid. He intends to do this twice a year. He also "takes 100 supplements a day, religiously follows a low-carb, high fat diet, bathes in infrared light, chills in a cryotherapy chamber, and relaxes in a hyperbaric oxygen chamber."[10]

In a TED talk, British researcher Aubrey de Grey said that "the first human beings who will live to 1,000 years old have already been born."[11] Futurist and Inventor Hall of Fame inductee Ray Kurzweil and antiaging physician Terry Grossman ask in *Fantastic Voyage: Live Long Enough to Live Forever*, "Do we have the knowledge and the tools today to live forever?" They write, "The answer to our question is actually a definitive *yes*—the knowledge exists, if aggressively applied, for you to slow aging and disease processes to such a degree that you can be in good health and good spirits when the more radical life-extending and life-enhancing technologies become available over the next couple of decades."[12]

Whole Foods Markets are full of such hopefuls.

Sociologist and philosopher Zygmunt Bauman put in perspective our quest to live a very long time—if not forever. "Modernity did not conquer mortality," writes Bauman. "Having failed to achieve the ultimate, it zeroed in its effort instead on second best solutions and surrogate targets...It replaced the big worry about survival with many small—manageable—worries about the assorted causes of dying."[13] Now, writes Bauman, "one need no more stand idle waiting for impending doom. One can *do something*, something 'reasonable' and 'useful.'"[14] Mortality has been deconstructed "into an infinite series of individual causes of death, and of the struggle against death into an infinitely extendable series of battles against specific diseases."[15]

Frequently at the end of an obituary, we'll see "In lieu of flowers, give to the American Cancer Society," or the American Heart Society, or whatever organization the now dead person hoped would cure the thing that killed them.

Not long ago I attended a reunion with some friends, and several of them passed around a 600-plus-page hardbound volume entitled *How to Not Die: Discover the Foods Scientifically Proven to Prevent and Reverse Disease.* This book lists the 15 major causes of death—heart disease, lung disease, brain disease, digestive cancers, and so on—and gives dietary guidelines for avoiding each of them. Trying to implement the 600-plus pages will keep you busy, and it makes your mortality manageable—sort of. Over the years, Jean E. and I have known some people with whom every conversation eventually turned to which foods were healthy and which were not. We've heard about colon cleanses, the perils of genetically modified organisms (GMOs), juice fasts, exercise routines, what hygiene products to use or avoid, and on and on and on and on. Of course, not all of this is bad—some of these things are helpful to living a healthy life—but for some, it becomes all consuming. And why not? After all, their lives depend on it! Or so they think. Although all of us should strive to be physically healthy, for many this is another way to ignore the inevitable.

No wonder gym memberships increase every year and non-GMO foods, vitamins, and this or that diet are the rage. This hope in health care and lust for longer life drives much of human behavior. Jessica E. Brown put it well: the fear of death is "strong enough to compel us to force kale down our throats, run sweatily on a treadmill at 7am on a Monday morning, and show our genitals to a stranger with cold hands and a white coat if we feel something's a little off."[16] One recent health hope is parabiosis, where the blood of 16- to 25-year-olds is transfused into older people. About this "vampire therapy," cell and molecular biologist at the University of California, Berkeley Michael Conboy says, "It just reeks of snake oil." But for many, that doesn't matter because if there's even the slightest chance to defy death, they are going to take it.[17]

Focusing on the thousands of more manageable health threats

creates craziness. Coffee is bad for you; coffee is good for you. Eggs are bad for you; eggs are good for you. Many ate hockey puck-like bran biscuits to avoid colon cancer until the American Cancer Society concluded that it made no difference. This contradictory craziness showed up at a women's retreat where Jean E. was salting her lunch. A 30-something woman at her table warned that salt wasn't good for her. Jean E. replied, "I have low blood pressure, so my doctor told me to eat more salt." Aghast, her tablemate exclaimed, "Don't they have a drug they could give you?!" It's funny because salt is as natural as it gets, but she wasn't laughing—she'd been so propagandized that salt was bad, she believed an artificial combination of chemicals must be healthier. People will do just about anything to squeeze a few months, or weeks, or even days out of life *here*. Sadly, I knew of one hospitalized pastor who was hooked up to a ventilator. He couldn't talk or eat on his own, but he was adamant that every medical means be used to keep him alive for just a few more days or hours. And that's what happened: he lived a miserable—and expensive—few more days. Thus the fear of death is the reason that health care costs skyrocket.

People place so much hope in diet and exercise to stave off death that when someone is stricken with a serious disease, we often see Christians and non-Christians alike start blaming the sickness on some unhealthy or unwise habit of the sufferer.[18] People do this because they desperately want to believe that if they live rightly, then tragedy won't strike them.[19] This is well illustrated by a comic strip called *Pearls Before Swine* by Stephan Pastis. In one strip, we find two of the main characters, Rat and Goat, talking. Goat mentions a friend named Fred who died at age 42. Rat then quizzes Goat as to whether Fred was a heavy smoker or obese or used drugs, but Goat says no to all. Then Rat, eyes bulging, gets in Goat's face and says, "It can't be nothing, because nothing could happen to me! Meaning that fate is whimsical! That I, too, could die anytime! Give me something about Fred that made him different than me!!" Goat offers, "He collected stamps?" At that, Rat is calmed and says, "High-risk hobby. He was doomed."[20]

You get the point. Many Christians desperately want to believe that when others suffer severely or die slowly or suddenly, they deserved to suffer because they did something wrong. Years ago when I was an associate pastor at a large church and Jean E. miscarried, a young woman told her, "*We* know your miscarriage happened because you didn't have enough faith." A guy told her, "God knew you wouldn't be a good mother" (he later apologized for that nonsense). So much for weeping with those who weep! This belief that some Christians suffer because they deserve it comforts others who are desperate to believe that early death won't strike them. Thus the Lord allows some people who do everything right to suffer so that no one can be secure in this world. When a famous apologist, who was a husband and father, died young from cancer, some Christians said his death had damaged their faith. In response, I wrote on Facebook that his death carried with it a major lesson for everyone: "You. Are. Not. Safe." Do not think you are too important to die at any time. You're not! Our hope needs to be in the eternal life available through Jesus.

The dramatic increase in life expectancy confuses people. In the United States at the turn of the twentieth century, the average life span was about 45 years. Now people are expected to live up to 78.5 years.[21] That has spurred an unwarranted optimism, when in truth, the overwhelming majority of the increase is the result of a decrease in infant mortality. At the turn of the twentieth century, about 10 to 15 percent of all children died before their first birthdays, mostly from infectious diseases. But because of medical advances, today less than 1 percent of children die before their first birthdays. Thus S. Jay Olshansky and Bruce A. Carnes point out in their book *The Quest for Immortality: Science at the Frontiers of Aging*, "The rise in life expectancy has slowed to a crawl."[22]

Another thing that confuses people is thinking that if we could cure cancer, most of us would live many more years. Not true. In fact, Harvard demographer Nathan Keyfitz (1913–2010) calculated that if researchers cured *all* forms of cancer, people would live only a measly 2.265 years longer before they died of something else![23] Unless science cures the majority of *all* diseases, as Stephen Cave writes, "Then the result is not a utopia of strong-bodied demigods but a plethora of care homes and hospitals filled with the depressed, the diseased and the incontinent old."[24] In that case, adds Cave, "it is not so much about living longer but dying slower."[25]

Consider that many health gurus didn't themselves see the promise of a long life. In 1969, Lucille Roberts (1943–2003) opened New York's first gym for women and turned it into a health club empire. The *New York Times* reported that Roberts was "a fitness fanatic who wouldn't touch a French fry, much less smoke a cigarette," but she died from lung cancer at age 59.[26] Nutrition author, natural foods advocate, and Grape-Nuts spokesman Euell Gibbons (1911–75) died of an aneurysm at 64.[27] Whole grains and cereals advocate Adelle Davis (1904–74—my mother was a huge fan), author of *Let's Eat Right to Keep Fit*, preached the dangers of refined foods but died at 70 of bone cancer.[28] Long-distance runner Jim Fixx (1932–84), who advocated the health benefits of running, died of a heart attack after a run at age 52.[29] Daniel Rudman (1927–94), the first scientist to test the antiaging properties of growth hormones, died at age 67 from a pulmonary embolism.[30] Juice fasting advocate Paavo Airola (1918–83), who argued against meat and fish consumption, was president of the International Academy of Biological Medicine, and authored 14 books (two became international bestsellers), died of a stroke at 64.[31] Nathan Pritikin (1915–85), charismatic exercise advocate and founder of the low-cholesterol Pritikin diet, committed suicide by slashing his wrists in his hospital bed. Pritikin was 69 and dying of leukemia.[32]

Diet promoter Michel Montignac (1944–2010), whose diet was the basis for the South Beach diet, died of prostate cancer at age 66.[33] Robert E. Kowalski (1942–2007), author of many nutrition books—including *The NEW 8-Week Cholesterol Cure* (which was on the *New York Times* bestseller list for a remarkable 115 weeks) and *8 Steps to a Healthy Heart*—died at the age of 65 from a pulmonary embolism.[34] Henry S. Lodge (1959–2017) , coauthor of the bestselling *Younger Next Year: Live Strong, Fit, and Sexy—Until You're 80 and Beyond*, died of pancreatic cancer at 58.[35] Jerome Rodale (1898–1971), founder of *Prevention* magazine, declared he would live to 100 unless he was killed by accident. But during a 1971 interview with Dick Cavett on the health and longevity benefits of organic foods, the 72-year-old Rodale dropped dead of a heart attack (needless to say, that episode never aired).[36] International medical leader and Rockefeller Foundation president John H. Knowles (1927–79) advocated a "doctrine of personal responsibility" for one's health. Knowles railed that "the cost of sloth, gluttony, alcoholic intemperance, reckless driving, sexual frenzy, and smoking is now a national, not an individual responsibility."[37] Nonetheless, Knowles died of pancreatic cancer at 52.[38]

Fereidoun M. Esfandiary, or FM-2030 (1930–2000, he legally changed his name to FM-2030—2030 would be the date of his one-hundredth birthday), was an outspoken, lifelong vegetarian who wouldn't eat anything that had a mother. He was a futurist who thought "death was tyrannical...He wanted to do away with death."[39] Like Benjamin Franklin, FM-2030 rued that he had been born too early: "I am a 21st-century person who was accidentally born into the 20th," he said. "I have a deep nostalgia for the future."[40] But unlike Franklin, FM-2030 was optimistic that he wasn't too early for science to deny his death: "If you are around in 2010," he told Larry King in a 1990 interview, "there's a very good chance you'll be around in the year 2030 and if you are around in 2030 there's an excellent chance you can coast to immortality—indefinite life spans."[41] But FM-2030 didn't make it to 2010; he died of pancreatic cancer in 2000. His body is now submerged in liquid nitrogen at the Alcor Life Extension Foundation in Scottsdale, Arizona. We'll talk about cryonics shortly.

I imagine some readers are thinking that all of these health gurus did something wrong: they must not have eaten quite right, they must have eaten something quite wrong, or their exercise regimen wasn't quite right. Like Rat, we chase something—anything—so we can reassure ourselves that an early death won't happen to us. Perhaps some are thinking, "Yes, but medical science has advanced so far since most of these people died so this won't happen to me." But even if our diet does help us live a little longer, we could still die at any time. My point isn't that their diets or exercise didn't help them—they may even have added to their longevity—but that they died anyway. I'm not suggesting we shouldn't eat healthy foods (whatever that means to you) or exercise—we should. But do not put confidence in the flesh, because until the Lord returns, diet and exercise *may* let us live *a little* longer, or live a *little* healthier, but we're all going to die.[42]

Or are we?

Transhumanists say we don't have to.

Transhumanism

Two weeks after 17-year-old Mary's baby died, she wrote in her diary, "Dream that my little baby came to life again; that it had only been cold, and that we rubbed it before the fire and it lived. Awake and find no baby. I think about the little thing all day. Not in good spirits."[43] Mary's own mother died of an infection a few days after giving birth to Mary, so death haunted her. At the time Mary lost her child, demonstrations of the power of galvanism were popular. Galvanism, named after scientist Luigi Galvani (1737–98), was the process of giving electric shocks to parts of a dead body that resulted in the muscles contracting. One such experiment on an executed murderer brought this result: "On the first application of the process to the face, the jaws of the deceased criminal began to quiver, and the adjoining muscles were horribly contorted, and one eye was actually opened. In the subsequent part of the process the right hand was raised and clenched, and the legs and thighs were set in motion." Some feared "that the wretched man was on the eve of being restored to life."[44]

About galvanism, Mary wondered, "Perhaps a corpse would be reanimated; galvanism had given token of such things: perhaps the component parts of a creature might be manufactured, brought together, and endued with vital warmth."[45] Mary wasn't a scientist, but she turned out to be a good writer. In 1818, at age 21, Mary Shelley (1797–1851) published the book that would make her famous: *Frankenstein*.

Since *Frankenstein*, science fiction has been abuzz with genetically altered humans, or transhumans. Some of them possess terrific powers, and some of them are even immortal. This is seen in movies such as *Spiderman*, *Captain America*, *X-Men*, *Limitless*, *Lucy*, and so on. But many now argue that immortality isn't just science fiction because science is now on the brink of bestowing true immortality through transhumanism (often represented as H+, as in "human plus"). The basic idea is simple: If unguided, random matter—via natural selection—is capable of evolving humans into the marvelous beings that we are, then what happens if we humans use our intelligence to take the chance out of natural selection by modifying our DNA? Those who think this sometimes call it "unnatural selection."[46]

Enthusiasts

Tech executives are betting on it: the founders of PayPal, Google, Facebook, eBay, Napster, and Netscape are spending hundreds of millions to defeat death entirely—or at least to radically increase human longevity. Oracle cofounder Larry Ellison has donated more than $430 million to antiaging research.[47] In Mike Wilson's biography of Ellison, *The Difference Between God and Larry Ellison*: Inside the Oracle Corporation* (*God Doesn't Think He's Larry Ellison), Wilson recounts that Ellison told him, "Death has never made any sense to me. How can a person be there and then just vanish, just not be there?" Then Ellison added, "Death makes me very angry. Premature death makes me angrier still."[48] Similarly, Alphabet CEO Larry Page started Calico (short for California Life Company) with an investment of up to $750 million from Google for the purpose of life-extension research.[49] Tech investor Peter Theil writes, "I stand against confiscatory taxes, totalitarian collectives, and the ideology of the inevitability of the death of every individual."[50]

Once we get this all figured out, we'll be able to "reverse aging," writes Ray Kurzweil. This will be accomplished through biotechnology "methods such as RNA interference for turning off destructive genes, gene therapy for changing your genetic code, therapeutic cloning for regenerating your cells and tissues, smart drugs to reprogram your metabolic pathways, and many other emerging techniques." If that doesn't do it, "whatever biotechnology doesn't get around to accomplishing, we'll have the means to do with nanotechnology."[51] Kurzweil explains that

> nanobots will be able to travel through the bloodstream, then go in and around our cells and perform various services, such as removing toxins, sweeping out debris,

correcting DNA errors, repairing and restoring cell membranes, reversing atherosclerosis, modifying the levels of hormones, neurotransmitters, and other metabolic chemicals, and a myriad of other tasks. For each aging process, we can describe a means for nanobots to reverse the process, down to the level of individual cells, cell components, and molecules.[52]

Of course, we're not even remotely close to accomplishing these things, but that's why Kurzweil's book is entitled *The Singularity Is Near*. The singularity will save us. We'll talk more about the singularity shortly.

Brain Uploading

Another way we could live forever is through brain uploading or mind uploading—also known as "whole brain emulation." Brain uploading is a kind of transhumanism in which the mind—a collection of memories, personality, mental state, and attributes of a specific individual—is transferred from its original biological brain to a computer. If you could upload your consciousness into a computer, then you could load yourself into a new body or a digital avatar. You could be She-Ra or the Hunk-Ra, and if those names are already taken (and they are), don't worry; there are avatar name generators to help you.

Sci-Fi Brain Uploading

Brain uploading is illustrated in many movies, such as *Transcendence* (2014), *Selfless* (2015), and *Avatar* (2009).[53] Brain uploading was even in an episode of *The Simpsons*, in which Homer's antics result in his death. But to the relief of everyone, we learn at Homer's funeral that he has been cloned by Professor Frink. This encourages the brain-uploaded and cloned Homer to be ever more careless, since he knows he can come back to life. But after 30 years of Homer dying and coming back as a clone, Frink announces at Homer's umpteenth funeral that he has run out of clones. All is not lost, however, because Frick had uploaded Homer onto a flash drive, which is ultimately uploaded into Marge's home entertainment system.[54] The episode is hilarious until Homer only exists in digital form. From then on, the episode is sad, and ultimately, because she misses being with Homer, Marge electrocutes herself so she can be uploaded and join him forever in the flash drive.

The Not-Kidding Proponents of Brain Uploading

For some, brain uploading isn't science fiction; it's achievable science. This belief is enabled by the philosophy of materialism, which states that humans are no more than material stuff—that is, humans don't have souls; we are only molecules in motion. Brain uploaders argue that because humans are no more than molecules, there's no reason the synapses of our brains can't be replicated with components and circuitry that are *yet to be invented*. When these electronic whizbangs are created, brain uploaders believe there's no reason a computer, which is also just material stuff, can't become a vessel into which a person can upload their consciousness.

Once we are able to upload our consciousnesses, we could then be avatars in a computer world or we could download our consciousnesses into a different body or into a robot. As Kurzweil puts it, "We will have plenty of options for twenty-first-century bodies for both nonbiological humans and biological humans who avail themselves of extensions to our intelligence. The human body version 2.0 will include virtual bodies in completely realistic virtual environments, nanotechnology-based physical bodies, and more."[55] Futurologist Ian Pearson predicts that "realistically by 2050 we would expect to be able to download your mind into a machine, so when you die it's not a major career problem."[56]

One brain-uploading true believer is David J. Chalmers, a professor of philosophy and neural science at New York University and codirector of the Center for Mind, Brain, and Consciousness. Chalmers writes that there are two views of brain uploading: "Suppose that I can upload my brain into a computer? Will the result be me? On the optimistic view of uploading, the upload will be the same person as the original. On the pessimistic view of uploading, the upload will not be the same person as the original."[57] Let's examine the pessimistic view first.

Pessimistic View

In this pessimistic view, if you uploaded your brain to a computer, it would not be you. Chalmers uses identical twins as an example. Let's suppose you have a "perfect identical twin whose brain and body are molecule-for-molecule duplicates." Let's suppose your parents raised you in every way identically to each other (I know that's not possible in real life, but this is a thought experiment). Your mother breastfed you and your twin at exactly the same time and even regularly switched breasts in case that made any difference. You were given exactly the same toys. You went to the same classes and sat side by side and even switched sides regularly. If you had such a twin, then she would be "qualitatively identical" to you, but she wouldn't be "numerically identical" to you—she would not be you. As Chalmers puts it, "If you kill the twin, I will survive. If you kill me (that is, if you destroy this system) and preserve the twin, I will die. The survival of the twin might be some consolation to me, but from a self-interested point of view this outcome seems much worse than the alternative."[58] Therefore, in this scenario, if you die, the fact that an identical consciousness to yours still exists doesn't change the fact that you're still dead—your twin might enjoy a grande, quad, nonfat, one-pump, no-whip mocha, but *you* will never experience that again.[59] Thus I'm not going to spend any more time on the pessimistic view of brain uploading because it doesn't offer literal immortality.[60]

Optimistic View

But Chalmers and a host of others hold to the optimistic view of brain uploading: you can upload your consciousness into a computer and it will still be you. Some of those who believe this are giddy at the prospect of an electronic immortality. One such giddy fellow is philosopher Mark Walker, who writes in the *Journal of Evolution and Technology*, "If one is uploaded to a computer, then it seems that it would be a relatively routine matter to enhance one's memory or cognition: just add more computer memory or processing power. The sky is literally the limit here." He enthuses, "In short, and without too much hyperbole, those who upload may well be on their way to godhood."[61]

Throughout the ages, we humans have made our own gods, but now some think we can make our*selves* gods.

But how could you possibly upload your *consciousness* onto a computer? One popular explanation is gradual uploading.[62] Chalmers explains,

> Suppose that 1% of Dave's brain is replaced by a functionally isomorphic [similar in form and structure] silicon circuit. Next suppose that another 1% is replaced, and another 1%. We can continue the process for 100 months, after which a wholly uploaded system will result. We can suppose that functional isomorphism preserves consciousness, so that the system has the same sort of conscious states throughout.[63]

Chalmers believes this gradual uploading is the "safest" way to upload your brain, and he is "reasonably confident that gradual uploading is a form of survival." Thus Chalmers writes, "So if at some point in the future I am faced with the choice between uploading and continuing in an increasingly slow biological embodiment, then as long as I have the option of gradual uploading, I will be happy to do so. Unfortunately, I may not have that option. It may be that gradual uploading technology will *not be available in my lifetime*."[64] Or any lifetime!

Science Isn't Even Close

Brain uploading won't be available in Chalmers's lifetime because the computer into which the brain is uploaded must have circuitry that is identical to the connections one finds in a human brain. Your brain needs to be mapped neuron by neuron and then replicated neuron by neuron along with the other relevant components. Chalmers writes about three ways of doing this, and I think you'll see why this won't be happening anytime soon.

Destructive Uploading

The first way is "destructive uploading," in which the brain is frozen and then analyzed "layer by layer" until all the "neurons and other relevant components" are mapped. Then all this information is loaded into a "computer model that includes an accurate simulation of neural behavior and dynamics." Chalmers says, "The result *might be* an emulation of the original brain."[65]

Gradual Uploading

Then comes "gradual uploading," and I need to quote everything Chalmers says about it so you'll appreciate its complexity. He begins, "The most widely discussed method is that of nanotransfer":

> Here one or more nanotechnology devices (perhaps tiny robots) are inserted into the brain and attach themselves to a single neuron. Each device learns to simulate the behavior of the associated neuron and also learns about its connectivity. Once it simulates the neuron's behavior well enough, it takes the place of the original neuron, perhaps leaving receptors and effectors in place and offloading the relevant processing to a computer via radiotransmitters. It then moves to other neurons and repeats the procedure, until eventually every neuron has been replaced by an emulation, and perhaps all processing has been offloaded to a computer.[66]

The trouble is, this is also a destructive method. You wouldn't survive it except—if it worked—as consciousness in a machine, but it's not clear if it would be your consciousness.

Nondestructive Uploading

But all is not lost. There is "nondestructive uploading: The nanotransfer method might in principle be used in a nondestructive form. The holy grail here is *some sort of* noninvasive method of brain imaging, analogous to functional magnetic resonance imaging but with fine enough grain that neural and synaptic dynamics can be recorded." But, writes Chalmers, "no such technology is currently *on the horizon*, but imaging technology is an area of rapid progress."[67] In other words, science isn't close to replicating your brain—much less to making circuitry conscious.

In fact, we can't even make artificial intelligence (AI) that acts like a person. Stanford University neuroscientist and HBO's *Westworld* advisor David Eagleman explains,

> AI is not any good at the sort of broad intelligence that, for example, a 3-year-old has. A 3-year-old can do things like pick up a dish from the sink and put it in the dishwasher and communicate with people and manipulate people and navigate a complex room without falling down or running into the furniture—all kinds of things that AI really stinks at currently. We are not really close to having AI that seems like a human.[68]

Eagleman says computers lack the "broad intelligence" of even a three-year-old. The problem is that humans possess a type of intelligence that is foreign to computers. Philosopher and strong AI detractor Hubert L. Dreyfus (1929–2017), in his book *What Computers Still Can't Do: A Critique of Artificial Reason*, points out "that metaphors like 'Sally is a block of ice' could not be analyzed by listing features that Sally and a large, cold cube have in common."[69] If you said that phrase to most humans, they would immediately understand your low opinion of Sally, but a computer would have no idea. Philosopher John R. Searle gives another example: "'Juliet is the sun,' does not mean 'Juliet is for the most part gaseous,' or 'Juliet is 90 million miles from earth,' both of which properties are salient and well-known features of the sun."[70] Artificial intelligence scientist Erik J. Larson points out that children know "when Barack Obama is in Washington, his left foot is also in Washington," but a computer wouldn't know that without being instructed. Larson says, "Simple knowledge like this seemed endless; even worse, the bits and pieces that became relevant kept changing, depending on context." Larson also gives the now famous example by mathematician Yehoshua Bar-Hillel (1915–75): "Little John was looking for his toy box. Finally he found it. The box was in the pen. John was very happy." Larson writes that the basic problem regards the question "What meaning do we assign to the English word 'pen'?"

As Bar-Hillel explains, there are at least two candidates: (1) a certain writing utensil or (2) an enclosure where small children can play. But the difference between these definitions matters, of course, because one object has to "fit" into the other in the example. Can little John's toy box fit in a writing utensil? Well, no. A person can see what's meant—an enclosure—but our appreciation of word meaning is the very deficit of automated systems. Since the computer has no actual knowledge of the relative sizes of objects, it can't decipher the correct meaning and gets stuck (or produces the wrong answer). Relying only on shallow statistical facts about the words in the sentences, it lacks this deeper understanding. And without it, how is it to properly translate Bar-Hillel's example and countless other sentences in natural language?[71]

Problems like this are endless because new things are always being created, already created things often change, and the terms we use to describe things are constantly in flux.

The Wiring Problem

The problem with producing a brain, writes Eagleman, is that "there are almost a hundred billion neurons—those are the specialized cell types in the brain—and each one of those has about 10,000 connections to its neighbor. So there are almost a thousand trillion connections in the brain and we just haven't figured out all the secrets to it yet."[72] So we haven't figured out the "secrets" to "a thousand trillion connections" of our "hundred billion neurons." Strong AI proponents say they will one day emulate the brain on a computer, but that's not the same thing as making a brain. Searle explains,

> The computational emulation of the brain is like a computational emulation of the stomach: we could do a perfect emulation of the stomach cell by cell, but such emulations produce models or pictures and not the real thing. Scientists have made artificial hearts that work but they do not produce them by computer simulation;

they may one day produce an artificial stomach, but this too would not be such an emulation. Even with a perfect computer emulation of the stomach, you cannot then stuff a pizza into the computer and expect the computer to digest it. Cell-by-cell computer emulation of the stomach is to real digestive processes as cell-by-cell emulation of the brain is to real cognitive processes. But do not mistake the simulation (or emulation) for the real thing. It would be helpful to those trying to construct the real thing but far from an actual stomach.[73]

But we haven't even figured out how a brain with *only* 302 neurons works. McGill University neuroscientist Michael Hendricks writes in the *MIT Technology Review,*

> I study a small roundworm, *Caenorhabditis elegans,* which is by far the best-described animal in all of biology. We know all of its genes and all of its cells (a little over 1,000). We know the identity and complete synaptic connectivity of its 302 neurons, and we have known it for 30 years. If we could "upload" or roughly simulate any brain, it should be that of *C. elegans.* Yet even with the full connectome in hand, a static model of this network of connections lacks *most* of the information necessary to simulate the mind of the worm. In short, brain activity cannot be inferred from synaptic neuroanatomy.[74]

We can't even replicate a 302-neuron worm brain!

The Harvard-educated MIT neuroscientist Sebastian Seung explains that the "bottleneck" for reproducing a brain involves "analysing the images." Seung says, "Suppose we can image a cubic millimetre of brain in two weeks. To trace the neurons through those images manually we estimate would take 100,000 years. For one cubic millimetre. The challenge is to speed up that process. One of the ways is to automate the process. But artificial intelligence (AI) is not perfect. It can speed people up, but it can't replace them. Even if AI does 99% of the work, that would only reduce 100,000 years to 1,000 years."[75] In other words, unless something changes drastically, they wouldn't be able to map anyone's brain within the lifetimes of those who are reading this.

Of course, because of the naturalist's *philosophical* commitment to materialism—a commitment that has nothing to do with science—naturalists go on whistling in the grim reaper's shadow, believing that one day, science will figure how to replicate a brain. But those who seek literal immortality have a last, best hope: the Singularity.

The Singularity

Those who hope for transhuman immortality (again, brain uploading is a type of transhumanism) recognize they aren't even close to having the computer power necessary to save them, but they trust in a coming superintelligence they call the Singularity. Cue the angels! But seriously, I'm not exaggerating: for many, the Singularity *is* their savior (or maybe their destroyer, or enslaver, or puppet master—we'll talk more about this shortly). Ray Kurzweil explains the Singularity: "It's a future period during which the pace of technological change will be so rapid, its impact so deep, that human life will be irreversibly transformed."[76] Kurzweil and others believe that computers will soon be smarter than people, and when that happens, these computers will exponentially start improving themselves.[77] And when that happens—yee-haw!—computers will help humans transcend biology. In the movie *Transcendence* (2014), scientist Will Caster (Johnny Depp)—who, among others, is trying to make a self-aware computer—is asked by an audience member, "So you want to create a god? Your own god?" Will replies, "Isn't that what man has always done?" Indeed it is!

Many think that when the Singularity happens, computers will become conscious. Kurzweil is bullish: "Clearly, *nonbiological* entities will claim to have emotional and spiritual experiences, just as we do today. They—we—will claim to be human and to have the full range of emotional and *spiritual* experiences that humans claim to have. And these will not be idle claims; they will evidence the sort of rich, complex, and subtle behavior associated with such feelings."[78] Notice the blurring of man and machine: "They—we—will claim to be human."

This may seem impossible, but Singulatarians—those who have pondered and "get" the significance of the Singularity—like to point out that in 1992, world chess champion Gary Kasparov "scorned the pathetic state" of computer chess, but just five years later, an IBM computer named Deep Blue beat Kasparov.[79] Therefore, give computers a chance, and as they get faster and faster, they'll become self-aware and start thinking on their own. When that happens, we'll be able to upload our brains. Kurzweil explains the glories of how this computer salvation will result in our own immortality:

> Our version 1.0 biological bodies are likewise frail and subject to a myriad of failure modes, not to mention the cumbersome maintenance rituals they require. While human intelligence is sometimes capable of soaring in its creativity and expressiveness, much human thought is derivative, petty, and circumscribed. The Singularity will allow us to transcend these limitations of our biological bodies and brains. We will gain power over our fates. Our mortality will be in our own hands. We will be able to live as long as we want (a subtly different statement from saying we will live forever). We will fully understand human thinking and will vastly extend and expand its reach. By the end of this century, the nonbiological portion of our intelligence will be trillions of trillions of times more powerful than unaided human intelligence.[80]

In other words, the Singularity will enable us to be transhuman and thus immortal. Our savior comes! Forget the angels—cue the theme music for *2001: A Space Odyssey*!

Destroyer, Enslaver, or Puppet Master?

One problem with the Singularity is that when a self-aware computer develops a mind of its own, who knows what that mind might do? In 1965, mathematician Irving Good warned that "the first ultra-intelligent machine is the *last* invention that man need ever make, provided that the machine is docile enough to tell us how to keep it under control."[81] Similarly, in 1993, mathematician Vernor Vinge, who first used the word "singularity" about strong AI computers, warned that if the Singularity could not be prevented, then it "would not be human-kind's 'tool'—any more than humans are the tools of rabbits or robins or chimpanzees."[82] Singularity advocates express concern that the Singularity might be our destroyer, enslaver, or puppet master. After all, if computers truly begin to think on their own and really are, as Kurzweil puts it, "trillions of trillions of times more powerful than unaided human intelligence," then that's where all the dystopian sci-fi movies come in. Thus Apple cofounder Steve Wozniak asks, "Will we be the gods? Will we be the family pets? Or will we be the ants that get stepped on?"[83]

Destroyer

What if, after the Singularity, the machine decides you're in the way, or using up and polluting valuable resources, or dangerous because at any moment, you might destroy the world with nuclear war—or even worse, you might switch it off? This Singularity savior might just be your murderer. We've seen this in *Star Trek: The Motion Picture* (1979), in which the "carbon unit's infestation" must be removed (you're a carbon unit). This idea is also present in the many films of the *Terminator* franchise (1984, 1991, 2003, 2009, 2015, 2019), where the system Skynet becomes self-aware and considers humans hostile to its existence and decides to destroy them.

Serious scientists share these concerns. Cambridge physicist Steven Hawking (1942–2018) warns, "The development of full artificial intelligence could spell the end of the human race."[84] Similarly, SpaceX and Tesla founder Elon Musk says that when it comes to making AI safe, "Maybe there's a five to 10 percent chance of success."[85] Philosopher Nick Bostrom, director of the Future of Humanity Institute at the University of Oxford, writes that "when the AI has gained sufficient strength to obviate the need for secrecy," then the "overt implementation phase might start with a 'strike' in which the AI eliminates the human species." Bostrom continues, "This could be achieved through the activation of some advanced weapons system" like "self-replicating biotechnology or nanotechnology" and might produce "nerve gas or target-seeking mosquito-like robots," which "might then burgeon forth simultaneously from every square meter of the globe."[86] Bostrom says, however, that "more effective ways of killing could probably be devised by a machine with the technology research superpower."[87] This could result in a "society of economic miracles and technological awesomeness, with nobody there to benefit. A Disneyland without children."[88] Bostrom seems to have overlooked the fact that conscious computers would benefit themselves, and they would have the time of their lives!

Enslaver

So the Singularity might kill us, but if it doesn't, there's another problem. What if it enslaves us? We've seen this in the *Matrix* films (1999, 2003, 2003), where humans are farmed to produce bioelectrical energy, and their minds are trapped in a virtual world to pacify them. Elon Musk thinks that our computer overlords might decide to keep us around as their pets. In a dialog between Musk and astrophysicist Neil deGrasse Tyson, Musk says, "We won't be like a pet Labrador [to the AI] if we're lucky." A couple moments later, Tyson says, "So we'll be lab pets to them." Musk agrees, and then Tyson says, "They'll keep the docile humans and get rid of the violent ones...And then breed the docile humans."[89]

But it gets worse. Musk and Tyson both think it's possible that we are presently living in a virtual reality. An audience member asks Musk if he'd ever thought about whether we are, right now, living in a computer simulation, and Musk replies that he has thought about it "a lot," adding, "The odds that we are in base reality is one in billions."[90] By saying it's one chance in *billions* that we are in "base reality," Musk means that odds are, we are presently in a simulation. Later, talk show host Larry King asked Tyson if Musk was right that we may be living in simulation, and Tyson replied, "I find it hard to argue against it, that possibility." Tyson continued, "Statistically...it's hard to argue against the possibility that all of us, are not just the creation of some kid, in a parent's basement, programming up a world for their own entertainment." Tyson goes on to say that his kid might get "bored" and throw in some "disruptive leader" for his own "entertainment."[91] You might be tempted to write off Musk and Tyson as just a couple of whiz kids, but in 2016, Bank of America sent a note to clients, stating, "It is conceivable that with advancements in artificial intelligence, virtual reality, and computing power, members of future civilizations could have decided to run a simulation of their ancestors."[92] Now, I do agree with Hawking, Musk, and Tyson that if the Singularity does occur, it probably will either destroy us or enslave us, but thankfully, I don't believe for a nanosecond that a Singularity will occur any more than pigs will start making cotton candy. The Singularity has problems, two of them fatal.

The Singularitarians' Optimism Mistaken

Because of our accomplishments with computers, some think a computer can go from a series of zeros and ones (how everything is programmed today—electrical ons and offs) to computers possessing consciousness.[93] That's quite a leap! This has been dubbed by Bar-Hillel as the "fallacy of the successful first step." Erik Larson sums up Bar-Hillel's point: "Early progress does not imply that *subsequent steps of the same kind* guarantee an eventual solution."[94] Just because computers are becoming faster and faster, it doesn't mean they will be able to think on their own one day. There's nothing inherent in the concept of "faster" that would cause a computer to become conscious. As Hubert L. Dreyfus in *Minds and Machines* puts it, "Climbing a hill should not give one any assurance that if he keeps going he will reach the sky."[95] So for the Singularitarian, how does a computer become conscious? Again, they've got nothing! But if you're desperate to escape death and you don't want to submit to the Creator, none of this matters—you must believe the Singularity will save you.

Naturalists Don't Even Know What Consciousness Is

But it gets worse. Even if we could produce something that is wired *exactly* like your brain, naturalists like Chalmers admit, "It is true that we have *no idea* how a nonbiological system, such as a silicon computational system, could be conscious. But the fact is that we also have *no idea* how a biological system, such as a neural system, could be conscious. The gap is just as wide in both cases." So those who concede they have "no idea" about how consciousness even works tell us that computers can become conscious. But, Chalmers opines, we should assume they can because "we do not know of any principled differences between biological and nonbiological systems that suggest that the former can be conscious and the latter cannot. In the absence of such principled differences, I think the default attitude should be that both biological and nonbiological systems can be conscious."[96] There it is. They believe that our own consciousness arose from purely material stuff, so it must be the case that machine consciousness can somehow arise from purely material stuff. Chalmers's conclusion isn't based on science because, again, he has "no idea" how a computer could become conscious. What makes it seem possible to Chalmers is the *philosophical assumption* that materialism/naturalism is true.[97]

Also, even if materialism were true, perhaps it's possible that only biological systems, as opposed to nonbiological systems, have what's inherent to consciousness. If that were true (again, I hold that materialism is false), then it would be impossible to make a nonbiological system conscious. But if that's the case, there's a further problem: to date, no scientist has been able to make any biological system without beginning with an already existing biological system. They can't even make algae. You pick up a rock in a field, and there's organic life underneath it, but scientists, with all their brainpower and resources, have never been able to make anything organic—ever.[98] Nothing. Nil. Zip. Nada. But those desperate to not die don't care and cling to the notion that one day, science will find a way. As machine learning researcher Larson puts it, "Singularity enthusiasts apparently presuppose that some vague notion of technological progress sweeps all this under the carpet. But how? Surely just helping oneself to 'progress' can't prop the argument."[99]

Science Can't Explain the Origin of Consciousness

As noted above, Chalmers admits that "we also have *no idea* how a biological system, such as a neural system, could be conscious." And this is one of the arguments for the existence of God. How does that which isn't conscious—purely material stuff—produce consciousness? Chalmers, who spends his professional life on this subject, says we "have no idea." In other words, science cannot explain, in principle, how nonconscious stuff becomes conscious. By "in principle," I mean that someone needs to explain how faster processing speeds and more advanced programming could in any way, shape, or form suddenly become self-aware and have a will of its own—that is, become conscious. C.S. Lewis explains the naturalist's dilemma:

> If naturalism is true, every finite thing or event must be (in principle) explicable in terms of the Total system. I say "explicable *in principle*" because of course we are not going to demand that naturalists, at any given moment, should have found the detailed explanation of every phenomenon. Obviously many things will only be explained when the sciences have made further progress. But if Naturalism is to be accepted we have a right to demand that every single thing should be such that we see, in general, how it could be explained in terms of the Total System.[100]

But naturalists cannot even explain in principle how consciousness arose or how a computer might become conscious. They just *know* it must be able to happen because we are conscious.

Or there's a God!

Singularity Advocates Are Doing Metaphysics, Not Science

The idea that humans could create something conscious is based on the notion that our brains, with their "hundred billion neurons" and "thousand trillion connections" that became conscious, evolved into the creative creatures we are—by luck.[101] Extreme luck. Supercalifragilisticexpialidocious luck.[102] Singulatarians believe that the material came from the nonmaterial, that life came from nonlife, that complexity came from disorder, and that consciousness came from that which had no consciousness. This and only this enables the notion that the technological whizbang called the Singularity can spring from molecules in motion and one day give them immortality! As Searle puts it, many people who argue for strong AI aren't doing science but "metaphysics."[103] We aren't the result of extreme luck. Thus David writes in Psalm 14:1, "The fool says in his heart, 'There is no God.'"

In the meantime, Kurzweil realizes that the Singularity might not come in his lifetime—he was born in 1948—so when he dies, he intends to be kept in a liquid nitrogen thermos at Alcor.[104]

Cryonics

In the 2013 movie *Star Trek into Darkness*, the Enterprise crew finds Khan (Benedict Cumberbatch) cryonically frozen and revive him (Trekkies knew this was going to turn out badly). In *The Empire Strikes Back* (1980), Han Solo (Harrison Ford) was frozen in carbonite and then revived in the next movie, *The Return of the Jedi* (1983). In *Austin Powers: International Man of Mystery* (1997), after Austin Powers's (Mike Myers) nemesis, Dr. Evil (also played by Mike Myers), escapes in a space rocket and cryonically freezes himself, Powers volunteers to be placed into cryostasis in case Dr. Evil returns in the future.[105]

But it's not just fiction. Baseball Hall of Fame player Ted Williams (1918–2002) is cryonically frozen at Alcor (his head and body are in two different tanks of liquid nitrogen). Williams's daughter, Claudia Williams, explains why they froze her father: "It [cryonics] was like a religion, something we could have faith in."[106] At the cost of more than $100,000 a whack, not a lot of people will be doing that, but Simon Cowell, Larry King, and Seth MacFarlane all say they want to be frozen.[107] In an interview with Larry King, talk show host Conan O'Brien asks King, "You plan to be cryogenically frozen...why?" King replies, "I don't believe in an afterlife. I just never accepted it. I never made the leap of faith. So, that means when you die, it's bye, bye, baby...So the only hope, the only fragment of hope, is to be frozen, and then someday they cure whatever you died of, and you're back." Later King asks, "If, on the presumption that there is nothing more after this, why is it stupid?"[108] When asked about his fear of death, Jordan Sparks, the director of the Oregon Cryonics Institute, replies, "Yeah, I'm afraid of death in all ways, and I will never give up...I want to yell at the entire world, 'Don't you get it, you're going to die. Here's an option, the only option.'"[109]

But there are a host of problems with being frozen.

Will Anyone Want to Defrost You?

First, there's the problem of whether anyone would want to hit the defrost button in the first place. Who needs another rich guy around using up precious resources? Sure, you might want to try to defrost some people as an interesting science experiment, but once you figure it out, wouldn't it be like watching another rocket lift off? Nobody cares. After all, in the distant future, if humankind learns to cure all diseases, then earth will become overpopulated, and we might not want to honor those contracts after all! As McGill University neuroscientist Michael Hendricks says, "Burdening future generations with our brain banks is just comically arrogant. Aren't we leaving them with enough problems?" He continues, "I hope future people are appalled that in the 21st century, the richest and most comfortable people in history spent their money and resources trying to live forever on the backs of their descendants. I mean, it's a joke, right? They are cartoon bad guys."[110] David Chalmers asks, "If reconstructive uploading will eventually be possible, how can one ensure that it happens?" Chalmers suggests, "Keeping a bank account with compound interest to pay them for doing so." He says, "My own strategy is to write about the singularity and about uploading. Perhaps this will encourage our successors to reconstruct me, if only to prove me wrong."[111] Notice the kinds of thoughts people contrive to avoid death.

Freezer Burn

It gets worse. When I think of cryonics, I think of meat I've left in my freezer for too long. You know what I mean: it seemed like a good idea to freeze those chicken breasts, but months later they're covered with this crystalized crust, and you throw them out. Mehmet Toner, cryobiologist at Massachusetts General Hospital, points out that the human body is mostly water: "You can only slowly freeze and slowly warm large things. Ice is going to form inevitably during warming."

Then Toner says, "The chances that you will bring a frozen head back is the same as when you go home tonight, open the freezer, get the ground beef out, and make a cow out of it." It's a "ridiculous concept." Toner continues, "I've spent thirty-three years...day in and day out thinking about how to freeze things, and I know it's not going to work." After all, if ice crystals form in the brain, synapses will be shattered. Think freezer burn.[112]

It's Never Been Done on Even a Small Animal

On the Alcor Life Extension Foundation website, there is a curious Q & A:

Q: Has an animal ever been cryopreserved and revived?
A: Small roundworms (nematodes) and possibly some insects can survive temperatures below –100°C. However, since scientists are still struggling to cryopreserve many individual organs, *it should be obvious* that no large animal has ever been cryopreserved and revived. Such an achievement is still likely decades in the future.[113]

Maybe it's just me, but "it should be obvious" sounds snarky. Apparently not even what's touted as the nuclear-war-survivable cockroach can survive –100°C!

Acoustic Fracturing

One of the reasons scientists haven't been able to revive anything is that they haven't "conquered the ultimate bane of cryonics practitioners everywhere: the unfortunate phenomena known in the trade as 'acoustic fracturing events.'"[114] Acoustic fracturing events are the "audible cracking noises made by the brain and other internal organs as they shatter from the effects of the extreme cold," writes Howard Witt. "It's exactly that kind of noise when you drop an ice cube into a glass of Coke," explains Tanya Jones, Alcor's director of technical operations. She says, "In the best-case scenario we've ever had, it was only five fracture events. We are working on the engineering to see how to eliminate this problem." After I told Jean E. about this, we needed to quickly cool some just-boiled eggs, so we listened and watched as we dropped ice cubes into a bowl of water. Crack. Crack. Crack. Listen for the fracturing sound the next time you put ice in a warm Diet Coke, and you'll not be too impressed about being deep frozen. You wouldn't want the children to be there when their father is frozen: "Why's daddy making that sound, mommy?" So in the reviving process, how does one fix shattered brains? "'It should *just* be a matter of stitching them back together," Jones says. "You might be able to glue them together, but we don't have repair technologies on that scale yet.'"[115] Sure, that's how you do it—you just glue it back together. Your insides will be reminiscent of how Frankenstein's monster looked on the outside. Alcor hopes to one day discover the Elmer's brain superglue, but when glue bonds, doesn't it also create a barrier?

Must Be Frozen Immediately

There's another problem if you're going to be frozen: when you die, you need to have the personnel and equipment at your bedside because if you wait too long, then your brain will be so damaged, there may not be much to bring back. As we all know, brain cells begin to die in less than five minutes. Thus Alcor says on their website, "Cryonics procedures should ideally begin within the first one or two minutes after the heart stops, and preferably within 15 minutes. Longer delays place a greater burden on future technology to reverse injury and restore the brain to a healthy state."[116] One to two minutes? You'd better spend your last days at Alcor. So real is this problem that some argue we should allow people to be frozen while they are still alive! Oddly, even Christian apologist John Warwick Montgomery has argued that freezing someone *while still alive* wouldn't be suicide:

> And cryonics? What about the recent effort (both in real life and on television) of the patient with a terminal brain tumor to have himself frozen now so that on being revived (hopefully!) at a later stage of medical knowledge his brain will have a better chance of treatment?

> Assuming that this patient's brain would be destroyed
> by the time of his natural death, one could well argue
> that pre-death freezing would not in fact be suicide in
> the ordinary sense, since the object here is not cessation
> of life but the (admittedly remote but nonetheless scien-
> tifically responsible) chance of restoring it.[117]

But don't forget, future humans not only have to restore and reanimate your fractured brain; they still have to be able to cure what killed
you in the first place! And since they've often frozen the body separately
from the head (as in the case of Ted Williams), they'll have to figure out
how to sew a head onto a body.

Perhaps the biggest problem is that, as I've mentioned, we're not
just material stuff—we have souls, and when your body is dead, your
soul is no longer there (we'll talk more about this in chapter 8). And if
we have souls, then even if scientists are able to one day reanimate your
frozen cadaver, then *you* still wouldn't be walking and talking again on
earth because the most essential *you*—the conscious you—wouldn't
be there when the defrost happens. As skeptic Michael Shermer puts
it, "Cryonics is kind of like a scientific search for immortality." But,
says Shermer, "Today the idea of reanimating heads or bodies in a century or two, or five, is wishful thinking. Because we don't even know
if in principle, how you could reanimate a brain." This is because "we
still don't know the basis of consciousness. We're going to conquer the
technology of bringing it back after it's gone. That's wishful thinking
at the moment."[118]

And if we have souls, then brain uploading will never happen for
anyone because the soul is nontransferable. And if we have souls, then
the Singularity will never happen because consciousness springs from
the soul. And if we have souls, then all these things are no more than
scientific mumbo jumbo gumbo for those hungry for eternal life but
unwilling to come to Him who will give them eternal life and the water
with which they will never thirst again.

The Evil of Literal Immortality Projects

Useless

Literal immortality projects—living until science finds a way to make us live forever—are useless and vain. They are useless because from a biblical standpoint, there is nothing you can do that will keep you from dying. As it says in Hebrews 9:27 (NIV), "People are destined to die once, and after that to face judgment." We've all known people who do everything wrong, from a modern medical science point of view, but live a long time. On the other hand, we've all known people who do everything right but die young. Even if you do stumble upon the healthiest diet (I won't argue it is healthiest, but I like low carb for weight-loss purposes), you're still going to die when God has appointed it. Robert Atkins (1930–2003), the founder of the low-carb Atkins diet, slipped on ice in New York, went into a coma, and died nine days later from a blood clot in his brain—he was 73.[119] I feel like I need to write this again: I'm not saying the exercise and healthy eating aren't valuable, but forget making them into any kind of a literal immortality project!

Selfish

Literal immortality projects are innately selfish. Of course, there's nothing wrong with taking care of our bodies. After all, our bodies enable our souls to interact with the physical world. But some people waste an immense amount of time and money on trying to live significantly longer, if not forever. To give an extreme example, Ray Kurtzweil spends "about $1.6 million a year of pretax income devoted to nutritional supplements alone!"[120] Similarly, although it's true that bodily exercise is "of some value" (1 Timothy 4:8), people who spend *hours* every day working out are wasting time that could be spent in service to our Lord and others.

Idolatrous

Literal immortality projects are idolatrous. Adherents hope these projects will save them from death. For too many, their hearts are first and foremost about the extension of their earthly existence. It consumes them: "I love me, I love me, my picture's on the shelf. I love me, I love me—oh, how I love myself." However, Moses says in Psalm 90:10, "The years of our life are seventy, or even by reason of strength eighty; yet their span is but toil and trouble; they are soon gone, and we fly away." So let's accept what should be obvious: we're all going to die, and absolutely nothing but the Lord's return will prevent that. In the meantime, let us not ruin the life we have left by worrying about it. Indeed, Philosopher Michel de Montaigne (1533–92) says he pities "several gentlemen who, by the stupidity of their doctors, have made prisoners of themselves, though still young and sound in health...We should conform to the best rules, but not enslave ourselves to them."[121] I've known such people who were obsessed with their health. But as Jesus says in Luke 12:25, "And which of you by being anxious can add a single hour to his span of life?" I'm not saying you shouldn't pay attention to qualified medical expertise, but don't obsess over it and especially don't see it as a sort of pseudo-salvation.[122]

Not long ago, there was a series of "Get Rid of Cable" Direct TV commercials you may have seen. So I've been kidding my friends: "When you don't trust Jesus to give you eternal life, you feel desperate about death. When you feel desperate about death, you trust inventions to give you immortality that won't happen in your lifetime. When you trust inventions to give you immortality that won't happen in your lifetime, you choose to be cryonically frozen. When you choose to be cryonically frozen, liquid nitrogen fractures your brain.

"Don't fracture your brain with liquid nitrogen. Trust Jesus to give you eternal life."[123]

Seriously—trust Jesus to give you eternal life.

3

Symbolic Immortality Projects

M ost people who don't believe that they are going to obtain literal immortality will strive to obtain symbolic immortality. As
philosopher Sam Keen puts it in the foreword to Ernest Becker's *The
Denial of Death*, to cope with mortality, humans try to "transcend
death by participating in something of lasting worth. We achieve
ersatz immortality by sacrificing ourselves to conquer an empire, to
build a temple, to write a book, to establish a family, to accumulate a
fortune, to further progress and prosperity, to create an information
society and a global free market."[1] Since Becker's book, many psychologists have argued that trying to transcend death motivates much of
human behavior. Sheldon Solomon, Jeff Greenberg, and Tom Pyszczynski claim, "The search for symbolic immortality and the expression
of heightened worldview defense represent personal attempts by people to align themselves with something that will survive beyond their
own death: a reputation, a family, a cultural group, a nation, or even
an abstract ideal to be upheld by others for generations."[2]

Edwin Shneidman (1918–2009) was the first professor of thana-
tology (the study of death) at UCLA, chief of the first national suicide prevention program at the National Institute of Mental Health,
founder of the American Association of Suicidology, and author of
many books about death and suicide. In other words, Shneidman
wasn't a philosopher who spent a year on the subject while writing
a book about death—studying death was his occupation; he has

contemplated death for most of his life.[3] So how does Shneidman deal with his own death? In *A Commonsense Book of Death: Reflections at Ninety of a Lifelong Thanatologist*, he writes, "I have a keen investment in my postself, my reputation after I am dead. I take a special pleasure, narcissistic delight, in the thought that these words will live in a future that is not mine, what Melville called 'a posthumous glory to come.' That's not bad." Then Shneidman gets rapturous: "I'll tell you my answer to Romeo's question 'What's in a name?' Plenty: Investment in self. Pride. Identity. A lien, in some kind of mystical way, on a future. Self-worth. Fulfillment (antidote to emptiness and nothingness and despair)." But there's more: "I now have deposits in two banks: the gene bank and the library. Apropos the first, the object of which I am *most proud* on my son's military uniform is not the eagles on his shoulders nor the four rows of ribbons on his chest, but the blue tag on his right breast pocked with my name on it. That is one of the ways we attempt to tame death."[4] Wow, right? "Son, you've excelled in the military, you're a decorated colonel, but what really makes me proud is that my name is on your jacket!" But if that's all you have, if you can't have literal immortality, go with symbolic immortality through accomplishment and the gene pool. Later Shneidman enthuses, "A positive postself is a most worthy goal of life. To live beyond one's own breath. To be lauded in the obituary pages of *The New York Times*. To have a future in the world yet to come; to have a gossamer extension beyond the date of one's death. To escape oblivionation; to survive ones' self is a lofty and reasonable aspiration."[5]

Many atheists think similarly. Pro-euthanasia advocate Arthur Koestler (1905–83) writes, "If the word death were absent from our vocabulary, our great works of literature would have remained unwritten, pyramids and cathedrals would not exist, nor works of religious art—and all art is of religious or magic origin. The pathology and creativity of the human mind are two sides of the same medal, coined by the same mintmaster."[6] Similarly, Auschwitz survivor Viktor E. Frankl says, "At any moment, man must decide, for better or worse, what will be the monument of his existence."[7] Consider this dialog between astrophysicist Neil deGrasse Tyson and Larry King on *Larry King Now*:

Neil deGrasse Tyson: If you could live forever, would you?

Larry King: Yes!

Tyson: [Laughs] Okay, we're done with the interview!

King: [Incomprehensible]

Tyson: Yes! No, okay, sure. That's an attractive idea, but the way I look at it is, it is the knowledge that I'm going to die that creates the focus that I bring to being alive. The urgency of accomplishment, the need to express love now, not later. If we live forever, why ever even get out of bed in the morning? Because you always have tomorrow. That's not the kind of life I want to lead.

King: But why? Don't you fear not being around?

Tyson: I fear living a life where I could have accomplished something and didn't. That's what I fear. I don't fear death.

King: You don't fear the unknown?

Tyson: I love the unknown! I loved it. You know what I want on my tombstone? My sister has this in her notes, just in case I can't tell anyone after I die. On my tombstone, a quote from Horace Mann, a great educator: "Be ashamed to die, until you have scored some victory for humanity." That's what I want on my tombstone.[8]

There is it. For Tyson not to fear death, he must believe he's scored some victory for humanity!

Although, as you'll soon see, some atheists say symbolic immortality is useless in the face of a universe going dark. Michael Shermer is unabashed about this kind of "immortality":

> Although immortality has not yet been vouchsafed to us in this universe, we *live on* nonetheless through our genes and our families, our loves and our friends, our work and our engagement with others, our participation in politics, the economy, society, and culture, and our contributions—however modest—to making the

world a little bit better today than it was yesterday. Pro-
topian progress is real and meaningful, and we can all
make a mark, however small.[9]

We can "live on," writes Shermer.[10]

Similarly, atheist Stephen Fry on Richard Dawkins's website says,
"When we do die, we will live on in the work we have done and in the
memories of the other people whose lives we have been a part of."[11]
Atheist Corliss Lamont (1902–95) concludes his book *The Illusion of
Immortality* with "We can make our actions count and endow our days
on earth with a scope and meaning that the finality of death cannot
defeat." Lamont says we can "give our best to the continuing affirmation of life on behalf of the *greater glory of man*."[12] Shneidman writes
of the horror of leaving no legacy: "To cease as though one had never
been, to exit life with no hope of living on in the memory of another,
to be expunged from history's record—that is a fate literally far worse
than death. That's what's in a name, in a postself. Only a feral child or a
deeply autistic person might not be capable of conceptualizing a postself. Everyone else wants to beat death."[13]

This isn't new. In his *Symposium*, Greek philosopher Plato (ca. 425–
ca. 348 BCE) writes that his muse, Diotima, says that if we think of
"the ambition of men," we "will marvel at their senselessness" unless we
"consider how they are stirred by the love of an immortality of fame."
Plato's muse tells him that those seeking symbolic immortality "are
ready to run risks greater far than they would have run for their children, and to spend money and undergo any sort of toil, and even to
die for the sake of leaving behind them a name which shall be eternal."
Later Diotima says, "For I am persuaded that all men do all things for
the sake of the glorious fame of immortal virtue, and the better they
are the more they desire this; for they are ravished with the desires of
the immortal."[14]

The Spanish philosopher, playwright, and novelist Miguel de Unamuno (1864–1936), in his *Tragic Sense of Life*, has words for those who
say they don't desire fame: "The man of letters who shall tell you that he
despises fame is a lying rascal."[15] Later he adds, "Neither is this wish to

leave a name pride, but terror of extinction. We aim at being all because in that we see the only means of escaping from being nothing. We wish to save our memory—at any rate, our memory. How long will it last? At most as long as the human race lasts."[16]

People strive for symbolic immortality in many ways based on what they perceive as their most promising internal and external resources. For example, if you consider yourself smart, then your symbolic immortality projects will involve studies, writing, speaking, invention, and so on. If you're rich, you might become a captain of industry or a land baron or adorn buildings with your name through philanthropy. If you're beautiful, then you might win pageants and become a model or an actor. If you're smart, beautiful, and rich, then you might seek symbolic immortality in all of the above. But if you perceive yourself as having nothing going except that you are of a certain race, then you can make the success or purity of that race your own personal success. And there's more.

Procreation and Adoption

The most common symbolic immortality attempts are through giving birth to or adopting children. Plato's muse, Diotima, instructs him, "Marvel not then at the love which all men have of their offspring; for that universal love and interest is for the sake of immortality."[17] Similarly, philosopher Luc Ferry points out that "by having children, humans assure their 'continuity': becoming in a sense a part of the eternal cycle of nature, of a universe of things that can never die. The proof lies in the fact that our children resemble us physically as well as mentally. They carry forwards, through time, something of us."[18]

Albert Einstein (1875–1955) writes, "Our death is not an end if we can live on in our children and the younger generation. For they are us; our bodies are only wilted leaves on the tree of life."[19] As Nathan A. Heflick puts it in *Psychology Today*, "So why do people have children? One reason is to transcend the great specter of death."[20] Humanist Lawrence Rifkin gives it a scientific spin in *Scientific American*: "So is making babies—and having genes survive through the generations—the meaning of life? The answer is yes—from an evolutionary gene's eye view."[21]

Academy Award–winning actor, author, and comedian Sir Peter Ustinov (1921–2004) writes, "Children are the only form of immortality that we can be sure of."[22] In response to *Parade Magazine*'s question "What do you feel is your biggest achievement?" actress Jada Pinkett Smith (wife of actor Will Smith) replies, "Motherhood is the most important job I've had on this planet and it's something that never stops. Will and I have done a hell of a job laying a foundation for Jaden, who's 19, and Willow, who's 16, and I'm very proud of them. I'd say that I made a pretty awesome contribution to this planet. I always thought it would be something else, but it's Willow and Jaden."[23]

I think Plato's mistaken to say that *all* love for offspring is in the interest of one's own immortality, but who can deny that for the overwhelming majority of people, this is a part of it? Of course, most people prefer procreation to adoption because biological offspring don't just carry on your name and influence (whether good or bad); they carry on your genes. But whether their offspring are biological or adopted, parents have a sense of continuance through their children and children's children's children. Philosopher Samuel Scheffler is right that for many, "The coming into existence of people we do not know and love matters more to us than our own survival and the survival of people we do know and love."[24] One only child told me that when she informed her parents that she and her husband had decided not to have children, both of her parents started crying. The need for a sense of continuance at least partly explains why so many parents proclaim they would die for their children.

Thus the family unit isn't *just* about a loving relationship (hopefully, much of the time it is that!); hugely, it is about transcending death. For many, then, "my family" means much more than "the recipients of my love and affection." Rather, "my family" often means "the people through which I gain immortality." Thus for those who seek immortality through their children, killing their children is akin to killing themselves. Kill their children, and you have taken away their immortality. In Greek mythology, Medea kills Jason's children because that is "better than killing Jason himself—it is killing his chance for the immortality that comes through children."[25]

Oxford biologist Richard Dawkins writes, "The genes are the immortals...We, the individual survival machines in the world, can expect to live a few more decades. But the genes in the world have an expectation of life that must be measured not in decades but in thousands and millions of years."[26] Notice that Dawkins says only "thousands and millions of years" because he knows the universe will freeze, completely lightless and lifeless, and our genes then will not be going anywhere or doing anything—ever.

But suppose your genes do go on for millions of years through procreation—what does that really accomplish? Dawkins points out that "sexual reproduction is not replication. Just as a population is contaminated by other populations, so an individual's posterity is contaminated by that of his sexual partner. Your children are only half you, your grandchildren only a quarter you. In a few generations the most you can hope for is a large number of descendants, each of whom bears only a tiny portion of you—a few genes—even if a few do bear your surname as well."[27] Here's the math: the contribution of your genes to your posterity in the following generation averages 12.5 percent, then 6.25, then 3.125, then 1.6 (I'm now rounding), then .78, then .39, then .19, then .09, and so on. By the tenth generation, your gene contribution is a miniscule .05 percent! Another ten generations: .000004 percent. And on you hardly go. There wouldn't be enough of your genes to feed a mosquito! But if that's all you've got, woo-hoo!

Also, as King Solomon asks, what if your children are fools? He writes in Ecclesiastes 2:18-21, "I hated all my toil in which I toil under the sun, seeing that I must leave it to the man who will come after me, and who knows whether he will be wise or a fool? Yet he will be master of all for which I toiled and used my wisdom under the sun. This also is vanity."[28] Indeed, the foolishness of King Rehoboam, Solomon's son, led to the fracturing of the nation of Israel. Would you be happy to "live on" through your descendants if you knew they would be no more than cellblock idiots?

Further, your descendants rarely care. I've enjoyed asking classrooms full of students if they knew the names of their great-great-grandparents, and so far, only one student said he did. I then ask, "Do you care?" *No one cares.* One twentysomething student, however, volunteered that she was glad her great-great-grandparents "got together" or she wouldn't exist. But there are many whose desire for some sense of eternal life leads them to pursue ancestor veneration or to do genealogy research (I probably haven't had a student into those yet), and we'll talk about them shortly.[29]

There's a sad problem related to this. So many mothers base much, if not all, of their existence on their children. Many a mother's world revolves around her kids (of course, the more kids you have, the more this happens). But what happens when her kids leave the nest? If her immortality project was about raising children, then her project has come to an end, and what does she do? Ernest Becker writes about this:

> I saw that often menopausal women in psychiatric hospitals were there because their lives were no longer useful. In some cases their role as wives had failed because of late divorce; in others this circumstance combined with the expiration of their role as mothers because their children had grown up and married, and they were now alone with nothing meaningful to do. As they had never learned any social role, trade, or skill outside of their work in the family, when the family no longer needed them they were literally useless.[30]

I've seen this many times, and it saddens Jean E. and me. How much worse divorce makes this. Malachi 2:16 (NIV) tells us, "'The man who hates and divorces his wife,' says the Lord, the God of Israel, 'does violence to the one he should protect,' says the Lord Almighty." Indeed, divorce devastates, and anyone who bases their value on their children, even if married, will be disappointed when those children no longer need them. Oh, the need to have an identity of service to Jesus! No one and nothing can ever take that away from you, and it's eternally valuable. We'll talk more about this in chapter 7.

But even if you have lots of children and grandchildren, when you die, *you're* still dead. Your consciousness of this world ceases, and whether your descendants survive or not—or would even give a rat's hiney about you—is not in your control. Immortality through procreation fails because, as Ferry points out, "this way of accessing eternity really only benefits the species" because the individual still dies. Thus the individual "fails to rise above the condition of the rest of brute creation." Ferry continues, "To put it plainly: however many children I have, it will not prevent me from dying."[31] And ultimately, worms are going to eat all your children's and your children's children's bodies.

But in Jesus, you can have eternal life and be renowned for your faithfulness to Him!

Ancestor Worship/Veneration and Genealogy Research

Practiced throughout much of the world, ancestor veneration is a popular immortality project.[32] After all, if your religion requires that you must venerate your ancestors, then your children, your children's children, and so on will have to venerate you! Of late, there is a Western version of ancestor veneration: genealogy research.[33] What drives genealogy or family history research, at least in part, is the sense that if ancestors are remembered, then they symbolically live on. And surely the researcher believes subsequent generations will remember the person who, as *Roots* author Alex Haley puts it, is the "family historian."[34]

There's nothing wrong with studying a family tree to quench your curiosity about from whence you came (I'm curious); but some develop ancestry charts to place themselves on an immortality timeline. Many, of course, hope that their offspring will look back and remember them. Ah, to be remembered forever as the first family historian! In an online forum, one genealogy researcher writes, "People come into this world and struggle for their whole lives...then they die and most are forgotten. Genealogy is my attempt to make sure that doesn't happen *in my family*."[35] In *Legacy News*, Lorine McGinnis Schulze states, "I do genealogy because I want my children and grandchildren to know and recognize the individuals over the centuries whose lives helped make us who we are today." Schulze continues, "They also *deserve* to be remembered, and to *continue* to be part of our lives. Our children and grandchildren need to hear about those ancestors. They need to speak of them to their children, and to carry on the stories they hear *from me.*"[36] This is a type of symbolic immortality that's within everyone's reach— everyone who has children, that is. Thus there's a need to have some- one to at least carry on your name, if not your genes.

Of course, there's a dark side to this. As Stephen Cave points out, the preservation of our family lines or communities "might sound like innocent values, but they are intimately linked with the struggle to preserve our legacy at the expense of others. Indeed, raising one's own group to the status of 'chosen' or somehow superior to others is a sure way of strengthening that group's myth of immortality—whether that group is an aristocratic family or a billion-strong nation."[37]

The really dark side of these symbolic immortality projects is that they motivated some of the worst horrors in human history. Consider one of the prophets of German nationalism, Johann Gottlieb Fichte (1762–1814), who wrote that for the good German, immortality lay in "the hope of eternal continuance of the people without admixture of, or corruption by, any alien element." Of course, this thinking led to Germany's Third Reich, the deaths of millions of those from "impure" races, and the deaths of more than 50 million in the Second World War. But it's much more than this. Consider how many wars have been at least *partly*—usually completely—about "my country" thriving at the expense of "your country."[38] *My* culture, *my* tribe, must continue for *me* to have immortality, and the better my culture or tribe thrives, the more my symbolic immortality is assured. Our wanting our kids to inherit our stuff isn't simply that we want to make them comfortable, it's often so they will remember us. As Yalom put it, "A last will and tes- tament is one's final effort to lunge into the future."[39]

Although the most common way to obtain symbolic immortal- ity is through having children, there are many other methods. Cave approvingly quotes psychologist Roy Baumeister: "The most effec- tive solution to this threat [of death] is to place one's life in some context that will outlast the self. If one's efforts are devoted to goals and values that project many generations into the future, then death does not undermine them."[40] As philosopher Luc Ferry puts it, "The second strategy" for immortality is more "elaborate." It consists of "performing heroic and glorious deeds to become the subject of an epic narrative, the written trace having as its principal virtue the conquest of transitory time."[41]

Atheist Daniel Dennett thinks legacy helps one face death. In somber tones, Dennett muses to Richard Dawkins, "A dear professor of mine just died, a few days ago, and I've been thinking quite a bit about it...The idea that his memory lives on with his children, with his friends, his colleagues, and, of course, he has his work, or, he had his work, which will live on, not everybody gets that kind of legacy...Yeah, we suffer but, uh..." At that, Dennett sounds forlorn, so Dawkins cuts in: "You're right, it is a consolation to have a few books behind one, or musical compositions, or I suppose a great family life, or there are plenty of things of that sort."[42] In other words, symbolic immortality consoles Dawkins.

Creation

Right up there with striving for immortality through having children is striving for immortality through creating something lasting. Many children have been neglected or even abandoned by parents in such pursuits. People are desperate to create something of lasting worth as a means of symbolic immortality, such as writing a book, inventing a vaccine or an artificial heart, building a temple, painting a masterpiece, and so on. Miguel de Unamuno is characteristically blunt: "If the man who tells you that he writes, paints, sculptures, or sings for his own amusement, gives his work to the public, he lies; he lies if he puts his name to his writing, painting, statue, or song. He wishes, at the least, to leave behind a shadow of his spirit, something that may survive him."[43]

Psychoanalyst Otto Rank (1884–1939) writes, "The creative impulse in the artist, springing from his tendency to immortalize himself, is so powerful that he is always seeking to protect himself against transient experience, which eats up his ego."[44] Michelangelo (1475–1564) says, "No thought is born in me that has not 'death' engraved upon it."[45] Similarly, one of Michelangelo's contemporaries, sculptor Benvenuto Cellini (1500–1571), writes, "Before I die I will leave such a witness to the world of what I can do as I shall make a score of mortals marvel."[46]

What drove Sigmund Freud? Irvin D. Yalom writes that "the core of Freud's consuming determination was his unquenchable passion to obtain greatness."[47]

The most astounding man-made ode to self that Jean E. and I have ever seen is the French king Louis XIV's Palace of Versailles. It's the world's largest palace. The palace is 721,206 square feet, and its grounds cover more than 87,728,720 square feet, or 2,014 acres, which include 230 acres of gardens decorated by lavish fountains and canals (by comparison, the White House is a paltry 55,000 square feet on 18 acres of land). The salons are many, and gold leaf abounds. Just the famous Hall of Mirrors took 11 years to build and is more than 8,000 square feet and 40 feet high. The Hall of Mirror's ceilings lavishly depict the glorious history of Louis XIV. What a symbolic immortality project! And indeed, that's what Louis XIV had in mind: "In my heart I prefer fame above all else, *even life itself*...Love of glory has the same subtleties as the most tender passions...In exercising *a totally divine function* here on earth, we must appear incapable of turmoils which could debase it."[48] In an address to the Academie Royale, Louis XIV was unabashed: "I entrust to you the most precious thing on earth, my fame."[49] In addition to wanting everyone in the world to know of his greatness while he was alive, Louis XIV had secured an amazing symbolic immortality.

Of course, most creations aren't so glorious as the Sistine Chapel or the Palace of Versailles, but the point is clear: create something that transcends your death—paint a masterpiece, cure cancer, build a skyscraper, put a man on Mars. You could have a successful blog or YouTube channel. Or you could write a book. Author Samuel Johnson (1709–84), who "was arguably the most distinguished man of letters in English history," writes, "No place affords a more striking conviction of the vanity of human hopes than a public library."[50] And no, the irony of my writing this book isn't lost on me, but I strive to remember the Audience of One. I'm not saying that symbolic immortality is the only motive for these things—people are more complex than that (again, I strive to remember the only One whose opinion really matters; 1 Corinthians 4:5)—but this sense of doing something of worth that will transcend your personal date with death can certainly play a large part.

We've already seen that atheists Dennett and Dawkins take comfort about their own mortality in creating things that they consider are of lasting worth, and so did atheist Stephen Hawking. In an interview with the *Guardian*, Hawking says the "belief that heaven or an afterlife awaits us is a 'fairy story' for people afraid of death."[51] But Hawking tells *Vanity Fair*, "I never expected to reach 75, so I feel very fortunate to be able to reflect on my legacy...I think my greatest achievement will be my discovery that black holes are not entirely black."[52] You get the point.

Of course, if you're rich enough, you can always buy yourself some immortality by putting your name on a building at a university, or on a hospital, or on a center for the performing arts. Yalom talks about "leaving one's name on buildings, institutes, foundations" in glowing terms.[53] But even this is fleeting. Political journalist Michael Kinsley points out that

> when New York's Lincoln Center for the Performing Arts opened in 1962, its auditorium for orchestra concerts was called, simply, Philharmonic Hall. A few years later, dissatisfied with the acoustics, officials solicited a large gift from Avery Fisher to redo the place and, in return, agreed to change the name to Avery Fisher Hall. Who's Avery Fisher? That's exactly the point. He owned a speaker-manufacturing company, but almost no one knows that. What they know is that the concert hall is called Avery Fisher Hall. But in 2015, Lincoln Center announced that it was, once again, redoing the hall to improve the acoustics and henceforth it would be named David Geffen Hall, after the media mogul who bought the naming rights. The family of Avery Fisher sold them back for $15 million. So much for immortality.[54]

I suspect Avery Fisher would have been disappointed to know his kids would rather buy more stuff than have their dad's name on a building.

Heroism

Heroism is another way to obtain symbolic immortality. The heroic escapades spun in Homer's *Iliad* inspired Alexander the Great (356–323 BCE), who was said to have slept with a dagger and a copy of the *Iliad* under his pillow.[55] The *Iliad* is jam-packed with heroics. In one Homeric dialog, we find "Ah, my friend, if the two of us could escape from this war, and be both immortal and ageless for eternity, then neither would I myself be among the foremost fighters nor would I send you out into battle that wins men honor." But since the "death-spirits around us are myriad, something no mortal can flee or avoid—let's go on, to win ourselves glory, or yield it to others."[56] Achilles says there are two ways he might die: "If I stay here, and fight around the Trojan's city I'll lose my homecoming but gain imperishable renown. On the other hand, if I return to my own dear country, my fine renown will have perished, but my life will long endure."[57] Achilles chooses imperishable renown rather than a longer life at home without renown.[58]

The abolitionist and martyr John Brown (1800–1859) assessed his own coming execution: "I am worth inconceivably more to hang than for any other purpose." Indeed, Ernest Becker writes that a fellow who may "throw himself on a grenade to save his comrades" must "feel and believe what he is doing is truly heroic, timeless, and supremely meaningful" and says this striving for heroics in "passionate people" is "a screaming for glory as uncritical and reflexive as the howling of a dog."[59] By the way, jumping on a grenade is the only guaranteed way of being awarded the Congressional Medal of Honor. A former Marine, in telling about a Marine who jumped on a grenade and survived, writes, "*Anyone who has ever served* in the armed forces has at times fantasized about performing a heroic deed and receiving the Medal...The Medal is a symbol of the nation's gratitude toward those who have risked, or have given, all for the American ideal."[60] But heroics may be less obvious. Becker writes that for most people—for the more "passive masses"—heroism is "disguised as they humbly and complainingly follow out the roles that society provides for their heroics and try to earn their promotions within the system," which allows them to "stick out, but ever so little and so safely."[61] You know what else is heroic? Being a famous atheist and proclaiming to a world terrified by death that you can stare at the jaws of death unafraid.[62]

But it's not easy to find a drowning child to save, so some people do extremely dangerous things to broadcast their heroism. One study reported that more than 250 people have been killed while taking selfies in dangerous situations.[63] This is known as "dying for the 'gram" (short for Instagram). Many may have seen the photo on social media of the fellow who backflipped on the edge of a skyscraper, only to miss the ledge and fall to his death. Then there's the pregnant mother of a three-year-old who shot her boyfriend, who was holding a book in front of his chest, with a 50-caliber pistol. Before she did it, she tweeted they were going to "Shoot One of the Most Dangerous Videos Ever...HIS Idea Not MINE." But the book wasn't thick enough, so he died at the scene. She said they performed the stunt to have a famous YouTube channel.[64] I could relate many more of these look-at-me stories, but you get the point.

Activism

Activism is another way to transcend our fear of mortality. Saving the environment, protecting the downtrodden, and fighting discrimination are all good things in themselves (obviously there's also a lot of activism for evil causes like abortion), but if people see their participation in these causes as a means of accomplishing something supremely meaningful, like saving the planet, then they will see their activism as transcending their deaths. The energy available for such immortality is virtually limitless. In "Activism as a Heroic Quest for Symbolic Immortality," Julia Elad-Strenger writes in the *Journal of Social and Political Psychology*, "According to the existential point of view, personal identity concerns and group identity concerns are intertwined: To gain a sense of symbolic immortality most effectively, individuals must pursue the satisfaction of their need for self-distinction within the context of their cultural meaning system [how your culture finds meaning in life]."[65] This works, says Elad-Strenger, because "leaving a personal mark on one's meaning system by acting to advance and protect its values and goals allows the individual to stand out as heroic and unique, and at the same time preserve the anxiety-buffering function of the meaning system that satisfies his or her need for inclusion."[66] It's no surprise, then, that parents who have lost a child may crusade for legal changes. Thus there is now the Amber alert for missing children and Megan's law, which mandates sex offender registration. This provides symbolic immortality for the child and the activist parent.

Elad-Strenger points out that "numerous" studies have "found that death reminders and threats to one's group or the validity of its worldview increase support for violence against worldview-threatening others, including support for terrorist violence."[67] If I can't live on, at least the culture to which I have contributed can, and anything that hinders that must be destroyed, or it will destroy my legacy. Now, I'm not saying that striving for immortality is the only thing motivating the activist—often their causes are worth striving for—but seeking immortality through activism will often be a motivating factor.

Trying to obtain symbolic immortality through activism explains why many people aren't just concerned about global warming—they're absolutely militant (I'm *not* getting into the merits of global warming activism, only some possible motives). If saving the planet becomes your symbolic immortality project, then those who ignore or reject your project threaten your symbolic immortality. This is doubly true because most people have children, and as we've seen, having children is the most popular symbolic immortality project. Thus if your children's children's children's children are all underwater, then when you die, you've failed at protecting the planet, and you've failed at living on through your children. You're dead-dead. Is this effort really an altruistic love for people you'll never meet? Protecting strangers is *always* an honorable thing to do—think of the good Samaritan—but protecting strangers through political activism may also, and maybe sometimes only, be about loving yourself.

Making a Difference

Activism on a smaller scale is just making a difference in the lives of those around you. In other words, helping them through their difficulties means that you are leaving a legacy even if you never hold a bullhorn or CNN never interviews you. The fear of death causes people to strive for a sense of symbolic immortality, and one way to do this is to make a difference in the lives of others. In other words, as you help others, you're changing their world, and that will impact those they influence. This underlies the plot of *A Christmas Carol* by Charles Dickens. It was only when the selfish Scrooge, led by the Ghost of the Future, "crept towards" his grave, "trembling as he went; and following the finger, read upon the stone of the neglected grave his own name, EBENEZER SCROOGE." In response, Scrooge cries, "Hear me! I'm not the man I was. I will not be the man I must have been," and from then on Scrooge is a changed man and helps others.[68] Why? Because Scrooge didn't want his legacy, his postmortem existence, to be no more than a neglected gravestone.

Irvin D. Yalom writes about how making a difference can counter a person's anxiety about death:

> Of all the ideas that have emerged from my years of practice to counter a person's death anxiety and distress at the transience of life, I have found the idea of *rippling* singularly powerful. Rippling refers to the fact that each of us creates—often without our conscious intent or knowledge—concentric circles of influence that may affect others for years, even for generations. That is, the effect we have on other people is in turn passed on to others, much as the ripples in a pond go on and on until they're no longer visible but continuing at a nano level. The idea that we can leave something of ourselves, even beyond our knowing, offers a potent answer to those who claim that meaninglessness inevitably flows from one's finiteness and transiency.[69]

But Yalom doesn't stop there. Once you die and are ultimately decomposed, you can look forward to "rejoining nature through one's scattered molecules, which may serve as building blocks for future life."[70]

Of course, you'll be indistinguishable from pond scum, but at least you're something!

Sociologist and philosopher Zygmunt Bauman writes in glowing terms about making a difference as a sort of immortality: "I should act as if the alleviation of suffering of every being depended upon my action. Only when dedicated to such action, my *life* counts; its termination, its being-no-more, my *death*, is no more a senseless, absurd, unjustifiable occurrence: not that sinking into the emptiness of nonexistence it once was—the vanishing which changes nothing in the world."[71] So far, this doesn't sound so bad, but it often takes a dark turn: "Through making *myself* for-the-other, *I make myself for myself*, *I* pour meaning into *my* being-in-the-world, *I* refuse the world the license to disdain and dismiss *my* presence; *I* force the world to note, and to dread in advance *my* passing away, and to bewail it when it comes."[72] Yikes! "I'm helping you so that you'll need me, so that you'll revere me, and so that you'll dread my dying!" Codependent evermore! I don't want that person's help, do you?

Psychiatrist R.D. Laing is right: "Who is not engaged in trying to impress, to leave a mark, to engrave his image on others and the world—graven images held more dear than life itself." Our trying to gain a sense of immortality through leaving a "mark" on others results in no more than "graven images." Laing continues, "We wish to die leaving our imprints burned into the hearts of others. What would life be if there were no one left to remember us, to think of us when we are absent, to keep us alive when we are dead?" But Laing acknowledges that this fails: "And when we are dead, suddenly or gradually, our presence, scattered in ten or ten thousand hearts, will fade and disappear. How many candles in how many hearts? Of such stuff is our hope and despair."[73]

But, dear Christian, when we serve others not for worldly legacy but out of love, we can take comfort in Revelation 14:13: "And I heard a voice from heaven saying, 'Write this: Blessed are the dead who die in the Lord from now on.' 'Blessed indeed,' says the Spirit, 'that they may rest from their labors, for their deeds follow them!'" The service you did here, no matter how small, will be remembered in heaven!

Correct Belief

Thinking you have correct beliefs can also be a symbolic immortality project—even when one's beliefs are incorrect![74] Christians, of course, believe that a person must have a minimal amount of correct beliefs about the gospel to obtain literal immortality through Jesus, but here we're only talking about how people cling to what they think are "correct" beliefs to obtain symbolic immortality. As Ernest Becker puts it, "Each person nourishes his immortality in the ideology of self-perpetuation to which he gives his allegiance; this gives his life the only abiding significance it can have. No wonder men go into a rage over fine points of belief: if your adversary wins the argument about truth, *you die.* Your immortality system has been shown to be fallible."[75] I don't think you will find this surprising because most of us have argued with people whose lives seemed to depend on their being right—even on small points. Once people give up true immortality, then whatever god they trust for their secular salvation must be correct or they will not even have that paltry symbolic immortality.

To stand out, some people seek special insight into Scripture—such as double meanings—that no one else sees even after they attempt to explain it (I've been on the receiving end of this). Others see themselves as correcting this or that doctrine of historic Christianity. To get attention, some war over peripheral doctrines (of course, if you tell them the doctrine over which they war is peripheral, they'll find a way to promote its significance to a near essential). Some go so far as to publicly denounce this or that pastor, teacher, theologian, church, or Christian institution. The more famous the person or institution, the more attention the denouncer can garner for themselves. Now of course, sometimes a Christian leader or institution needs correction, but often these rebukes sound like gleeful grandstanding. James in 3:13-14 warns about this: "Who is wise and understanding among you? By his good conduct let him show his works in the *meekness of wisdom.* But if you have bitter jealousy and selfish ambition in your hearts, do not boast and be false to the truth."

Haven't we all seen criticism that appears to spring from jealousy?

Building your immortality project on what one considers to be correct belief explains a lot of human evil. As Solomon, Greenberg, and Pyszczynski put it, "Suddenly, we had a way to understand *why* we so desperately crave self-esteem, and *why* we fear, loathe, and sometimes seek to obliterate people who are different from ourselves."[76] They discovered that "subtle, and even subliminal, reminders of death...amplify our disdain toward people who do not share our beliefs even to the point of taking solace in their demise."[77] Indeed, if you're building your symbolic immortality on being right about this or that point of belief, then that fosters jealousy and selfish ambition, and as James warns, "Where jealousy and selfish ambition exist, there will be disorder and every vile practice" (3:16). But if we see that our belief in Jesus gives us true immortality—actual eternal life—then that perspective enables us to possess the meekness of wisdom and not worry about whether someone is more famous than we are.

We've just seen symbolic immortality projects that actually *might* have intrinsic value. Making something helpful (creation), saving a drowning child (heroism), working to make the world a better place (activism), helping those around you (making a difference), and helping people see the truth (correct belief) *might* all be inherently valuable.[78] In what follows, we'll focus on symbolic immortality projects that aren't inherently valuable.

Celebrity

In his book *Illusions of Immortality: A Psychology of Fame and Celebrity*, David Giles talks about the "Christian image of eternal salvation" and says that "the decline of religious faith in the West is in sharp contrast with the meteoric rise of celebrity culture."[79] Exactly! If you don't believe there is a God who can give you true immortality, then you'll try to live on in some other way. Thus many fantasize about becoming a celebrity to give themselves symbolic immortality.[80] Celebrities realize that people will talk about them for some time—depending on their success, maybe a long time after they're gone (think Babe Ruth; there's even a candy bar named after him). Stardom isn't inherently valuable because there isn't anything *inherently* valuable about how well someone catches, throws, hits, or kicks a ball. Now, I'm not saying there's anything wrong with playing or watching sports—sometimes I do—I'm only saying that these things aren't inherently valuable. Similarly, acting or singing well isn't inherently valuable. This being said, celebs may use their celebrity to further the kingdom of God, and that is eternally valuable.

In Irene Kara's song "Fame," she says that through fame, she will "live forever"—that she is going to be so wonderful, so famous, and so desirable, people "will see me and cry" (presumably because they would want to be her or be with her or have her). The song's refrain calls for people to remember her name. In class, I show a photo of a crowd of girls, cell phone cameras ready, screaming and crying at a Justine Bieber concert. One beautiful redhead at the front of the barricade has a large "JB" written on her face, and the back of her cell phone says "I ♥ Justin." She sobs, mouth agape. What a worldly high! Hedy Lamarr (1914–2000) was a movie star and inductee into the National Inventor's Hall of Fame (she invented frequency hopping, which your cell phone, Wi-Fi, and GPS use) and was promoted by cofounder of MGM studios, Louis B. Mayer, as "the most beautiful woman in the world." Lamarr said, "To be a star is to own the world and all the people in it. After a taste of stardom, everything else is poverty."[81] Similarly, the singer Morrissey said, "I always had a religious obsession with fame. I always thought being famous was *the only thing worth doing in human life*, and anything else was just perfunctory."[82]

As I said above, one can use celebrity for godly purposes, but being a star isn't *inherently* valuable. After all, when it comes to being a movie or TV star, you're just really good at acting like someone else. But many stars disagree. Consider Alec Baldwin at the sixty-ninth Annual Primetime Emmy Awards (2018). In his acceptance speech for winning Outstanding Supporting Actor in a Comedy Series, he says, "I *always remember* when someone told me, that is when you die, you don't remember a bill that Congress passed, or a decision the Supreme Court made, or an address made by the president." Instead, says Baldwin, "you remember a song, you remember a line from a movie, you remember a play, you remember a book, a painting, a poem. What we do is important, and for all of you out there in motion pictures and television, don't stop doing what you're doing. The audience is counting on you." Notice that for Baldwin, portraying a congressman, a Supreme Court justice, or a president *might* be more valuable to the dying than actually doing those things!

Of course, some people aren't particularly skilled at anything, but they find fame anyway. In 2007, Kim Kardashian came to fame because a tape of her having sex with her boyfriend was leaked to the public (how did it ever get "leaked" to anyone other than her boyfriend?). Since then, she has maintained her celebrity through a variety of things, including a reality TV show. In 2014, Kardashian posed for a nude photo of her substantial derriere that was said to "break the internet." One day after her break-the-internet photo appeared, *Paper*'s website saw 6.6 million page views. The next day, the site generated nearly 15.9 million page views and reached more than 11 million unique visitors.[83] As of this writing, Kardashian has more than 59 million Twitter followers and 129 million followers on Instagram. Now, I'm not saying that Kardashian doesn't have any real talents; I'm only saying she isn't widely known for any particular talent. She's known for being Kim Kardashian.

Millions of people wish they were famous like Kim Kardashian. Leo Braudy, in *The Frenzy of Renown: Fame and Its History*, puts this in perspective: "This immediate and self-centered fame has become the goal for many who want their characters (or their personalities) appreciated more than their achievements, whose self-centeredness runs ahead of any discernible talent. Stoked on a diet of the names and faces of others, I wonder why I shouldn't be famous too."[84]

Fandom

Being a fan can also help you transcend your death. Even though you die, what you're a fan of goes on. As a fan, you're a part of something larger than yourself. Philosopher and spiritual formation professor Dallas Willard (1935–2013), in his book *Renovation of the Heart*, is insightful: "Fanaticism—in art, politics, sports, or religion, to name some of the main kinds—is the result of inherently meaningless lives becoming obsessed with performance and then trying to take all of their existence into it. Being a fan…is treated as something deep and important."[85] Indeed, not just important but transcendent. Although there is nothing wrong with enjoying sports, for some it becomes much more than that. That's why, especially when it comes to sports, the more one suffers, the more one is really, truly a fan—not a "fair-weather fan" (like me) but a true believer. Thus fans brag about sitting in rain or snow, hot or cold, hanging in there and hoping that one day, *their* team will win. Of course, with rare exception, their team has no idea who they are, but win or lose, as true fans, if their team goes on, so do they.

"Just Spell My Name Right"

It was probably P.T. Barnum (1810–91), the ultimate promoter of all things Barnum, who was first to say, "I don't care what the newspapers say about me as long as they spell my name right."[86] Indeed, countless others look for that kind of symbolic immortality in often bizarre ways. Consider the *Guinness Book of World Records*, which "awards" people for being the world's best at something. There's the man with the longest fingernails on one hand (a combined length of 358.1 inches—ick). Of course, that makes his left hand not useful for anything other than getting attention, but "his dedication has *paid off* since he is officially recognised by Guinness World Records as the person with the longest fingernails on a single hand ever."[87] Wow, his not cutting his nails on his left hand since 1952 has *paid off*? Then there's the fellow who ate the most Big Macs in a lifetime (28,788 by August 24, 2016),[88] the record holders for the most milkshake dispensed through the nose (1.82 ounces—gross), the largest collection of garden gnomes (2,010—oh, but why?), the largest collection of toothpaste tubes (2,037—again, why?), the largest bubblegum bubble (20 inches—okay, that's kind of cool, but I'd want to pop it), the most toilet seats broken by one's head in one minute (46—what originally came into his mind that made him think he'd have a talent for this?), most apples held in the mouth and cut by chainsaw in one minute (8—yikes!), and so on.[89] See the desperation in trying to make a name for yourself?

Or you can get negative attention through a myriad of things that horrify people. Some get attention from ever more bizarre piercings, tattoos, and surgeries (like the people who have their tongues surgically divided to look like a serpent's tongue). Other psychological issues aside, you can get *a lot* of attention by telling everyone you're transgender. Or you can get even more attention by telling everyone you're trans-species, like the woman who says she's really a cat and crawls around on all fours. People need to be noticed, and at the very least, they need to believe they are having an effect on those with whom they come into contact. As William James puts it, "No more fiendish punishment could be devised, were such a thing physically possible, than that one should be turned loose in society and remain absolutely unnoticed by all the members thereof."[90] Everyone needs to feel, if nothing else, that they are affecting their culture. In so doing, they will know that as culture goes on after they are dead, it will have been shaped by them. This kind of fame reminds me of the Steve Martin comedy *The Jerk* (1979), where Martin's character, gas station attendant Nathan Johnson, rushes up to the phone book delivery man and grabs a book out of the man's hands. He rips through the pages to find his own name. When he does, he triumphantly exclaims, "I'm somebody now! Millions of people look at this book every day!"

"Want Me"

Once people no longer have the immortality promised through belief in God, what are they to do? Well, one attempted salvation is seeking love from another by putting hope in a romantic and sexual partner, on a love object—"a cosmology of two." Ernest Becker writes that "the self-glorification that he needed in his innermost nature he now looked for in the love partner. The love partner becomes the divine ideal within which to fulfill one's life. All spiritual and moral needs now become focused in one individual." He continues, "Man reached for a 'thou' when the world-view of the great religious community overseen by God died."[91] If you can't conquer death, well, maybe you can conquer (i.e., seduce) another person.

But how, you might ask, does having sex with someone give you a sense of symbolic immortality? Strictly speaking, there is no such thing as a meaningless sexual encounter. Jason K. Swedene, in his book *The Varieties of Immortality*, is right: "Love, I argue, is a desire to extend a relationship on into the indefinite future. Love is always projecting itself into the future. The rational, decision-making, love vows its continuation into the future and the passionate, erotic love of the flesh seeks to secure a future in the passing on of life."[92] Sex with another person *always*, for good or bad, marks that person emotionally, and sometimes sex makes literal marks on another person in pregnancy or disease. In sex, you change the world, but unless sex is done within the parameters God ordains, it always changes the world for the worse.

But even if the romantic relationship transcends the one-night stand or the shared apartment, even if it ends in marriage, it's not enough. Becker asks, "What is it that we want when we elevate the love partner to the position of God? We want redemption—nothing less. We want to be rid of our faults, of our feeling of nothingness." But Becker is right: "Needless to say, human partners can't do this. The lover does not dispense cosmic heroism; he cannot give absolution in his own name."[93] Becker, in discussing the perspective of psychologist Otto Rank (1884–1939), writes, "Sex is a 'disappointing answer to life's riddle,' and if we pretend that it is an adequate one, we are lying both to ourselves and to our children."

Becker says sex education can become a "kind of wishful thinking, a rationalization, and a pretense: we try to believe that if we give instruction in the mechanics of sex we are explaining the mystery of life. We might say that modern man tries to replace vital awe and wonder with a 'How to do it' manual."[94] Thus many people have made it their life's work—their immortality project—to indoctrinate teens on sexual practice. Here's just one example in *Teen Vogue*: "Anal Sex: What You Need to Know: How to do it the RIGHT way."[95] *Teen Vogue*!

But what if you can't have the person of your dreams for real? Well, having people *want* you is what sexual fantasy is all about. Sexual fantasy can temporarily make you feel good—until you open your eyes and are again confronted by your mortality. Of course, sexual fantasy, if indulged long enough, can make you want to do it "for real," and that's trouble. Adultery is rampant in our *Desperate Housewives* culture. If you can't get the object of your fantasy, then there's prostitution. Or worse, there's rape. In an interview with James Dobson of Focus on the Family, serial rapist/killer Ted Bundy (1946–89) said that he began looking at soft porn, but to satisfy his urges, he needed something "more potent," so he started "craving something that [was] harder." This led him to look at violent pornography "until [he reached] the point where pornography only goes so far."[96] Well, then he raped and killed at least 30 women. He claimed to have since become a Christian. I hope that's true. We'll all see. Now, I'm not saying the fear of death led Bundy to rape and murder. I'm only saying people can resort to sexual fantasy in an attempt to escape their fear of death, and under the wrong circumstances, that can lead to rape and murder.

Victimhood

Then there's victimhood. If you have nothing else, you can stand out from the crowd by playing the victim card. As Miguel de Unamuno puts it, "Man habitually sacrifices his life to his purse, but he sacrifices his purse to his vanity. He boasts even of his weaknesses and his misfortunes, for want of anything better to boast of, and is like a child who, in order to attract attention, struts about with a bandaged finger. And vanity, what is it but eagerness for survival?"[97] If you can't stand out for being wonderful, you can stand out for being a victim.

Of course, there are millions upon millions of people who really have been victimized—and we are told to weep with those who weep, and we are commanded to help them—but it is also true that some wear their victimization, whether real or imagined, like a badge of honor.

Infamy

If you can't get attention and thus somehow obtain a symbolic immortality through doing something good—or at least in some sense, neutral—then you can always do evil. The Temple of Artemis of the Ephesians was 380 feet long, 180 feet wide, and 60 feet tall and took

120 years to build. But in 356 BCE, a man destroyed the temple by setting its wooden roof ablaze. The Ephesians caught that man right away and tortured him on the rack. He confessed he burned the temple so that he would be famous. Well, the Ephesians weren't going to let that happen, so they prescribed what was later to be called a *damnatio memoriae*: anyone who mentioned the arsonist's name would be executed. The arsonist was to be scrubbed from history—a fate the Romans considered worse than death. But we know the arsonist's name: it's Herostratus. Fiction and nonfiction books, plays, poems, films, and even works of art have been created about Herostratus, but none of those things have been created about the architect of the temple. Such is the human lust for fame. Everyone would agree that fame for doing something wonderful surpasses fame, or infamy, for doing something horrible, but doing something wonderful takes skill and hard work—it's easier to become famous for doing evil.

What people will do for infamy is hard to read (this is a warning about what follows), but why they do what they do tells us much about the human quest for immortality. We noted earlier the literal immortality attempts of the first emperor of China, Qin Shih Huang, who buried alive 460 scholars who failed to fulfill their promise of bringing him an elixir of eternal life. Well, China's communist revolutionary Mao Zedong (1893–1976), who became the first chairman of communist China, certainly didn't want to be outdone by the legacy of the first emperor of China! Thus Mao Zedong boasted in a 1958 speech to the party functionaries, "What's so unusual about Emperor Shih Huang of the Chin Dynasty? He had buried alive 460 scholars only, but we have buried alive 46,000 scholars."[98] As I mentioned in my book *Why Does God Allow Evil?*, when I first read this, I thought "buried alive" must be a metaphor for something less horrible—I could hardly believe it!—but then I kept reading. Live burial became a common method of execution in China.

Charles Lindberg became the first person to complete a solo nonstop flight across the Atlantic Ocean on May 20–21, 1927. But Lindberg and his wife were struck with tragedy when their first child was kidnapped and murdered. The kidnapping garnered the attention of the entire nation, and it was called "the crime of the century." But before police captured the actual killer, more than 200 people confessed to the crime.[99] Such is the desire for attention—even bad attention.

Another infamy seeker was the BTK killer (for bind, torture, kill). He murdered at least ten people from 1974 to 1991. But the BTK killer wasn't getting the attention he craved, so in 1978, he sent a letter to Wichita's KAKE-TV, complaining, "How many do I have to kill before I get my name in the paper or some national attention?"[100] Similarly, in 1988, John Miller abducted eight-year-old April Tinsley while she was playing outside her home and subsequently raped and murdered her. Miller taunted police for the next 30 years. One note Miller left tied to a bicycle read, "Hi Honey, I been watching you. I am the same person that kidnapped [and] rape [and] kill April Tinsley. You are my next victim if you don't report this to police [and] I don't see this in the paper tomorrow or on the local news."[101] John Lennon (1940–80) was killed by Mark David Chapman, who said, "I committed this act for attention...to, in a sense, steal John Lennon's fame."[102] In his parole hearing, Chapman said, "That bright light of fame, of infamy, notoriety was there. I couldn't resist it. My self-esteem was shot, and I was looking for an easy way out. It was a bad way out but it was the way I chose, and it was horrible."[103] Recently, German nurse Niels Hoegel admitted "to injecting patients with drugs that can cause heart failure or circulatory collapse so he could then try to revive them and, when successful, shine as a saviour before his medical peers."[104] Police estimate he may have killed as many as 180 patients.

People still ask why the October 1, 2017, Las Vegas shooter killed 58 people and wounded 851 others. In today's (as I'm writing this) *Los Angeles Times*, a front-page article is titled, "Portrait of Vegas Gunman Missing a Motive." The article states that law enforcement had been unable to determine the motive. That's an odd conclusion, since the article quotes the gunman's brother as saying the shooter "would have planned the attack to kill a large amount of people because he would want to be known as having the largest casualty count. Paddock [the shooter] always wanted to be the best and known to everyone."[105] We may not know all his reasons in this lifetime, but he knew he'd be infamous! He went out in an infamous blaze of gory (that's not a typo).

The Parkland school shooter, who murdered 17 people, recorded a video prior to his crime in which he said, "It's gonna be a big event...When you see me on the news you'll all know who I am." Then on the day of the massacre, he said, "Today is the day. The day that it all begins. The day of my massacre shall begin...All the kids in school will run in fear and hide. From the wrath of my power they will know who I am."[106]

The US Secret Service examined the "thinking and behavior of the 83 American attackers and near-lethal approachers" and identified eight major motives for their attacks or planned attacks. What topped the list? Attackers desired "to achieve notoriety or fame."[107] It's better to go out in a blaze of glory than have no glory at all. As people in the West continue to cast off God and the literal immortality offered through Jesus, how many more will kill if they think that's the only immortality available?

Seeking Symbolic Immortality Is Often Evil and Always Futile

Evil

Ernest Becker is largely correct "that man's natural and inevitable urge to deny mortality and achieve a heroic self-image are the root causes of human evil."[108] Or, to put it in Christian terms, seeking to make a name for yourself apart from the Creator is idolatry. Instead of worshipping the only true God, we can attempt to become our own gods. It causes people to ignore relationally and spiritually essential things. For example, workaholics ignore their families, sexaholics hurt their loved ones (not to mention those they cheat with and the cheater's loved ones), and those who despair of a way to obtain symbolic immortality may become alcoholics or addicts to who knows what.

The quest for symbolic immortality drives us to slander, ridicule, and gossip about those we perceive as being equally or more glorious than ourselves. The quest for symbolic immortality drives us to outshine other people. We want others to live in our shadow. This is the quest for human glory. That's where gossip and slander come in. Put down the competition. As the old saying goes, "If you want to know a man's faults, praise him to his peers." Decades ago, when I first heard that, I tried it and I am embarrassed to say that it works (I've repented)! We should never do this intentionally, but the next time you find yourself praising someone, pay attention to the response of that person's peers.

Symbolic immortality projects foster a profound selfishness as people strive to surpass their fellows. After all, if others have more successful children than you, have more successful careers, or are more acclaimed for whatever you value, then their symbolic immortality is more assured than yours. Thus we work ever harder to be and even to humiliate the competition! Steve Kroft of *60 Minutes* interviewed Chobani yogurt founder Hamdi Ulukaya:

> **Hamdi Ulukaya:** I love innovation, I love competing. I hate my competitors.
> **Steve Kroft:** You hate your competitors?
> **Ulukaya:** Of course I do. I wanna beat them up.
> **Kroft:** You want to make Dannon yogurt and Yoplait suffer?
> **Ulukaya:** [I want them to go] back to France. Just kidding aside. What I mean is you cannot be in the world of business when you don't have this consciousness of winning.[109]

Was he kidding?

We see this everywhere—business, sports, academics, child raising, beauty. When your symbolic immortality is on the line, it's not enough to do as well as the next guy—you need to best him. As C.S. Lewis puts it, "We say that people are proud of being rich, or clever, or good-looking, but they are not. They are proud of being richer, or cleverer, or better looking than others. If every one else became equally rich, or clever, or good-looking there would be nothing to be proud about. It is the comparison that makes you proud: the pleasure of being above the rest."[110] As Becker states, "Obviously it is not very convincing about one's worth to be better than a lobster, or even a fox; but outshine 'that fellow sitting over there...'—now that is something that carries the conviction of ultimacy."[111] And when it comes to symbolic immortality, if someone builds a better mousetrap, then the world stops using your mousetrap. If that happens, then you're forgotten except perhaps as a footnote. This leads to tribalism, where *my* family, *my* tribe, *my* country, *my* company must succeed over your family, tribe, country, or company.

Of course, we typically disguise, or at least understate, our lust for greatness because admitting this lust makes us look selfish. But when someone does succeed in beating all competition (at least in their own minds), they find little need to hide. We saw this with King Louis XIV, but it's also illustrated by Ashur-Nasir-Pal, the ruler of ancient Assyria, when he had it inscribed on his palace walls that he is the

> chosen one of the gods Enlil and Ninurta, beloved of the gods Anu and Dagan, destructive weapon of the great gods, strong king, king of the universe, king of Assyria...great king, strong king, king of the universe, king of Assyria...and has no rival among the princes of the four quarters, marvellous shepherd, fearless in battle, unopposable mighty floodtide, king who subdues those insubordinate to him, he who rules all peoples, strong male who treads upon the necks of his foes, trampler of all enemies, he who smashes the forces of the rebellious.[112]

About this, Herbert Schlossberg, in *Idols for Destruction: The Conflict of Christian Faith and American Culture*, writes, "Sometimes we have revealed to us what most people learn to camouflage."[113]

Second, if we do achieve a symbolic immortality—if we become great before men and women—this engenders jealousy, a loss of friendships, and even sometimes physical harm. Indeed, as novelist and political commentator Gore Vidal (1925–2012) puts it, "Whenever a friend succeeds, a little something inside me dies."[114] When someone seeking symbolic immortality succeeds, his or her success highlights what others perceive as their own failures to achieve the same. And this has dire consequences. As Solomon says in Proverbs 27:4, "Wrath is cruel, anger is overwhelming, but who can stand before jealousy?" The jealous King Saul obsessed with trying to kill the innocent but successful David. This is why some kids stomp on others' superior sandcastles. This is why tabloid journalism succeeds—we like our stars taken down a notch...or ten. The Germans call this Schadenfreude, or the enjoyment of another's misfortune. If you want a lot of people to hate you— succeed! Sadly, this is often true in Christian circles. As Paul says in Philippians 1:15, "Some indeed preach Christ from envy and rivalry, but others from good will."

The following appeared in the 1858 *Times* of London:

> There is no vice of which a man can be guilty, no meanness, no shabbiness, no unkindness, which excites so much indignation among his contemporaries, friends, and neighbors, as his success. This is the one unpardonable crime, which reason cannot defend, nor humility mitigate. "When heaven with such parts blest him, have I not reason to detest him?" is a genuine and natural expression of the vulgar human mind. The man who writes as we cannot write, who speaks as we cannot speak, labours as we cannot labour, thrives as we cannot thrive, has accumulated on his own person all the offenses of which man can be guilty. Down with him! Why cumbereth he the ground?[115]

Of course, the Lord forbids envy. Number ten of the Ten Commandments is "You shall not covet...anything that is your neighbor's." Further, in Proverbs 24:17-18, Solomon warns that rejoicing in your neighbor's troubles is also a sin: "Do not rejoice when your enemy falls, and let not your heart be glad when he stumbles, lest the Lord see it and be displeased, and turn away his anger from him." But those seeking symbolic immortality won't be able to keep themselves from being jealous when others succeed or gloating when they fail.

Thus if someone believes you hinder their perceived immortality machine, they can justify anything. After all, if one's immortality is at stake, then lying here or there, cheating now and then, or even killing all makes self-interested sense. If there is no God who will one day judge us, who will give us the crown of life, then everything becomes subservient to our own immortality. Zygmunt Bauman was correct to write, "All too often...the audacious dream of killing death turns into the practice of killing people."[116]

Futile

Symbolic immortality doesn't work. After all, *symbolic* immortality is only symbolic—when you die, you're still dead. Symbolic immortality is a far cry from the real thing. Comedian Woody Allen puts this serious truth in a funny way: "I don't want to achieve immortality through my work; I want to achieve immortality through not dying."[117] In a *Rolling Stone* interview, Allen says, "Someone once asked me if my dream was to live on in the hearts of my people, and I said I would like to live on in my apartment."[118] Allen, who famously obsesses with death, recognizes that *symbolic* immortality leaves much to be desired—like not dying! Homer is dead. Homer is not presently enjoying the fact that people know his name.

The fleeting nature of symbolic immortality is captured by Roman emperor Marcus Aurelius (121–80 BCE): "What is the advantage of having one's own name on the lips of future generations when their overriding concern will be the same as ours: to have their names on the lips of successors...How does that confer any reality on us?"[119] If you do achieve symbolic immortality, the chief concern of those who recognize it will be to outshine you or even diminish you. One famous Christian author wondered out loud as to why so many Christians were so impressed with C.S. Lewis. (Answer: Lewis was a better writer than he, or I, or just about anyone will ever be.) The trouble is that when you're set to achieve symbolic immortality, then you'll also want to knock down your peers—even if they're dead!

Then you have to maintain your symbolic immortality, and that's hard to do! As Bauman puts it, "Success is always an 'until further notice' success; it is never final. It must be repeated over and over again. The effort can ever grind to a halt."[120] Journalist Maureen Orth interviewed Madonna in 1992 and "found a tough, middle-class, ex-Catholic girl who craved to be really, really bad so that she could be noticed even more. I also found a woman who represents, perhaps more than anyone else, one of the truths about fame today. It is not only hard to get famous; it is even harder to stay cutting-edge." Orth points out that "the pursuit and nurturing of fame is a job that can occupy the seeker twenty-four hours a day, seven days a week—and that doesn't count doing actual work. Fame takes endless maintenance, fine-tuning, damage control. It is a never-ending task, and Madonna has tackled it with a steely determination and zeal."[121] But how long can Madonna be famous? How many times can she reinvent herself? We will all see.

Stardom is intoxicating, and when it's gone, the problems begin. By the age of 29, novelist Jack London (1876–1916) had published *The Call of the Wild*, *White Fang*, and *The Sea Wolf*, but psychologist Orville Gilbert Brim, author of *Look at Me! The Fame Motive from Childhood to Death*, writes that afterward, London was "unable to match the success of his earlier works" and was "plagued by alcoholism and rheumatism." Eventually, London "died of an overdose of morphine at age forty."[122] Jack Kerouac (1922–69) became a household name by publishing *On the Road* (1957) but died of alcoholism at age 47. F. Scott Fitzgerald (1896–1940) wrote *This Side of Paradise* in 1920 and *The Great Gatsby* in 1925, but his subsequent work was panned by the critics and didn't sell well. He struggled with alcoholism much of his life and felt like a failure.[123] He died of a heart attack at the age of 44.

Hedy Lamarr was married six times, and as "movie offers began to dwindle, her finances did, too. She was arrested in 1966 for shoplifting at a Los Angeles department store. She had plastic surgery that her son, Anthony Loder, said left her looking like 'a Frankenstein.' She became angry, reclusive and litigious."[124] I've seen pictures of Lamarr toward the end of her life, and "Frankenstein" is too far, but her surgeries were disfiguring. But we all understand her. If you're told you're the most beautiful woman in the world, you don't want to lose that. I wonder if building your fame on your beauty is the cruelest of all, because unless you die young, you will absolutely not be able to keep your beauty. After her disfiguring surgeries, Lamarr largely hid until she died. Of course, it's not just female stars that struggle with losing the limelight.

Chevy Chase was one of the original cast members of *Saturday Night Live* (SNL); starred in such films as *Caddyshack*, *National Lampoon's Vacation*, and *Fletch*; and had made a comeback in the 2009– 15 NBC show *Community*. But when he appeared on SNL's fortieth anniversary show in 2015, "It wasn't pretty," wrote Geoff Edgers in the *Washington Post*. "He was bursting out of his tux, drinking too much and depressed."[125] Since then, Chase has lost weight and stopped drinking, but when he called SNL's executive producer, Lorne Michael, to ask if he could again host SNL, Michaels replied, "No. You're too old." Chevy said, "It's like they're taking it all away from me." After making a racial crack at *Community* star Donald Glover, Glover said, "I just saw Chevy as fighting time...A true artist has to be okay with his reign being over."[126] Do they? Can they? We'll see how Glover fares when his reign is over. Remember Lamarr's line that compared to fame everything else is "poverty"? If so, then how many stars will be okay with poverty?

I considered giving more examples of fading stars—they are legion—but they have enough problems. (And I'm sad for them. Really.) They don't need another person discussing their fading beauty, face-lifts, divorces, and descents into addiction and suicides. No wonder that one study reported that sports, singing, and movie stars died a full 13.2 years younger than the average American! But the news is bleaker for female stars. Whereas male stars died 8.3 years younger than the average population, female stars died an astounding 21.5 years younger than average.[127] That female stars die so young is unsurprising, as few maintain their stardom anywhere near as long as male stars. Consider how few female actresses have careers past age 40.[128]

Further, once the famous are dead, soon dies their fame. Andy Warhol (1928–87) coined the now famous phrase, "In the future, everyone will be world-famous for fifteen minutes." Ironically, at the 2004 Hollywood Oscars ceremony, Allstate Insurance ran an advertisement that began, "Someone once said, 'Everyone will be famous for fifteen minutes.'" Warhol himself had been reduced to a "someone."[129] I often use popular culture to illustrate my teaching, but I've realized that once world-famous fare is now just a footnote to many, if even that. In 1977, I didn't know anyone my age who hadn't seen *Star Wars*. But even though the saga has been rebooted, many younger adults haven't seen the original film—or an Indiana Jones movie—and they don't care!

It's no wonder, then, that death terrifies even the famous. In a touching interview, the then 17-year-old pop star Katy Perry confesses, "I'm really afraid of death actually, too. I'm afraid that I'll be eighty, one day, and everyone I know will be passed on and I'll just be waiting."[130] Perry then makes a soft cry. Similarly, the 71-year-old Arnold Schwarzenegger complains, "I have always been extremely [angry] about the idea of death." He says, "It's such a waste. I know it's inevitable...Your whole life you work, you try to improve yourself, save money, invest wisely, and then all of a sudden—poof. It's over...Death [angers me] more than ever."[131] Comedian and actress Sarah Silverman told Ellen DeGeneres that she was once a "really social kid" and "was the class clown," but suddenly depression hit her, and she "didn't see any reason to be with people." She said she would "watch my friends at school just existing, carefree, you know, and I would be so jealous that they're just so unaware that we're all alone, and *going to die*, and alone behind our eyes." She said that to deal with her depression she's been on a "low dose of Zoloft since 1994 and that's really kept "me from the total paralysis of depression." Nonetheless, she says, "I still have lows. I still am like a ball on my bathroom floor every once in a while."[132]

But there's a much darker, colder, unrelenting problem for all symbolic immortality projects: if you believe there is no God, then—and this isn't open to debate—all the stars in the entire universe will burn out, and the universe will go to absolute zero. As atheist Bertrand Russell (1872–1970) acknowledges, "All the labours of the ages, all the devotion, all the inspiration, all the noonday brightness of human genius, are destined to extinction in the vast death of the solar system, and that the whole temple of Man's achievement must inevitably be buried beneath the debris of a universe in ruins."[133] If there is no God, then what's the point? But even Russell had to find some meaning in life. Russell needed something to hold on to, so he wrote, "Through the greatness of the universe which philosophy contemplates, the mind also is rendered great, and becomes capable of that union with the universe which constitutes its highest good."[134] This is weird because Russell thinks, rightly, that the universe will be dead, so why bother even doing that? Because it's all he's got. As Stephen Cave puts it, "No matter how great our glory, it could only ever be a postponement of oblivion."[135]

Poet W.H. Auden (1907–73), in his 1967 National Medal for Literature acceptance speech, sheds some light on why Russell and others embrace vain hopes:

> To believe in the value of art is to believe that it is possible to make an object, be it an epic or two-line epigram, which will remain permanently on hand in the World. The probabilities of success are against him, but an artist must not attempt anything less...In the meantime, and whatever is going to happen, we must try to live as E.M. Forster recommends that we should: "The people I respect must behave as if they were immortal and as if society were eternal. Both assumptions are false. Both must be accepted as true if we are to go on working and eating and loving, and are able to keep open a few breathing holes for the human spirit."[136]

In other words, if one were to live in unblinking acknowledgment of the stark reality that the universe is going to go beyond-liquid-nitrogen cold, then it would be harder to get up in the morning—if not impossible! Thus in the meantime, they must ignore the inevitable and believe what is obviously false.[137]

Kumbaya, my lifeless, lightless, freezer-burned ruin of a universe!

As if that isn't bad enough, it gets worse—much worse. The ultimate emptiness of these symbolic immortality projects will be exposed when we all stand before the Creator to give an account of ourselves. In 1 Corinthians 4:5, Paul tells us that when the Lord comes, He will bring to light the things hidden in darkness and will disclose the purposes of the heart." In the Creator's opinion, doing a good act for selfish reasons profits nothing. Jesus says in Matthew 6:2, "When you give to the needy, sound no trumpet before you, as the hypocrites do in the synagogues and in the streets, that they may be praised by others. Truly, I say to you, they have received their reward." Many wealthy Christians need to rethink putting their names on buildings. Similarly, Paul says, "If I give away all I have, and if I deliver up my body to be burned, but have not love, I gain nothing" (1 Corinthians 13:3). Thus Paul says you can give everything you have to the poor and die in their service, but if you don't have love—if you do it to make a name for yourself—it's worthless!

In Romans 2 we are told, "He will render to each one according to his works" (verse 6), and "for those who are self-seeking and do not obey the truth, but obey unrighteousness, there will be wrath and fury" (verse 8). But "to those who by patience in well-doing seek for glory and honor and immortality, he will give eternal life" (verse 7). He will give *you* eternal life. Jesus says in John 5:24, "Truly, truly, I say to you, whoever hears my word and believes him who sent me has eternal life. He does not come into judgment, but has passed from death to life."

Trying to live on through doing something wonderful that will be remembered only on earth is like rearranging the deck chairs on the Titanic after it had hit the iceberg. The deck chairs may indeed look nicer than they did before you employed your feng shui, but they're going to be a jumble at the bottom of the ocean, so who cares?

But live a life of loving the Lord and your neighbor as yourself, and your deeds will follow you into eternity.

4

Mortality Mitigation Projects

Since all our literal and symbolic immortality projects—"all our labours," as Bertrand Russell puts it—will be "buried beneath the debris of a universe in ruins," since neither literal nor symbolic immortality projects will keep the universe from becoming so cold that the slightest tap would shatter it into a gazillion pieces, how's an atheist going to cope with his or her impending death?

Parisian philosopher Luc Ferry is one of those who have decided there probably is no God, and he says this is exactly "where philosophy comes in."[1] "Philosophy," as Ferry puts it, is "well and truly a 'doctrine of salvation without god': an attempt to escape our fears without recourse either to belief or to a supreme being, but by exercising our reason and trying to pull through without assistance."[2] In fact, many philosophers conclude that the fear of death is what drives philosophy. As I mentioned in the introduction, Ferry writes, "The quest for a salvation without God is at the heart of every great philosophical system, and that is its essential and ultimate objective."[3] Ferry isn't alone in seeing philosophy as a way to cope with death.

Also in the introduction, I mentioned that Plato, in his *Phaedo*, which is the tale of Socrates's last hours before his death, writes that Socrates said, "Truly then...those who practise philosophy aright are cultivating dying, and for them, least of all men, does being dead hold any terror."[4] And later in the *Phaedo*, Socrates said, "Practicing philosophy in the right way" is "in fact, training to die easily."[5] As you'll soon see, Epicurus (341–270 BCE), the founder of Epicureanism, sought to help people escape the fear of death. One of the greatest representatives of Stoicism, Epictetus (55–135 CE), writes, "Will you realize once for all that it is not death that is the source of *all man's evils*, and of a mean and cowardly spirit, but rather the fear of death? Against this fear then I would have you discipline yourself; to this let all your reasonings, your lectures, and your trainings be directed; and then you will know that only so do men achieve their freedom."[6] Philosopher Michel de Montaigne, in an essay entitled "To Philosophize Is to Learn How to Die," says, "All the wisdom and argument in the world eventually come down to one conclusion; which is to teach us not to be afraid of dying."[7] Similarly, philosopher Arthur Schopenhauer (1788–1860) writes, "Indeed without death men would scarcely philosophise."[8] Thus the Humanist Manifesto II declares, "No deity will save us, we must save ourselves."[9]

But from whence does their secular salvation come? How can the secular person overcome his or her fear of death? As Sheldon Solomon, Jeff Greenberg, and Tom Pyszczynski ask in their book *The Worm at the Core: On the Role of Death in Life*, "How then can we learn to deal with our inevitable mortality in a way that does not provoke personal distress and hatred and killing of others? How can we, in short, learn to live better with death?"[10] Atheists have come up with a host of ways to mitigate the horror of death. What follows are the contortions and circumlocutions that atheists contrive to comfort themselves about their demise.

Immortality Would Be Boring

"The first step to undermining the will to immortality," writes philosopher Stephen Cave, "is to realize that genuinely unending life would most likely be a terrible curse."[11] This notion is ancient. For example, Ferry writes of the goddess Calypso offering Odysseus immortality if he marries her, but he refuses her. Ferry says Odysseus's "refusal is of epochal significance." It is "undoubtedly the most powerful and profound lesson of Greek mythology, which will subsequently be adopted by Greek philosophy for its own purposes"—namely, "a mortal life well lived is worth far more than a wasted immortality."[12] Cave and other philosophers argue that if we thought it through, we'd realize that our death is preferable to our living forever.[13] They argue that you would run out of pleasurable things to do because, given a limitless amount of time, you would have had done all of them countless times. If that's the case, then all you would have to look forward to was doing them all again and again and again. Thus they argue that in time, everything would become tedious.

As Brian Ribeiro puts it in *Ratio*, "To wit, we generally find that our pleasures wear out. At least many of them do. And the fact that so many earthly pleasures are in fact exhausted by us strongly suggests that any earthly pleasure is in principle exhaustible by sufficient repetition."[14] Similarly, in an interview, atheist Lawrence Krauss says, "I certainly don't find the idea of immortality that attractive, by the way." The interviewer then asks, "Why not?" Krauss continues, "Woody Allen said, 'eternity is a long time, especially near the end.' And, uh, the point is there's a big difference between living a long time and living forever…Eternity or an infinite lifespan does not seem to me to be likely or desirable."[15] Science fiction writer Isaac Asimov (1920–92) agrees: "Whatever the tortures of hell, I think the boredom of heaven would be even worse."[16]

Of all the books I have read on mortality mitigation projects, Andrew Stark's offers the most fervent and sustained argument that you wouldn't want to live forever. In fact, he titles part 3 of his book "Immortality Would Be Malignant." "Immortality," writes Stark, would take us to a "deathlike realm of stupefying boredom," where all our precious memories, "the moments of our lives," would "vanish into the past," which he likens to a kind of death.[17] Thus our physical deaths "may be the option that contains the least amount of death."[18] For Stark, "at that most fundamental level, the bundle of ego and anxiety that dwells within me feels consoled about our mortal condition. Not cheered. But consoled. I—you, we, humankind—got the *best deal imaginable*."[19]

Wow, that's quite a comparison—forgetting a cherished event is something akin to physically dying? Stark doesn't give much of an argument for why forgetting is like death other than to make an appeal to our experiences. But I find this bizarre because it's not my experience. I don't experience cherished events that vanish into the past as a kind of death. I suspect that Stark and others experience past events that way precisely because death looms in their consciousness. The fact that I'm going to have many wonderful events in my eternal future renders the wonderful events in my past as wonderful—I don't experience them as a loss because they are long over. For example, my mouth waters when I think about a well-seasoned, medium-rare prime rib end cut (getting an end cut cooked only to medium rare is hard to find), but my fading memory of having that in the past doesn't sadden me, because one of these days, I expect I'm going to have another well-seasoned, medium-rare prime rib end cut (hopefully with a loaded twice-baked potato—I could go on). Over the years, I've had many wonderful times with my brothers and sisters in Christ, but the fact that my memory might fade doesn't trouble me exactly because I expect to have even better times—much better times—with them in the future and for all time.

Now, it's true that there are some one-of-a-kind events, like my honeymoon, but I can experience the best parts of that again (if you know what I mean). There are some things I really shouldn't do anymore, like play racquetball (I'm having knee problems), and I miss that, but I look forward to complete restoration, as I'll talk about in the last chapter. I'm looking forward to having a body superior to any body that any athlete has ever had. In other words, I'm okay with the fact that racquetball is no longer a wise idea for me. If Stark actually believed that he was going to live in a joyful forever, then he wouldn't rue forgetting things in the past. My forgetfulness of a wonderful event isn't like dying, and when Stark writes that our getting to die is the "best deal imaginable," it sounds like we're all shrewd shoppers who scored by getting to die. Also, who says we're going to forget anything? There are people today who vividly remember almost everything that has ever happened to them.[20] Maybe we'll all be like that in the kingdom to come.

This you-wouldn't-want-to-live-forever-anyway isn't just the talk of philosophers. Jorge Luis Borges tells of a Roman soldier who hears there is a "secret river which cleanses men of death."[21] The problem with immortality, according to Borges's story, is that immortality leads to a reality where "there are no moral or intellectual merits. Homer composed the *Odyssey*; if we postulate an infinite period of time with infinite circumstances and changes, the impossible thing *is not to* compose the *Odyssey*, at least once. No one is anyone, one single immortal man is all men. Like Cornelius Agrippa, I am god, I am hero, I am philosopher, I am demon and I am world, which is a tedious way of saying that I do not exist."[22] Really? Given enough time, every one of us would sooner or later compose the *Odyssey*? Notice also how he changes immortality into the equivalent of "I do not exist." So being immortal is the same thing as nonexistence? See the desperation to make immortality undesirable?

Douglas Adams, in *Life, the Universe and Everything*, writes about a fellow who obtained immortality:

> To begin with it was fun; he had a ball, living dangerously, taking risks, cleaning up on high-yield long-term investments, and just generally outliving...everybody. In the end, it was the Sunday afternoons he couldn't cope with, and the terrible listlessness that starts to set in at about 2:55, when you know you've taken all the baths you can usefully take that day, that however hard you stare at any given paragraph in the newspaper you will never actually read it, or use the revolutionary new pruning technique it describes, and that as you stare at the clock the hands will move relentlessly on to four o'clock, and you will enter the long dark teatime of the soul.[23]

There are several reasons this isn't close to heaven, but for now, I'll only mention two. First, notice that this fellow is the only one with immortality. Everyone else dies. That would be sad. Second, notice that, as is typical for atheist arguments, immortality is presented as continuing on forever in this humdrum, finite existence. Watch for this as you keep reading. Atheists rarely talk about whether they would want to live forever in heaven because they don't believe in heaven. So their consolations about mortality not being so bad are because immortality on this earth—as we know it now—isn't that attractive to them. But we're not going to continue forever on this planet as it is now. For the Christian, Jesus is coming back and will make "all things new" (Revelation 21:5), and we'll live forever in the new heavens and new earth.

Novelist Susan Ertz (1894–1985) writes, "Millions long for immortality who don't know what to do with themselves on a rainy Sunday afternoon."[24] That's funny because she was a novelist, and reading on a rainy Sunday afternoon is one of my all-time favorite things. Similarly, novelist Natalie Babbitt (1932–2016) pushed this idea in her book *Tuck Everlasting*, twice adapted as a film and once as a musical. Angus Tuck explains to the young Winnie, "You can't have living without dying. So you can't call it living, what we got. We just *are*, we just *be*, like rocks beside the road."[25] Babbitt says she was inspired to write *Tuck* "when her 4-year-old daughter woke from a nap crying because she was scared of dying."[26] So Babbitt's comfort is "Don't cry, dear; death is a good thing." It would appear that Ertz and Babbitt have forgotten that many people would rather live in utter misery than die. We frequently see this when people choose to endure one chemo and/or radiation treatment after another even though a doctor has advised that those torturous procedures *might* only grant them a few more months.[27]

This I-wouldn't-want-to-live-forever-anyway may be the worst case of sour grapes in the history of created beings! "Oh, I wouldn't want to live forever in paradise anyway! You can just take your eternal life and shove it. My death is a good thing." In my book *Why Does God Allow Evil?*, I explain at length why this is mistaken, but because this is such a foundational atheist argument, I've adapted some of my answers from that book here. The last chapter of this book describes the eternal glory that awaits us.[28]

The sour grapes strategy is largely based on the notion that we would get bored of doing the same things again and again. Cave admits, "Of course, there are some pleasures we enjoy more than once. A good meal or conversation with friends or taking part in a favorite sport or hearing a favorite piece of music—these things seem at least as good the second, third or hundredth time."[29] Yes, that's correct—we can and do enjoy the same things again and again. Nonetheless, Cave then writes, "But a man who eats caviar *every day* will grow sick of it eventually, and we will one day—even if a million years hence—tire of all our friends' jokes." Now that was a clumsy sleight of hand: he went from talking about enjoying things occasionally to eating caviar "every day." Who would do that? Also, because of a vast eternity where the One we call Creator is still creating, if your friends were telling jokes, then I would expect them to come up with new jokes, wouldn't you? Cave continues, "After we have enjoyed them long enough, all luxuries become commonplace and dull. Given *endless repetition*, whatever activities we pursue we would eventually feel like Sisyphus, the ancient Greek king condemned by the gods to spend eternity pushing a boulder up a hill only for it continually to roll back down."[30] That is another sloppy sleight of hand: having a sumptuous meal with friends isn't anything like pushing a boulder up a hill.

Further, humans like repetitive things that change. For example, humans tend to enjoy the changes of seasons, the different days of the week, and the different times of day (for me, afternoons are for napping). I enjoy a varied menu, and although I've had it countless times, I cannot *ever* imagine tiring of a well-seasoned, medium-rare prime rib and a baked potato loaded with cheese, bacon, chives, and lots of butter (are you seeing a theme here?) or a purple-red-orange sunset. Now, it is true that I may not enjoy something wonderful that I've had hundreds of times as much as I enjoy something I've only had once, but although my enjoyment may be diminished, I still enjoy it. Of course, I would tire of prime rib if I had it *every single day*. For crying out loud, I would even tire of king crab if I had it *every single day*, but I wouldn't do that even if I could afford it!

That's why atheist Stephen Fry, speaking on Richard Dawkins's website, attacks a strawman: "If life were eternal, wouldn't it lose much of what gives it shape, structure, meaning and purpose? Think about reading a good book or eating a delicious cake. These may be great pleasures, but one of the things that makes them pleasures is that they end. A book that went on forever and forever and a cake that you never stopped eating would both soon lose their appeal."[31] As I said, comparing eternity to forever eating the same cake or forever reading the same book is a strawman (if you read atheists on the subject, you'll see they do this a lot). Sure, no one would want to eat the *same* cake—nonstop—forever. But if the menu was wide ranging, and the frosted chocolate cake is something you only had from time to time, especially if you couldn't gain weight, who wouldn't want the occasional chocolate cake? That's how we eat now, after all—we vary our menu. As for reading a book that never ended, no, who'd want to do that? After all, good fiction always has a climax and a conclusion, and that conclusion is often an implied happily ever after. Again, we have no reason to believe that the Creator of all things seen and unseen will stop creating, and if that is true, why should we not expect an infinitely changing variety of amazements, foods, pleasures, and stories?

Finally, there *is* a problem about non-Christians finding satisfaction in this life's pleasures, but it's with the non-Christians themselves: they are incapable of finding this world to be ultimately satisfying because this world, without God, isn't ultimately satisfying. Until a person comes to Jesus, he will forever resonate with the Rolling Stone's refrain, "I can't get no satisfaction." As Augustine says, "You have made us for yourself, and our heart is restless until it rests in you."[32] Life without a proper relationship with the Creator will never satisfy. Thus Jesus tells the woman at the well, "Everyone who drinks of this water will be thirsty again, but whoever drinks of the water that I will give him will never be thirsty again. The water that I will give him will become in him a spring of water welling up to eternal life" (John 4:13-14).

Death Is Necessary for Life to Go On

Then there's this cold mortality mitigation consolation—you need to die, you need to get out of the way so that others can live! Without death, as Sheldon Solomon, Jeff Greenberg, and Tom Pyszczynski, put it, "humankind would be unable to adapt to fluctuating environmental conditions. If nobody died, there would be no room for new humans to provide genetic variation, original discoveries, technological innovations, and artistic creations. Human biological and cultural evolution would come to a grinding halt. Each of us must die to ensure 'that future generations may grow,' Lucretius wrote."[33]

Atheist firebrand Christopher Hitchens (1949–2011), author of *God Is Not Great: How Religion Poisons Everything*, apparently agrees. After Hitchens was diagnosed with esophageal cancer, he began work on his last book, *Mortality*, in which he reflects on his impending death. The last chapter consists of "fragmentary jottings left unfinished at the time of his death."[34] Here is his final jotting:

> With infinite life comes an infinite list of relatives. Grandparents never die, nor do great-grandparents, great aunts...and so on, back through the generations, all alive and offering advice. Sons never escape from the shadows of their fathers. Nor do daughters of their mothers. *No one ever comes into his own...*Such is the cost of immortality. No person is whole. No person is free.[35]

In other words, if people lived forever, then later generations would never come into their own. They'd never be their own boss, so to speak. I could see that being an earthly problem—if our ancestors were forever with us giving their advice—but in heaven, there will be a realignment. In heaven, we will not be "under" the authority of our earthly parents, and they won't be under the authority of their parents. Additionally, we won't continue bearing children.

In a Stanford University 2005 commencement address, Apple cofounder Steve Jobs (1955–2011) echoes this sentiment: "No one wants to die. Even people who want to go to heaven don't want to die to get there. And yet death is the destination we all share. No one has ever escaped it. And that is as it should be, because death is very likely the *single best invention of life*. It is life's change agent. It clears out the old to make way for the new."[36] I wonder if six years later, as Jobs was dying, he really believed death was the "single best invention of life"? In her 2016 hit "We Die," poet and songwriter Kate Tempest says, "We die so others can be born."[37] But that's just poetic prattle. Part of sex-leads-to-babies isn't that someone must die before others can be born.[38]

Also, even if it were true that humanity's lifeboat was too full and someone needed to drown in the icy deep for others to survive, would that comfort us? The prospect of an overcrowded earth where millions will die due to the scarcity of resources is only going to make people wish it weren't so. I'm reminded of the old movie *Logan's Run* (1976), where everyone is vaporized at age 30. Those who are to be vaporized are promised that they will be reborn into a new life. Well, Logan 5 (Michael York) and Jessica 6 (Jenny Agutter) don't believe the rebirth promise and certainly don't want to be vaporized, so they escape from the city and learn that it's all a lie. Recently, in *Avengers: Infinity War* (2018), supervillain Thanos (Josh Brolin) threatens to destroy 50 percent of all life because in his mind, it is the only way to spare the universe from overpopulation. Of course, the Avengers do everything in their power to stop him. But why shouldn't half the people die to save the rest? Now of course, Thanos is evil and gets it all wrong—but could somebody make a believable movie where healthy people are willing to die so that others might live? I doubt it.

Ultimately, the consolation that you need to die so others may live is irrelevant today anyway. No one needs to die *today* because there aren't enough resources. If there was no God, then the lifeboat might one day be too full, but presently—and for the foreseeable future—there's plenty of room! So how could this comfort anyone today?

Further, why would it be true, as Solomon, Greenberg, and Pyszczynski write, that if no one died, then "original discoveries, technological innovations, and artistic creations[...] Human biological and cultural evolution would come to a grinding halt"? Naturalistic biological evolution aside (which I reject), it's not at all clear that if people never died, they wouldn't be interested in new discoveries or artistic creation. Symbolic immortality projects aside, people like making their lives more interesting and more comfortable. My wife's a math nerd (she let me call her that) and asked why mathematicians wouldn't continue working out formulas for the joy of it? She loves the exploration. Why would exploration stop? Now again, if we were only going to live on earth *as it is now*, then sooner or later we would discover everything there is to discover. But in the presence of the Creator who has created all the star clusters, black holes, and who knows what—and who we have no reason to expect will ever stop creating—why would we ever be bored with creation?

Further, some futurists like Ray Kurzweil don't think the population increase from immortality is a problem:

> Yes, radical life extension will enlarge the population. But soon, all of our products and foods will be manufactured by nanotechnology replicators that can make essentially any physical product at almost no cost. So this will lead to a radical increase in prosperity around the world. And we've seen that as nations become more prosperous, they lower their population growth. The most advanced countries have negative population growth...We're going to be able to keep up very easily.[39]

Nanotechnology replicators would be cool—we've seen them on *Star Trek*. Ultimately, of course, if there is a God, then there are no space limitations. Thus the maxim of Mark Twain (1835–1910), "Buy land, they're not making it anymore," will be passé because, as Peter writes, "according to his promise we are waiting for new heavens and a new earth in which righteousness dwells" (2 Peter 3:13). Also, as far as we know, space is infinite, and I don't see any reason we wouldn't be able to explore new planets in ages to come.

We're Just Lucky We Were Born

In the opening paragraph of his book *Unweaving the Rainbow: Science, Delusion and the Appetite for Wonder*, Richard Dawkins tells us that having the chance to die is like winning the lottery:

> We are going to die, and that makes us the lucky ones. Most people are never going to die because they are never going to be born. The potential people who could have been here in my place but who will in fact never see the light of day outnumber the sand grains of Arabia. Certainly those unborn ghosts include greater poets

than Keats, scientists greater than Newton. We know this because the set of possible people allowed by our DNA so massively exceeds the set of actual people. In the teeth of these stupefying odds it is you and I, in our ordinariness, that are here. We privileged few, who won the lottery of birth against all odds, how dare we whine at our inevitable return to that prior state from which the vast majority have never stirred?[40]

Dawkins read this as part of a speech at Berkeley to rapturous applause, and he wants it read at his funeral.[41]

Similarly, *Skeptic* magazine publisher Michael Shermer tells us that we can be "facing death—and life" with "gratitude for a chance at life, given the biological reality that those hundred billion people who lived before us were, in fact, only a tiny fraction of the many trillions of people who could have been born but were not. The chance encounter of sperm and egg that led to each of us could just as well have produced someone else." Thus "we are given this one chance to live," and "that is the most any of us can reasonably hope for. Fortunately, it is enough. It is the soul of life. It is heaven on earth."[42] These last two sentences conclude Shermer's book and say again, "You got a chance to live, so stop whining and be grateful you were born."

This is nothing new. The Epicurean philosopher Philodemus (ca. 110–ca. 40 BCE) writes that the "sensible man," having had "a happy life," doesn't consider it "surprising" when his life is "being taken away" but considers the time that he has had to be a "piece of good luck" and is "grateful" even in the face of death.[43] Similarly, Marcus Aurelius says we should "pass through this brief life as nature demands. To give it up without complaint. Like an olive that ripens and falls. Praising its mother, thanking the tree it grew on."[44] Do olives do that? If we're going to personify olives, then who is to say? Maybe they go screaming to their splats.

But is everyone lucky to be alive? Many don't think so. Consider the one-billion-plus Hindus and Buddhists who look forward to Nirvana, the snuffing out of their existence—a state where they will not have individuated consciousnesses. Also, the Greek dramatist Sophocles (ca. 496–406 BCE) writes,

> Never to have been born at all:
> None can conceive a loftier thought!
> And second-best is this: Once born,
> Quickly to return to the dust.[45]

Philosopher and historian Pliny the Elder (23–79) agrees: "There are so many kinds of dangers, so many diseases, so many apprehensions, so many cares, we so often invoke death, that really there is nothing that is so often the object of our wishes. Nature has, in reality, bestowed no greater blessing on man than the shortness of life."[46]

It's easy, however, to write off these ancients as, well, ancient—they never experienced our modern Western society with clean water, healthy food, and medical science. But they aren't the only ones who say this. Some present-day philosophers argue that it would be better to have never been born. In *Better Never to Have Been: The Harm of Coming into Existence*, philosopher David Benatar argues that "coming into existence is always a serious harm." He writes, "Although the good things in one's life make it go better than it otherwise would have gone, one could not have been deprived of their absence if one had not existed. Those who never exist cannot be deprived. However by coming into existence one does suffer quite serious harms that could not have befallen one had one not come into existence."[47] Indeed, for Dawkins and Shermer's argument that we are "lucky to be alive" to succeed, those who never came into existence must be in some sense unlucky. But surely Benatar is correct—it makes no sense to say that people who never actually existed can in any sense be deprived or unlucky. It is incoherent to talk about "most people" who "don't exist." After all, the ontology (i.e., fundamental nature) of "potential people" is this: they don't exist.

Although it is possible to believe that one is lucky to be alive, this rationalization tells us nothing about the badness of death. Even if I am lucky to be alive, why would that mean I shouldn't be sad and fearful about dying? After all, if I'm lucky to be alive, then doesn't that mean being alive is a good thing? And if being alive is a good thing, then why shouldn't I be depressed by the fact that I'm not going to be alive any longer? Is there really solace, while facing death, that others never got a chance to exist?

Also, surely Dawkins and Shermer don't believe that the two-year-old who dies of cancer was in any sense lucky to be alive? But why not? Isn't it because that child knew little other than suffering and wasn't able to accomplish anything meaningful? In other words, just being alive isn't lucky unless you have at least some pleasure in this life and accomplish something that will give you some sense of going on after you're dead.

This brings us to what I suspect is the real reason Dawkins and Shermer say it's enough to have had the chance to be alive: both of them, as we saw in the chapter on symbolic immortality, are counting on their own symbolic immortality! As Shermer wrote, "we *live on*" through "our families" and "our work" and "our culture, and our contributions."[48] So it's not only having the chance to be alive that's giving Dawkins and Shermer comfort; it's that they have had the chance to obtain symbolic immortality! Of course, in their own minds, Dawkins and Shermer believe they will live on because they have a legacy of doing the world a favor by trying to convince everyone that there is no God and thus no immortality.

But there is a God.

"Death Is Nothing"

Another mitigating strategy is to tell yourself that death is no big deal. In fact, death is nothing. The Greek philosopher Epicurus (341–270 BCE) writes, "You should accustom yourself to believing that death means nothing to us, since every good and every evil lies in sensation; but death is the privation of sensation."[49] Epicurus continues, "This, the most horrifying of evils, means nothing to us, then, because so long as we are existent, death is not present and whenever it is present we are not-existent."[50] This is often abbreviated "When we are here death is not. When death is here we are not." In other words, Epicurus rejects Socrates and Plato's belief in the immortality of the soul and defines "dead" to mean "does not exist." If you don't exist, then in a sense you are not dead—or at least, you can't experience death because you no longer exist.

Similarly, Sam Harris tells an audience of 4,000 atheists at a Big Think conference in Australia,

> The good news of atheism, the gospel of atheism, is essentially *nothing*, that nothing happens after death. There's nothing to worry about, there's nothing to fear, when after you die you are returned to that nothingness that you were before you were born. Now this proposition is very difficult to understand and most people seem to mistake nothing with something...If we are right and nothing happens after death, death therefore is not a problem. Life is the problem.[51]

Philosopher Victor Stenger (1935–2014), in his book *The New Atheism: Taking a Stand for Science and Reason*, agrees: "I made my own independent study of Eastern philosophy...I find that when stripped of any implication of supernaturalism I agree with Harris that Eastern philosophers uncovered some unique insights into humanity and the human mind...The *sages'* teachings are marked by selflessness and calm acceptance of *the nothingness after death*."[52] We will talk about these "sages" shortly.

Similarly, former Christian but now skeptic Bart D. Ehrman, in answer to someone who asked whether death was "terrifying" and how to "get over" that fear, replies on his Facebook page, "Now my view is that death is the end of the story. We didn't exist with consciousness before we were born. And we won't exist with consciousness after we die." Thus, continues Ehrman, the thought of death "does not greatly bother me anymore. It's the reality of life." In fact, he says the recognition of his death makes him "more inclined to live life to the fullest, now, *in the present*...We should enjoy life every bit as much as we can now, and see that others can do the same."[53] Irvin D. Yalom gushes about Epicurus, "The more I learn about this extraordinary Athenian thinker, the more strongly I recognize Epicurus as the proto-existential psychotherapist."[54] Yalom says, "Generally I introduce the ideas of Epicurus early in my work with patients suffering from death terror."[55]

Of course, most people will remain horrified by the idea of their nonexistence, but then Epicureans appeal to what is called the symmetry, or mirror, argument. The symmetry argument is that it didn't bother you to not exist before you were born, so why would it bother you to not exist after you're dead? These are, the Epicureans say, mirror images. Indeed, there was the popular Roman saying, found engraved on some ancient tombstones, "Non fui, fui, non sum, non curo" (I was not; I was; I am not; I do not care). Arthur Schopenhauer writes, "If what makes death seem so terrible to us were the thought of not being, we would necessarily think with equal horror of the time when as yet we were not. For it is irrefutably certain that not being after death cannot be different from not being before birth, and consequently is also no more deplorable."[56] The Epicurean philosopher Lucretius puts it this way: "Why do you not depart like a banqueter who is sated with life, and embrace untroubled quiet with a calm mind, you fool?"[57]

Mark Twain regularly mocked Christianity and put the best spin on the Epicurean argument:

> Annihilation has no terrors for me, because I have already tried it before I was born—a hundred million years—and I have suffered more in an hour, in this life, than I remember to have suffered in the whole hundred million years put together. There was a peace, a serenity, an absence of all sense of responsibility, an absence of worry, an absence of care, grief, perplexity; and the presence of a deep content and unbroken satisfaction in that hundred million years of holiday which I look back upon with a tender longing and with a grateful desire to resume, when the opportunity comes.[58]

Although we'll talk about this more later, notice that Twain and the philosophers hope for annihilation. The Epicurean answer is that you need to think differently about what it means to be dead. As Epicurus puts it, when death is "present we are not-existent." Indeed, if death is annihilation, then when you are dead, you no longer exist. Christians who abandon the doctrine of eternal punishment encourage the atheist that his desire for the future will be granted. But what if there is eternal punishment?

It's the Loss of Life That's Troubling

Even if there weren't eternal punishment, should the atheist be consoled? It's not surprising that many have challenged the philosophical illuminati that death is in no way bad for the one who dies. One common objection is that if the Epicurean doesn't think it is bad to be dead, then the Epicurean must have no objection to being *painlessly* murdered (Epicureans agree that pain while you're living is a bad thing). But almost everyone would object to being murdered even if it was painless. Philosopher Thomas Nagel is right to point out that if the Epicureans are correct that death is annihilation, where one has no negative sensations, it isn't "the state of being dead, or nonexistent, or unconscious, that is objectionable" but "the loss of life."[59]

I'm going to borrow from Nagel regarding the symmetry argument. Suppose you were told that you would soon be reduced to having the mental capacity of a contented infant, and you would be happy as long you had a full stomach and a dry diaper. If you were once a contented infant and soon you would again be a contented infant, how would you receive that news? I doubt you, dear reader, or anyone else, would find the symmetry argument any comfort whatsoever. Now, it's true that the contented infant—regardless of whether he or she was once a fully functioning, intelligent adult—would still be happy, but for you, the intelligent, purposeful adult, this would appear to be one of the greatest tragedies imaginable.

Nagel clarifies that "this does not mean that a contented infant is unfortunate. The intelligent adult who has been reduced to this condition is the subject of the misfortune. He is the one we pity."[60] Nagel continues, "It is true that both the time before a man's birth and the time after his death are times when he does not exist. But the time after his death is time of which his death deprives him."[61] A person's death "is an abrupt cancellation of indefinitely extensive possible goods."[62] Nagel is right that "it can be said that life is all we have and the loss of it is the greatest loss we can sustain."[63] Similarly, David Benatar says, "Each individual, speaking in the first person, can say: 'My death obliterates me. Not only am I deprived of future goods but I am also destroyed. This person, about whom I care so much, will cease to exist. My memories, values, beliefs, perspectives, hopes—my very self—will come to an end, and for all eternity.'"[64]

No wonder Vladimir Nabokov (1899–1977), the great Russian American novelist, begins his autobiography, *Speak, Memory*, with these lines: "The cradle rocks above an abyss, and common sense tells us that our existence is but a brief crack of light between two eternities of darkness. Although the two are identical twins, man, as a rule, views the prenatal abyss with more calm than the one he is heading for (at some forty-five hundred heartbeats an hour)."[65] Indeed, people like the idea of being alive, and if they didn't think they would ever die, then they would like being alive even more.[66] Death is the ultimate offense to godhood fantasies. Bauman calls death the "scandal, the ultimate humiliation of reason. It saps the trust in reason and the security that reason promises. It loudly declares reason's lie."[67] Bauman calls mortality the "ultimate offence against human omnipotence."[68] Indeed, that you can die and decay is the ultimate blow to your self-esteem.[69] It's hard to think you're "all that" when your body is going to be eaten by worms.

Consider that Epicurus made it his life's work to tell his disciples, and the world, that he didn't fear death and neither should anyone else. But did he succeed in not fearing death? Consider that Epicurus died horribly. Nonetheless, he writes, "Passing a delightful day, which will also be the last of my life, I write you this note. Dysentery and an inability to urinate have occasioned the worst possible sufferings. But a counterweight to all this is the joy in my heart when I remember our conversations."[70] People tell me that kidney stones (the probable cause) are one of the most painful things a person can endure. Imagine what not being able to urinate at all must have felt like! Add to that the severe diarrhea and abdominal cramps caused by dysentery. So I ask you, does it make sense for him to write "Having a delightful day"? Does that ring psychologically true, or does this sound like the philosophical propaganda of someone who is trying to secure a symbolic immortality by proclaiming to everyone that he didn't fear death like a true philosopher? After all, those who faced death boldly in ancient Greece were considered philosophical Jedis, so if Epicurus had these fears, would he have admitted them?[71] Who is to say that while he lay there, he didn't fear the loss of the only thing he had, which was his own existence? How often did he repeat, in mantra fashion, "Death is nothing to us, death is nothing to us, death is nothing to us"?

Solomon, Greenberg, and Pyszczynski write that although Epicurean arguments are "worthy of serious consideration," the

> Epicurean efforts to eliminate death anxiety on rational grounds have been spectacularly unsuccessful to date. People have not changed that much in the last three thousand years; they remain steadfastly disinclined to die, and passionately devoted to acquiring literal and symbolic immortality. Death—"the undiscovered country," as Hamlet portrayed it, from which "no traveler returns"—is, for self-conscious creatures, too terrifying to stop worrying about. Death anxiety may not be rational—but neither are we.[72]

Apparently his future nonexistence wasn't enough for Epicurus, since he formed his existence around his teaching, started a school to propagate it, and left a will providing for the school's continuance.[73] That's quite a symbolic immortality project. But as was pointed out above, maybe the fear of death is all too rational, since our being alive is the only thing we possess.

Death Does Not End Your Existence

There is a sense that *if* death is annihilation, you won't really suffer once you are annihilated. But if the Christian conception of God is true, then there's a serious problem with this thinking. Paul writes in 1 Corinthians 15:56 that "the sting of death is sin." The reason that sin makes death sting is that after we die, we are judged. Death, then, results not in a life of bliss but in having your selfish deeds broadcast to all creation at the Judgment. I doubt Nagel believes there will be life after death, but as he puts it, "If one thinks about it logically, it seems as though death should be something to be afraid of only if we *will* survive it, and perhaps undergo some terrifying transformation."[74] After all, as Nagel says elsewhere, "If there is life after death, the prospect will be grim or happy depending on where your soul will end up."[75]

Death Horrifies Because Eternity Is in Our Hearts

Christians understand that it *is* rational to want to live: humans have souls, and the Lord has imbued these souls with a sense of eternity. As Solomon puts it in Ecclesiastes 3:11 (NIV), "He has made everything beautiful in its time. He has also set eternity in the human heart; yet no one can fathom what God has done from beginning to end." C.S. Lewis beautifully captures this longing for eternity, this longing for a better place, in his novel *Till We Have Faces: A Myth Retold.* Lewis's favorite of his own works tells the story of a young woman who was going to her lover (i.e., Christ). The woman tells her sister, "The sweetest thing in all my life has been the longing—to reach the Mountain [i.e., heaven], to find the place where the beauty came from."[76] Then she says, "My country, the place where I ought to have been born...For indeed it now feels not like going, but like going back. All my life the god of the Mountain has been wooing me."[77] Lewis also writes of this in *Mere Christianity*:

> If I find in myself a desire which no experience in this world can satisfy, the most probable explanation is that I was made for another world. If none of my earthly pleasures satisfy it, that does not prove that the universe is a fraud. Probably earthly pleasures were never meant to satisfy it, but only to arouse it, to suggest the real thing. If that is so, I must take care, on the one hand, never to despise, or to be unthankful for, these earthly blessings, and on the other, never to mistake them for the

something else of which they are only a kind of copy, or echo, or mirage. I must keep alive in myself the desire for my true country, which I shall not find till after death.[78]

Your true country awaits, dear Christian!

Detachment

We've seen that one trouble with death is losing all we love. Well, that brings us to another atheist attempt to mitigate the horror of death: detachment. In other words, don't get too attached to anything or anyone because attachment to things only means that the loss of those things will hurt you. This is most famously associated with Buddhism and the Four Nobel Truths. Indeed, the first truth is "to live means to suffer," and the second truth is "the origin of suffering is attachment."[79] The Buddha (ca. sixth–fourth century BCE) taught that the basic cause of suffering is "the attachment to the desire to have (craving) and the desire not to have (aversion)."[80] Although some might think it odd that I would mention Buddhism in discussing how many atheists employ detachment to cope with their fear of death, atheists freely admit the similarities their views have with Buddhism. Also, Stoic nonattachment is, as Luc Ferry puts it, "remarkably close to that of Buddhism," and you'll see that all the remaining mortality mitigating projects share Buddhist beliefs.[81]

The historian of philosophy Pierre Hadot (1922–2010) writes, "In the view of *all* philosophical schools, mankind's principal cause of suffering, disorder, and unconsciousness were the passions: that is, unregulated desires and exaggerated fears."[82] This is certainly true of Epicureanism and Stoicism. There may be no greater example of the Stoic detachment than what happened at the Roman triumph. The Roman triumph was a parade through the streets of Rome held in honor of the return of a victorious general. As Harvard historian Mary Beard puts it, "To be awarded a triumph was the most outstanding honor a Roman general could hope for." In the parade, the general "would be drawn in a chariot—accompanied by the booty he had won, the prisoners he had taken captive, and his no doubt rowdy and raucous troops in their battle gear—through the streets of the city to the Temple of Jupiter on the Capitoline hill, where he would offer a sacrifice to the god."[83] It was the most lavish of all Roman rituals and was "celebrated more than three hundred times in the thousand-or-so-year history of the ancient city of Rome."[84]

The reason I said this was an amazing example of Stoic detachment is because as the crowd was roaring its acclamation, a slave would stand behind the general in his chariot, "holding a golden crown over his head and whispering 'Look behind you. Remember you are a man.'"[85] About this, early church father Tertullian (155/160–after 200) writes, "He is reminded that he is a man even while he is triumphing, in that most exalted chariot. For at his back he is given the warning: 'Look behind you. Remember you are a man.' And so he rejoices all the more that he is in such a blaze of glory that a reminder of mortality is necessary."[86]

This detachment is found in Rudyard Kipling's (1865–1936) stoic poem "If," where he tells his son that he will be a man "if all men count with you, but none too much."[87] Bertrand Russell writes that "the best way to overcome" the fear of dying "is to make your interests gradually wider and more *impersonal*, until bit by bit the walls of the ego recede, and your life becomes increasingly merged in the universal life."[88] Russell continues, "The man who, in old age, can see his life in this way, will not suffer from the fear of death, since the *things he cares for* will continue."[89] When Russell says "cares for," he doesn't mean people—people die—he means he cares for causes (e.g., Russell was an anti-nuclear crusader).[90]

Detachment Is Not Realistic for the Average Person

But is this detachment achievable by the average person? After all, how can you choose to go to college, choose a career, marry, and have children unless you really care about those things? How does one detach oneself from his or her spouse or children without hurting them? Can one be successful in business without caring to be successful in business? Certainly the Buddhists didn't think it was possible to escape desire, and thus achieve Nirvana, outside the monastic life.[91] Thus Buddhists take it as a given that those outside the monastic life will not achieve the detachment necessary to escape the cycle of rebirth and redeath.

Detachment Deadens Life

Jean E. and I visited a large Buddhist temple in Singapore, and on the third floor there was a lavish red-and-gold room filled with elaborately decorated idols. A monk sat in the lotus position facing a corner. He did not move. There was nothing for him to see. I suspect he really wouldn't mind dying all that much because that certainly wasn't living! Indeed, I would suspect that detachment could allay your fear of death if you're willing to ruin your life here! I mean, if you keep yourself from getting attached to people, or dogs, or cats, or filet mignon, or scallops, or king crab (I love vegetables too, but they're not the main event), or whatever. If you don't set your heart on accomplishing anything. If you just live your life as if your life doesn't matter, you can make it so that you don't fear death much because you're already dead.[92]

Although he doesn't call it detachment, Andrew Stark talks about a kind of detachment. Namely, he points out that some people regard life as a series of deaths:

> *Life, with its losses, is itself nothing but an imitation of death.* List all the evils that you think death inflicts. You will see that life, sooner or later, deals them out as well. If we were clear-eyed about this reality, then death would cease to be a source of terror. Think of one of death's most stinging deprivations: our having to part forever from the people and things we love. This happens in life all the time anyway. "Husbands walk out, wives walk out," says Joan Didion. We lose cherished jobs, beloved homes, treasured keepsakes, life-sustaining ideals and convictions all the time.[93]

In other words, if we focus on the horrors of this life, then death won't be that big a deal.

But Stark doesn't buy this counsel: "Yes, husbands walk out, wives walk out" but, he says, "those losses will never rival the ones that death imposes."[94] Now, again, if one were to constantly keep in mind life's miseries, then one might not mind dying so much. I suspect that Eeyore the donkey would face death easier than Winnie the Pooh or Tigger, but do we want to be the pessimistic, depressed Eeyore even if that helps us face death? To make life miserable so that when death comes you're glad to go is dying before you die. Apparently there are some who think this an acceptable trade—make your life comparatively miserable here so that you won't be made miserable by the fear of death. But if you are willing to make that trade, it is *precisely* because you fear death—you might say, "Because I fear death so much, I'll make myself miserable so I won't fear death so much."

Detachment Is Selfish

Even though Buddhists and the Greek philosophers say that in the midst of detachment, we should be compassionate toward others, detachment is still selfish. A little historical perspective might help. In her book *Buddha* in a chapter entitled "Renunciation," comparative religion author and 2008 TED Prize recipient, Karen Armstrong, tells of the beginning of the Buddha's path to enlightenment:

> One night toward the end of the sixth century B.C.E., a young man called Siddhatta Gotama walked out of his comfortable home in Kapilavatthu in the foothills of the Himalayas and took to the road. We are told he was twenty-nine years old. His father was one of the leading men of Kapilavatthu and had surrounded Gotama with every pleasure he could desire: he had a wife and son who was only a few days old. But Gotama had felt no pleasure when the child was born. He had called the little boy Rāhula, or "fetter": the baby, he believed would shackle him to a way of life that had become abhorrent. He had a yearning for an existence that was "wide open" and as "complete as a pure and polished shell," but even though his father's house was elegant and refined, Gotama found it constricting, "crowded" and "dusty." A

miasma of petty tasks and pointless duties sullied everything. Increasingly he had found himself longing for a
lifestyle that had nothing to do with domesticity.[95]

Armstrong writes that before he left, Siddhatta "stole upstairs, took
one last look at his sleeping wife and son, and crept away without saying goodbye."[96] Whoa. Siddhatta left his wife and child without saying
goodbye because he felt like chores and family life are shackles? Doesn't
this make Buddha just another deadbeat dad? How many American
men have left their wives and children to "find themselves"?

As Luc Ferry puts it, "We can be tempted by the counsels of Buddhism, which can be reduced to a fundamental principle: do not become
attached. Not from indifference—Buddhism, like Stoicism, speaks up
for human compassion and the obligations of friendship," but "if we
allow ourselves to be trapped by the net of attachments in which love
invariably entangles us, we are without doubt preparing the worst of
sufferings for ourselves...because...human beings are perishable."[97]

And even if your spouse doesn't leave you, can you imagine him or
her gathering you and the kids around to announce, "Hey, family, you
know how much I love you, but I'm not going to love you as much as I
used to because I'm afraid of death, and I won't be as afraid of death if I
don't love you so much." Now, it's hard to imagine that anyone would
really say that, but isn't that what they would be doing—detaching
themselves from their family so as not to hurt if they die? That's not a
good place to be! Of course, as Christians we are commanded to love
even though we know our family members will die. We must reject any
counsel that says we shouldn't care too much about them to protect
ourselves. We'd think that those who detached themselves from their
families because they wanted to mitigate their fear of death would be
no more than gravy-sucking pig dogs.

Detachment Is the Opposite of Loving
Your Neighbor as Yourself

Notice how contrary this don't-care-too-much-for-people attitude
is to Christianity, where the second-greatest command is to "love your

neighbor as yourself" (Matthew 22:39). This "I'm not going to love you too much so I won't be hurt" idea is all about loving yourself more than your neighbor. Ferry is correct that for the Christian, "attachment is not prohibited as long as it is correctly oriented." By "correctly," he means this must be done in the context of loving God. Ferry points to the Gospel of John and the death of Lazarus, where "Christ weeps when he learns his friend is dead—which the Buddha would never allow himself to do. He weeps because, having taken human form, he is experiencing separation as grief, as suffering. But he knows, of course, that he will soon be united once more with Lazarus: that love is stronger than death."[98] Instead, writes Ferry, "I find the Christian proposition infinitely more tempting—except for the fact that I do not believe in it. But were it to be true I would certainly be a taker."[99] This saddens me for Ferry. He sees the wonder of the promise of eternal life in Jesus but rejects its truth. Ferry considers Christianity to be "morally submissive and tedious."[100] In other words, Ferry likes the promise of Christianity but doesn't *want* to submit his will to God.

Detachment isn't the way to eternal life; rather, those on the way to eternal life will love God and their neighbor. In Luke 10:25-28, a lawyer asks Jesus, "Teacher what shall I do to inherit eternal life?" Jesus then asks him, "What is written in the Law?" The lawyer replies, "You shall love the Lord your God with all your heart and with all your soul and with all your strength and with all your mind, and your neighbor as yourself." Jesus then says to him, "You have answered correctly; do this, and you will *live*."

Live in the Present

One way to detach yourself is to practice "mindfulness" and "live in the moment," but few realize that through the ages, this has been considered a hardcore philosophical means of coping with the fear of death. Mindfulness concerns being present by being aware of who you are and where you are in the present moment. Mindfulness meditation encourages a person to ponder how they feel right now. I could go on to explain the differences between mindfulness and living in the moment (they're not identical), but for our purposes, I'm going to just say that they both emphasize living in the present.

As Roman emperor and Stoic philosopher Marcus Aurelius (121–80 BCE) writes, "And if you take care to live only what can truly be called life, that is, the *present moment*, you will be able to spend the time that remains until death undisturbed, with kindness and obedience to the divine spirit within."[101] Ferry points out that "for Stoicism as for Buddhism, the tense in which the struggle against anxiety is to be waged is indeed the 'future perfect.' In effect: 'When destiny strikes, I shall have been prepared for it.' When catastrophe—be it illness, poverty or death, all the ills linked to the irreversible nature of time—*will have taken place*, I shall be able to confront it thanks to the ability I have acquired to *live in the present*."[102] In other words, for the Stoic, if you have intellectually accepted that the worst can happen to you, then when something terrible happens, you will not be shocked by it. Therefore, stop thinking about the future and just live in the moment.

Ludwig Wittgenstein (1889–1951), who many consider the greatest philosopher of the twentieth century, writes, "Death is not an event in life: we do not live to experience death. If we take eternity to mean not infinite temporal duration but timelessness, then *eternal life belongs to those who live in the present.* Our life has no end in just the way in which our visual field has no limits."[103] Philosophers debate exactly all that Wittgenstein meant by this, but his comment "We do not live to experience death" is Epicurean and means that we cannot experience death because once we're actually dead, we don't experience anything at all because we no longer exist (in the view of most atheists, anyway). We've talked about this previously, and we'll talk about this again shortly. The idea that "eternal life belongs to the present" is not an unusual concept among philosophers. You can get "lost in the moment"—the past is over and the future is uncertain, so live in the present, and when you do, you're experiencing the flow of various moments of eternity.

Indeed, philosophy historian Pierre Hadot describes the goal of Epicureanism and Stoicism as allowing "people to free themselves from the past and the future, so that they [can] live within the present."[104] The Roman Stoic philosopher Seneca (4 BCE–65 CE) writes that if one ceased to hope, then one would cease to fear. If one hopes, then one also fears that their hopes will be dashed. Hopes and fears belong "to a mind that is in suspense, a mind that is worried by its expectation of what is to come."[105] Thus, writes Seneca, "no one is made wretched merely by the present."[106]

Hadot writes that both Epicureanism and Stoicism "posit as an axiom that happiness can only be found in the present, that one instant of happiness is the equivalent to an eternity of happiness, and that happiness can and must be found immediately, here and now."[107] Really? One instant of happiness is equivalent to an eternity of happiness? What this means is that we shouldn't think about the past or the future, and because we are only ever (currently) experiencing a single moment—that is, we never experience more than a single moment at a time, ever—if we live in that moment, we're living in eternity. But I want more than to live *in* eternity and then one day die and stop living *in* eternity: I want to live *for* eternity by never dying, don't you?

To an Australian atheist conference, in a lecture entitled "Death and the Present Moment," Sam Harris admits, "I do have existential worries. I, like I think everybody else, am concerned about death. You know...death is in some ways unacceptable. It's, it's just an astonishing fact of our being here. That we, that we die, but I think worse than that, we lose everyone we love in this world." A little later, Harris says, "I simply don't know about what, I don't know what I believe about death, and I don't think it's necessary to know, to live as sanely, as ethically, as happily as possible." Harris says that when it comes to death, "the reality of death is something we're all going to face...If you live long enough you're going to witness the death of everyone you love." Then Harris asks, "What does atheism have to offer in this circumstance?...How can people close to these tragedies make sense of them?"[108]

So what's Harris's answer? That we need to live in the present! "There are ways to really live in the present moment," says Harris. "What, what's the alternative? It is always now. However much you feel you may need to plan for the future, to anticipate it, to mitigate risks, the reality of your life is now." He admits that "most of us do our best not to think about death but we know that can't go on forever." Then he asks the audience to close their eyes and meditate on how they feel now, to think about what's happening to their bodies now, and so on. In other words, he leads them through a meditation exercise.

This goes on for almost eight minutes.

Then once he stops the exercise, he says, "I kind of smuggled mindfulness meditation into this talk and foisted it on 4,000 atheists—so you're now all Buddhists." He laughs and says, "I'm sorry to have done that to you. But it is an antidote to that kind of suffering. When you look closely at the mechanics of your own suffering, you find that when you're suffering you're lost in thought." Harris continues, "There's an antidote to the fear of death, and the experience of loss, that's compatible with reason, and I think it's to be found here." Harris says he has gone on retreats where he's been in "silence for eighteen hours a day." The result: "The truth is that it's possible to sink into the present moment in such a way as to find it sacred and to cease to have a problem. And that's just a fact to which there's so much testimony."[109]

Living in the Present Is Miserable While Suffering

If all is going well, then living in the moment isn't that hard. You might even be able to block out the suffering of those close to you. But if your pain now is severe, then "living in the moment" leaves a lot to be desired. If you are *presently* lying in a hospital bed—intubated, catheterized, and suffering—while dying from cancer, then that is the present moment. Do you want to be mindful of the catheter? IV? Feeding tube? After all, if those things are happening *now*, that is a pain-filled moment. You might choose to live in the present and push out of your mind that—present, active, indicative—you are dying in pain, but living in that moment *is* experiencing the tubes and the pain. Are we supposed to shut out that part of the present? Indeed, a study of randomized controlled trials only "found *low-quality evidence* that mindfulness meditation is associated with a *small* decrease in pain."[110] Well, that may be something, but it's not much if you're really suffering.

And here's a major folly: Earlier I quoted Hadot, who said that for the Epicureans and Stoics, "one instant of happiness is the equivalent to an eternity of happiness." Well, then, isn't the reverse also true? Isn't one instance of horror equivalent to an eternity of horror? I know what it's like to lie in bed in immense pain. I did that a lot when I had bone cancer, and the last thing on earth I would have wanted was to live in the moment. I thank God I was able to look forward to perhaps being cured (which happened)—and if not, to entering eternal life! I was "mindful" that I might not be healed, and eternal life was then my hope.

Living in the Present Hurts Tomorrow

But even if you are experiencing a time when you are well, is living in the present a good idea? No. As Daniel H. Pink writes in his book *When: The Scientific Secrets of Perfect Timing*, "Research has shown we plan more effectively and behave more responsibly when the future feels more closely connected to the current moment and our current selves. For example, one reason some people don't save for retirement is that they somehow consider the future version of themselves a different person than the current version." Later Pink writes, "As with nostalgia, the highest function of the future is to enhance the significance of the present."[111] That makes sense, right? How do we accomplish many—if not all—of the most valuable and enjoyable things in life without drawing from the things we learned in our pasts and using them to inform our futures? After all, training for a particular occupation, planning a honeymoon, planning to have a family, or planning for retirement requires thinking about the future, and those times can be amazingly enjoyable. The list of the things we might not accomplish if we only live in the moment is all but endless. Thus again, that's why the Buddhists hold that you can only achieve true detachment in the monastery.

Living in the Present Is Meaningless

In fact, there may be a cautionary tale about living completely in the present in the case of a fellow named Henry Gustav Molaison (1926–2008), widely known as "H.M." H.M. is probably the most studied individual in the history of neuroscience research. When H.M. was 27, he underwent an experimental lobotomy in an attempt to relieve his epileptic seizures. Although it decreased the frequency of his seizures, the experiment completely obliterated his ability to remember anything for more than a few seconds. Because of this, he couldn't plan for the future—even if it was just a few minutes into the future—because he couldn't hold anything in his mind for more than 30 seconds. MIT neuroscience researcher Suzanne Corkin, in her book on Henry entitled *Permanent Present Tense: The Unforgettable Life of the Amnesic Patient, H. M.*, writes, "Without the ability to travel consciously back in time from one episode to another, he was trapped in the here and now."[112] Because he had memories from times prior to his lobotomy, as Roman Krznaric puts it in *Carpe Diem: Seizing the Day in a Distracted World*, "he could talk, read, do basic arithmetic, and play bingo, but that was about it. When he went to a restaurant, he found it hard to order food, as he had no idea what he liked. He couldn't hold down a job because the moment he was taught to do something, he forgot it. He read and reread the same magazines." Krznaric continues, "He was pleasant and mild-mannered, but he couldn't make real friendships, as he couldn't recall anybody's name or anything about them." My father had dementia, which obliterated his short-term memory, and he often asked questions moments after we had answered them. He frequently called to ask when we would see him again, and I would remind him that we were there just minutes earlier. Krznaric is right that "we can read Henry's story almost as an allegory about how much we need the past in our lives."[113]

Besides, if you're only living in the moment, you might ignore future problems to which you should attend. Scheduling a mammogram or a colonoscopy are future events that might prevent you from having many painful future moments. Planning a lengthy vacation in Europe or Asia also requires much looking to the future in an enjoyable way. Again, research shows that people are happier when they are connected to the past and the future. As Pink writes, "Taken together, all of these studies suggest that the path to a life of meaning and significance isn't to 'live in the present' as so many spiritual gurus have advised. It is to integrate our perspectives on time into a coherent whole, one that helps us comprehend who we are and why we're here."[114] I couldn't agree more.

Of course, this is easier to do for the maturing Christian, as we see the Lord actually using all things, including suffering, for our good. Thus Christians can enjoy a sense of connection to the future not only because we know that God causes "all things [to] work together for good" (Romans 8:28) but because we know that "eternal life" awaits us (John 3:16).

Living in the Present Is Unrealistic

Also, like it or not, humans are not creatures who can simply keep their minds off their impending deaths. You might be able to do it for a short time, but you won't be able to do it for long because death is ever-present. Are you not going to attend the funerals of loved ones? Are you going to hide from suffering friends and family members? The folly of trying to live in the moment is that many suffer around us now, presently. We'll watch people we know die until our own deaths. One reason the Lord made it that way was so that we'd give up our failing immortality projects.

As I've been studying how non-Christians handle death, I've paid close attention to the last words in their books. Here are the last words in Stephen Cave's book on death:

> Our lives are bounded by beginning and end yet composed of moments that can reach out far beyond ourselves, touching other people and places in countless ways. In this sense, they are like a book, which is self-contained within its covers yet able to encompass distant landscapes, exotic figures and long-gone times. The book's characters know no horizons; they, like we, can only know the moments that make up their lives, even when the book is closed. They are therefore untroubled by reaching the last page. And so it should be with us.[115]

The characters in books "can only know the moments that make up their lives"? That's like Marcus Aurelius's olive talk. The characters in a book don't *know* the moments in their lives because the characters in a book don't *know* anything. They are "untroubled by reaching the last page" because they don't exist!

Poet and cleric John Donne (1572–1631) writes about how church bells ring when someone dies, and this ringing is a continual reminder of death. Thus because we are involved with our fellow man, each death diminishes us. So Donne advises, "Never send to know for whom the bells tolls; it tolls for thee."[116] And that bell always rings! People suffer and die all around us, and if we're going to bring them meals and pray for them at their bedsides, and if we're going to attend their funerals and comfort their grieving family members, then it's impossible to ignore our own impending deaths. We shouldn't be like children who don't want to hear bad news, putting our hands over our ears and shouting "La, la, la, la, la—I can't hear you!"

But if Christianity is true, suffering has meaning. Suffering unsettles our worldliness. Suffering humiliates our self-deification. Suffering drives us to find an end to suffering, and if we humble ourselves, suffering can drive us to focus on the end of all suffering that is available for all eternity for those who trust in Jesus's suffering and death for us on the cross.

Living in the moment isn't going to work now, and it hasn't worked in the past. As philosophy historian Hadot puts it, "It does seem, then, that the Greeks paid particular attention to the present moment. This, however, does not justify us in imagining" that "because they lived in the present moment," they "were perpetually bathed in beauty and serenity." Rather, "people in antiquity were just as filled with anguish as we are today, and ancient poetry often preserves the echo of this anguish, which sometimes goes as far as despair. Like us, the ancients bore the burden of the past, the uncertainty of the future, and the fear of death."[117] Bottom line: living entirely in the moment is impossible, and even if it were possible, it would lead to fewer happy "moments" in the future.

This live-in-the-moment notion reminds me of "The Serenity Now" episode of *Seinfeld*. In that episode, to keep his blood pressure down, Frank Costanza's doctor tells him that whenever he gets angry, he should say "Serenity now." This inspires Kramer to say "Serenity now" whenever he gets upset, but then the neighborhood kids pelt Kramer with eggs and cover his porch with toilet paper. Finally Kramer explodes and destroys 25 computers that George Costanza had been storing in Kramer's apartment while screaming, "SERENITY NOW! SERENITY NOW!" As a guest star in the episode puts it, "Serenity now, insanity later."

In a bizarre move, philosopher Stephen Cave appeals to the book of Ecclesiastes to bolster his philosophy:

> Ecclesiastes, for example, begins with a fine expression of the recognition of the fact of death: "For what happens to the children of man and what happens to the beasts is the same; as one dies, so dies the other" (3:19). The author goes on to make clear that neither glorious afterlife nor legacy awaits: "The dead know nothing; they have no more reward, and even the memory of them is lost" (9:5). And what *conclusion* does the author draw for what we mortals should then do? "Go thy way, eat thy bread with joy, and drink thy wine with a merry heart...Let thy garments be always white; and let thy head lack no ointment. Live joyfully with the wife whom thou lovest all the days of the life of thy vanity" (9:7-9).[118]

But this is not—not!—the conclusion of the book of Ecclesiastes. It's as if Cave either didn't finish reading Ecclesiastics or purposely didn't want to quote the book's final two verses: "The end of the matter; all has been heard. Fear God and keep his commandments, for this is the whole duty of man. For God will bring every deed into judgment, with every secret thing, whether good or evil" (12:13-14). And that's the biggest problem with living for today: the dead are raised, and then comes the Judgment. But as Jesus says in John 5:24, "Truly, truly, I say to you, whoever hears my word and believes him who sent me has eternal life. He does not come into judgment, but has passed from death to life." The poet/cleric John Donne, who wrote "Ask not for whom the bell tolls," preached his last sermon wearing a funeral shroud to impress upon the hearers the shortness of this life. He concluded that sermon telling the audience "to hang upon him that hangs upon the cross," as He has granted us "an ascension into that kingdom which He hath prepared for you with the inestimable price of his incorruptible blood. Amen."[119] Amen!

Individual Existence Is Unreal

Now we come to another Buddhist principle that most Westerners will consider absurd—everything is one (known as monism), and if everything truly is one, then your *individual* existence isn't real.[120] New Age alternative medicine guru Deepak Chopra says the next step in "conquering death," where you can be "as alive as you want to be," is "through a process known as surrender." Chopra says surrender is the act of entirely erasing the line between life and death: "When you can see yourself as the total cycle of death within life and the life within death, you have surrendered." When that happens, "the mystic gives up all need for boundaries and plunges directly into existence. The circle closes, and the mystic experiences himself as the one reality."[121] Although Buddhist, as we've seen with the other death-denial strategies, it has many Western adopters.

I expect many readers—Christian or not—will think it all but impossible to believe that intelligent, nonreligious people could believe such a thing, but they'd be wrong. Earlier I quoted Bertrand Russell as he spoke about a sense of detachment, of letting your interests become more impersonal, but Russell also embraces the notion of our individual existence being unreal: "An individual human existence should be like a river—small at first, narrowly contained within its banks, and rushing passionately past boulders and over waterfalls. Gradually the river grows wider, the banks recede, the waters flow more quietly, and in the end, without any visible break, they become merged in the sea, and painlessly lose their *individual* being."[122] Russell says this notion puts him at ease about his death. Russell's detachment would make the Buddha proud, but if Buddhism is taken to its logical conclusion, the Buddha has no individual consciousness and is literally (and I'm using "literally" correctly) indistinguishable from pond scum.

Another Westerner, Albert Einstein, wrote a letter to a father who had lost his son to illness:

A human being is a part of the whole, called by us "Universe," a part limited in time and space. He experiences himself, his thoughts and feelings as something separated from the rest—a kind of optical *delusion* of his consciousness. The striving to free oneself from this delusion is the one issue of true religion. Not to nourish the delusion but to try to overcome it is the way to reach the attainable measure of peace of mind.[123]

So here Einstein, perhaps the most respected scientist ever, writes that your individual existence is a delusion!

Einstein explains that this is different from the "anthropomorphic" religions of Judaism, Islam, and Christianity and their "conception" of a personal God. Einstein writes that "in general, only individuals of *exceptional endowments*, and exceptionally high-minded communities, rise to any considerable extent above this level."[124] But there is a "stage of religious experience...rarely found in a pure form: I shall call it cosmic religious feeling." This feeling, says Einstein, has "no anthropomorphic conception of God corresponding to it." Someone who is "high-minded" with "exceptional endowments" finds that "individual existence impresses him as a sort of prison and he wants to experience the universe as a single significant whole."[125] Of course, if your individual existence is a delusion, then your death is inconsequential, as you're no different than a mud puddle. Truly, "claiming to be wise, they became fools" (Romans 1:22).

It's Hard to Say Goodbye to Me

The *New York Times* described writer, filmmaker, philosopher, and activist Susan Sontag (1933–2004) as one of the "most lionized presences" in the twentieth century.[126] Unfortunately, Sontag spent her last couple of years battling cancer. Her son David reports that she once wrote in her journal, "Death is unbearable unless you can get beyond the 'I.'" But then he adds, "She who could do so many things in her life could never do that."[127] Instead, writes David, "she never really had a chance of freeing herself from her terrible fear of extinction, of not being."[128] So David says that through one torturous chemo treatment after another, he would keep encouraging her to have hope that she would survive. He admits, however, "I was fully conscious at the time that the more she hoped, the harder it would be for my mother to die. But to talk with her as if it were more likely that she was going to die than to live seemed certain to increase her fear and pain."[129] I suspect that there are deathbed testimonies of those who steadfastly say they don't exist and so their death is really nothing, but who is to say that for many (if not all), this is any more than bravado—a last-ditch symbolic immortality project intended to impress those around them?

Magic Mushrooms

Award-winning author and activist Barbara Ehrenreich, in her book *Natural Causes: An Epidemic of Wellness, the Certainty of Dying, and Killing Ourselves to Live Longer*, also thinks that removing the self is the key to facing death. She writes that she once "despaired" of removing "the self as an obstacle to a peaceful death without getting mired in the slippery realm of psychoanalysis or the even more intimidating discourse of postmodern philosophy." But she is encouraged that getting over a sense of self might be accomplished through "psychedelic drugs," specifically "psilocybin, the active ingredient in 'magic mushrooms.'"[130] When properly administered, "these drugs seem to act by suppressing or temporarily abolishing the sense of 'self.'"[131] As one 54-year-old TV news director who was undergoing psilocybin treatment puts it, "It all makes sense now, so simple and beautiful." Later he says, "Even the germs were beautiful, as was everything in our world and universe."[132] Well, sure, that's how you do it—get high on drugs and all your problems will float away! Let's all sing "Lucy in the Sky with Diamonds"! Please pass the Maui Wowie!

Monism, the idea that everything is one, is foundational to most Eastern religions and so rejects the basis for logic—the law of noncontradiction. After all, if everything is one, then hot and cold are one, day and night are one, hugging and pouring boiling oil on someone are one. If everything is one with everything else, then the AIDS virus and purple pansies are one. A is A, but everything is A—there's no non-A.

Inside and outside are the same. Now, I suppose someone could say, as others have, that he recognizes the law of noncontradiction, but he also doesn't recognize it. Perhaps when it comes to science he relies on the law of noncontradiction, but elsewhere he rejects it. Philosopher Stephen Cave states, "The idea of dissolving the self into a greater whole is also crucial to the Buddhist idea of nirvana and fundamental to some strands of Hinduism and to Taoism." Cave continues, "Indeed, recognizing yourself to be part of a deeper reality is for many the first step on the spiritual path. The Taoists say that the only difference between the immortals and the rest of us is that the former have recognized their unity with the underlying eternal reality, whereas we poor mortals still believe in individual death."[133]

As Chinese philosopher Chuang Tzu (ca. fourth century BCE) puts it, "That which makes things has no boundaries with things, but for things to have boundaries is what we mean by saying 'the boundaries between things.' The boundaryless boundary is the boundary without a boundary."[134] Ah, young grasshopper, do you see it now? Similarly, D.T. Suzuki (1894–1966), in *The Zen Doctrine of No Mind*, writes that *prajñā* (the process for reaching enlightenment) interrupts the "progress of logical reasoning, but all the time it underlies it, and without Prajñā we cannot have any reasoning whatever. Prajñā is at once above and in the process of reasoning. This is a contradiction, formally considered, but in truth, this contradiction is itself made possible because of Prajñā."[135] If you're scratching your head, maybe this will clear things up. Suzuki explains (or not!), "We generally think that 'A is A' is absolute, and that the proposition 'A is not-A' or 'A is B' is unthinkable...But now Zen declares that words are words and no more."[136] A little later, Suzuki writes, "The meaning of the proposition 'A is A' is realized when 'A is not-A.' To be itself is not to be itself—this is the logic of Zen, and satisfies all our aspirations."[137] Does this seem *illogical* to you, grasshopper? If so, you understand it correctly.

The folly of this thinking—that A can be non-A (rejecting the law of noncontradiction)—is well illustrated by Ravi Zacharias in his book *Can Man Live Without God?* Zacharias describes a discussion he had with a professor over lunch:

As the professor waxed eloquent and expounded on the law of non-contradiction, he eventually drew his conclusion: "This [either/or logic] is a Western way of looking at reality...The real problem is that you are seeing that contradiction as a Westerner when you should be approaching it as an Easterner. The both/and is the Eastern way of viewing reality..."

After he belabored these two ideas on either/or and both/and for some time and carried on his tirade that we ought not to study truth from a Western point of view but rather from an Eastern viewpoint, I finally asked if I could interrupt his unpunctuated train of thought and raise one question. He agreed and put down his pencil.

I said, "Sir, are you telling me that when I am studying Hinduism I *either* use the both/and logic *or* nothing else?"

There was a pin-drop silence for what seemed an eternity. I repeated my question: "Are you telling me that when I am studying Hinduism I *either* use the both/and logic *or* nothing else? Have I got that right?"

He threw his head back and said, "The *either/or* does seem to emerge, doesn't it?"

"Indeed, it does emerge," I said, "And as a matter of fact, even in India we look both ways before crossing the street—it is either the bus or me, not both of us."

Zacharias then asks the reader, "Do you see the mistake he was making? He was using the either/or logic in order to prove both/and. The more you try to hammer the law of non-contradiction, the more it hammers you."[138] These skeptics are teaching that the law of noncontradiction and even your individual existence are fake news!

You really exist (not fake news), and "whoever does the will of God abides forever" (1 John 2:17).

Our Particles Go On

Whether you believe in monism or not, there's a related comfort to help you accept your mortality—you still go on as particles! Evolutionary biologist Lynn Margulis (1938–2011) and Dorion Sagan explain, "Death is illusory in quite a real sense. As sheer persistence of biochemistry, 'we' have never died during the passage of 3,000 million years. Mountains and seas and even supercontinents have come and gone, but we have persisted."[139] Of course, by "we," they mean not that you and I go on but that the animal kingdom, of which we are a part, goes on. "When we do die," says Stephen Fry on Richard Dawkins's website, "our bodies will break up and become part again of the cycle of nature. The atoms that form us now will go on to form other things—trees and birds, flowers and butterflies."[140]

This idea that we go on in fragments that become other things is what the Stoics believed. As Luc Ferry puts it, "The Stoic doctrine of salvation is resolutely *anonymous* and *impersonal*. It promises us eternity, certainly, but of a non-personal kind, as an oblivious fragment of the *cosmos*: death for the Stoic, is a mere rite of passage, which involves a transition from a state of individual consciousness—you and I, as living and thinking beings—to a state of oneness with the *cosmos*, in the course of which we lose everything that constitutes our self-awareness and individuality."[141] Corliss Lamont writes that another way to "counteract the prospect of oblivion is that every man carries literally all eternity in his being." Lamont explains, "The indestructible matter that makes up our physical organisms was part of the universe five billion years ago and will still be part of it five billion years hence. The infinite past comes to a focus in our intricately structured bodies; and from them there radiates the infinite future."[142]

In one of the most bizarre attempts to make people feel good about their deaths, German philosopher Arthur Schopenhauer writes an ode to dust:

> "What!" it will be said, "the permanence of the mere dust,
> of the crude matter, is to be regarded as a continuance of
> our being?" Oh! do you know this dust, then? Do you

know what it is and what it can do? Learn to know it before you despise it. This matter which now lies there as dust and ashes will soon, dissolved in water, from itself as a crystal, will shine as metal, will then emit electric sparks...It will, of its own accord, form itself into plants and animals, and from its mysterious womb develop that life for the loss of which you, in your narrowness, are so painfully anxious. Is it, then, absolutely nothing to continue to exist as such matter? Nay, I seriously assert that even this permanence of matter affords evidence of the indestructibility of our true nature, though only as in image or simile, or, rather, only as in outline.[143]

But if you'll be only scattered dust, is that even an outline?

That we're going to go on in some sense existing as an undifferentiated part of the cosmos is also very much a part of Eastern religions. It might seem odd that a German philosopher would exalt ideas *resembling* Hinduism and Buddhism, but it's no accident. Schopenhauer considers the authors of the Upanishads and Vedas "sublime" people who could "scarcely be thought of as mere men," because these "wise men, standing nearer the origin of our race in time, comprehended the nature of things more clearly and profoundly" than we can today.[144] Perhaps these "wise men" would praise Schopenhauer's glorification of dust? The only appeal that I can see to Nirvana is that Nirvana ends the cycle of birth, death, rebirth, and redeath for those who believe in such things.

See their desperation?

So What?

This dust-is-really-something-wonderful idea doesn't wash with many skeptics. In his book *Death*, Yale philosopher Shelly Kagan writes about Schopenhauer's ode to dust: "Well, that's a very stirring passage, but I have to say, I don't buy it. I don't find any comfort at all in the thought that my atoms will still be around getting reused in something else...Schopenhauer was so *desperate* that he deluded himself into thinking, 'Oh, it doesn't matter that I'm about to turn into dust. Dust is really, really important.'"[145] Apparently the glory of being turned into dust wasn't all that satisfying even to Schopenhauer, as Ernest Becker says Schopenhauer "spent his lonely life scanning the footnotes of learned journals to see whether there was ever going to be recognition of his work."[146] In other words, Schopenhauer also sought symbolic immortality probably because while awake at night, staring at the ceiling, he realized that going on only as dust wasn't much solace.

The Spanish philosopher Miguel de Unamuno sums up this belief of Buddhism, Schopenhauer, Einstein, and a host of others—namely, when we live in the moment and realize that everything is one (monism), we gain eternal life:

> "That art thou!" they tell me with the Upanishads. And I answer: Yes, I am that, if that is I and all is mine, and mine the totality of things. As mine I love the All, and I love my neighbour because he lives in me and is part of my consciousness, because he is like me, because he is mine. Oh, to prolong this blissful moment, to sleep, to eternalize oneself in it![147]

He writes that those who "come seeking to deceive us with a deceit of deceits, telling us that nothing is lost, that everything is transformed, shifts and changes, that not the least particle of matter is annihilated, not the least impulse of energy is lost, and there are some who pretend to console us with this!" Not a chance! Unamuno writes, "Futile consolation! It is not my matter or my energy that is the cause of my disquiet, for they are not mine if I myself am not mine—that is, if I am not eternal. No, my longing is not to be submerged in the vast All, in an infinite and eternal Matter or Energy... *Tricks* of monism avail us nothing; we crave the substance and not the shadow of immortality."[148] That's right, right? Telling yourself that your individual existence isn't real, that everything is one, and that by this realization, you understand that you go on forever—although as dust—is a trick. Going on as dust isn't going on at all. In fact, in Genesis 3:19, we read this was precisely the Lord's judgment of Adam when he rebelled: "You are dust, and to dust you shall return." It is emblematic of human corruption that hundreds of millions of people (i.e., Hindus, Buddhists, and now many atheists) would take "to dust you shall return" and turn it into something noble!

Is it really glorious that you're just a bunch of particles eaten, digested, and then excreted by who knows what? I don't think dust wonderful—rather, dust is the reason I bought a Dyson vacuum. But when you die, you won't just go on as undifferentiated particles. Jesus says in John 5:28-29 that "an hour is coming when all who are in the tombs will hear his voice and come out, those who have done good to the resurrection of life."

The Misery of the Mortality-Mitigation Mind-Set

Skeptics say Christians constructed Christianity to assuage their fear of death, but notice the nonsense skeptics embrace to flee *their* fear. Also, the mere fact that Christianity provides hope doesn't mean it was invented (we'll talk more about that soon). It could be that the truth provides hope.

We've now reviewed the major mortality-mitigation projects employed by secularists, and we've seen problems with each. But how successful are all these attempts at mitigating the horror of death, even to atheists? In *Psychology Today*, physician Alan Lickerman writes, "I've tried to resolve my fear of death intellectually and come to the conclusion that it can't be done, at least not by me."[149] I wondered if Lickerman had learned something that might help him since his 2009 article in *Psychology Today*, so I checked out his 2012 book *The Undefeated Mind: On the Science of Constructing an Indestructible Self*. In his last chapter, Lickerman talks about his fear of death. He writes that he's "always surprised when someone tells [me] they're not afraid of death...I've always wondered if that answer hints at a denial so deeply seated it cannot be faced by most. Certainly, this has been the case with me. I love being here and don't want to leave." He admits, "Whenever I've tried wrapping my mind around the concept of my own demise, tried truly envisioning the world continuing on without me, the essence of what I am utterly gone forever, I've unearthed a fear so overwhelming it's turned my mind aside as if my imagination and the idea of my own end were two magnets of identical polarity, unwilling to meet no matter how hard I tried to make them."[150]

Sam Harris acknowledges,

> I do have existential worries. I, like I think everybody else, am concerned about death. You know, death is in some ways unacceptable. It's, it's just an astonishing fact of our being here that we die. But I think worse than that, if we live long enough, we lose everyone we love in this world. People die and disappear and we're left with this stark mystery, this shear not knowing of what happened to them.[151]

Harris says, "I think we can admit that atheism doesn't offer real consolation on this point...The thing that gets lost, the thing for which there is no substitute, is total consolation in the face of death."[152]

Psychiatrist Irvin D. Yalom, who offers his patients Epicurean counsel, writes, "I share the fear of death with every human being: it is our dark shadow from which we are never severed."[153] Likewise, Bauman states, "The horror of death is the horror of the void" and is "bound to remain, *traumatic*."[154] Similarly, Andrew Stark declares, "After all the reasoning and all the rationales, I'd still desperately prefer to be a conscious, healthy human being than a corpse. Who wouldn't?"[155]

Luc Ferry, after presenting his version of the "wisdom view," is honest about the puniness of this "salvation":

> You might object that, compared to the doctrine of Christianity—whose promise of the resurrection of the body means that we shall be reunited with those we love after death—a humanism without metaphysics is small beer. I grant you that amongst the available doctrines of salvation, nothing can compete with Christianity—provided, that is, that you are a believer.[156]

To compare his wisdom view of salvation as "small beer," a beer that contains little alcohol, with the enjoyment of Christian loved ones throughout eternity is like trying to quench a dying man's thirst with desert dirt. Let's recount the success of this naturalistic "small beer" salvation. When you die, your consciousness will cease. Your body will then decay, and as *The Hearse Song* goes, "The worms crawl in, the worms crawl out / The worms play pinochle on your snout." You have no hope of reuniting with your loved ones. You will never again enjoy other people, or sunsets, or beaches, or breakers, or mountains, or redwoods, or roses, or anything else for that matter. Soon *everyone will forget you* except as maybe a footnote of history. But even if you are a footnote of history, does that really matter?

Atheists, however, still hope that some enlightenment will save them from their fear of death. Ferry writes, "I am convinced, even if *I myself am still far from possessing it*, that this type of wisdom exists, and that it is the *crowning achievement of a humanism* released finally from the illusions of metaphysics and religion."[157] Wow, right? Ferry is *sure* the wisdom exists that would free him from his fear of death even as he admits that he is *far* from "possessing it."

Although he wasn't a Christian, Ralph Waldo Emerson understood the significance of a society giving up belief in immortality: "No sooner do we try to get rid of the idea of Immortality—than Pessimism raises its head...Human griefs seem little worth assuaging; human happiness too paltry (at best) to be worth increasing. The whole moral world is reduced to a point. Good and evil, right and wrong, become infinitesimal, ephemeral matters. The affections die away—die of their own conscious feebleness and uselessness. A moral paralysis creeps over us."[158] Thus Cave asks, "Can there be progress, justice and culture if we know that all our efforts will end in dust? Or should we for the sake of both our sanity and our civilization forget all our hard-won insights and attempt to recloak ourselves in the illusion of life everlasting?"[159] Sad.

Here is an amusing piece from Woody Allen about the philosophical success of mitigating the fear of death. Allen wrote himself into a dialog in which he plays the part of Socrates just prior to Socrates's execution. Allen, however, is trying to get out of dying:

Simmias: Is our wisest philosopher a coward?

Allen: I'm not a coward, and I'm not a hero. I'm somewhere in the middle.

Simmias: A cringing vermin.

Allen: That's approximately the spot.

Agathon: But it was you who proved that death doesn't exist.

Allen: Hey, listen—I've proved a lot of things. That's how I pay my rent. Theories and little observations. A puckish remark now and then. Occasional maxims. It beats picking olives, but let's not get carried away.

Agathon: But you have proved many times that the soul is immortal.

Allen: And it is! On paper. See, that's the thing about philosophy—it's not all that functional once you get out of class.[160]

Of course, Allen is being funny, but it's funny because there's a ring of truth here. Although I suspect that worldly philosophy *might* help some face death when they're not actually facing death, I'm skeptical about claims that it will help when death is imminent. Thus the saying, "There are no atheists in foxholes."[161] God has put eternity in our hearts, and we are all held in lifelong bondage to the fear of death (Hebrews 2:15). Philosophical mumbo jumbo won't fix that.

As we will see in chapter 6, there is compelling evidence that Jesus was raised from the dead, and so we have a logical reason to believe that we will have life everlasting. Indeed, Christians realize that no earthly wisdom will free the godless from their fear of death. That freedom only comes through Jesus, who will "deliver all those who through fear of death were subject to lifelong slavery" (Hebrews 2:15).

5

The Failure of All Secular Salvations

Although we humans employ a variety of secular salvation strate-gies to give us a sense of transcendence over death, they fail miser-ably, so we resort to unreal, wasteful, unhealthy, destructive, and even deadly measures to end the pain.

Denial, Distraction, and Dissipation

Over the years, I've many times said to Jean E. that I don't know how people endure this life without Jesus. But then I catch myself and tell her that I do know how they do it—in fact, that's what this book is about! And nothing is more often employed to compensate for the fear of death than denial and distraction.

You can't watch TV for long without seeing people talk as if death is unreal or the dead somehow go on living in some undefined way. It is a regular fixture of "reality" shows, talent and sporting competi-tions, interviews, and so on that otherwise nonreligious people will speak of the death of a loved one with words like these: "I know Mom's looking down on me," "Dad's with me," "My wife is proud of me," and so on. One study concludes, "In recent years, fewer Americans prayed, believed in God, took the Bible literally, attended religious services, identified as religious, affiliated with a religion, or had con-fidence in religious institutions."[1] But paradoxically, "Americans have become slightly more likely to believe in an afterlife." The study sug-gests, "One plausible, though speculative, explanation is that this is another example of the rise in entitlement—expecting special privileges without effort."[2] Well, no surprise there, right? Tell a generation that they are good unrelated to their behavior or performance, and they will think they should be able to live forever regardless of how they act or believe.

Sociologist Zygmunt Bauman explains that "reason" cannot free us from the shame of death; "it can only try a cover-up. And it does...Since the discovery of death...human societies have kept designing elaborate subterfuges, hoping that they would be allowed to forget about the scandal; failing that, they forbade speaking of it."[3] The morning after winning Emmys for being the producer and star of Veep, Julia Louis-Dreyfus said that the doctor called to tell her she had breast cancer. She said, "I howled with laughter, which turned into hysterical crying. I mean, it's a blow."[4]

Now cancer free, she was asked, does the "keen awareness of the dearness of life last?" She replied, "No. It comes and goes. But once you've walked through a life-threatening illness, there's this little nagging thing with you all the time. That fear doesn't completely go away because you've been face to face with it. But you know what?" asked Louis-Dreyfus, "We walk through our lives so oblivious to the fact that our lives are going to end. We really don't consider that. Ever. Almost ever. Maybe that's a good thing. But it's a cold, hard fact, and it is a strange thing to reconcile."[5] That's right. Most people go through their lives trying hard not to think about it!

Singularity hopeful Ray Kurzweil says death is "such a profoundly sad, lonely feeling that I really can't bear it." Then Kurzweil adds cheerfully, "So I go back to thinking about how I'm not going to die."[6] Robert Lanza, in a *Psychology Today* article, romanticized that death is "like a perennial flower that returns to bloom in the multiverse."[7] Notice the blooming banality employed to enable an ersatz eternity? Indeed, the first emperor of China prohibited—on pain of death—all mention of death in his presence. After a meteorite struck the earth and some "imperial officials arrived to inspect it, the stone from the sky had been inscribed with a graffito that implied the first emperor would die, and his empire would be divided back into the kingdoms of old. Although imperial investigators interrogated, and eventually executed everyone in the area, they were unable to locate the culprit."[8] One did not trifle with the first emperor.

Denial, however, does little without distraction. After all, *just* telling yourself that you're not going to die isn't possible. It's like the old brainteaser, "Think about whatever you want but for the next two minutes don't think about pink elephants."[9] Most everyone knows how this goes: the way you keep from thinking about pink elephants is to think about blue elephants. In other words, we need to distract ourselves. And we do![10]

"Most men spare themselves" the trouble of looking at death, writes Becker, "by keeping their minds on the small problems of their lives just as society maps these problems out for them...They 'tranquilize themselves with the trivial'—and so they can lead normal lives."[11] Thus we busy ourselves with careers, children, chores, and a host of other things to keep thoughts about our deaths at bay. Bertrand Russell thought this wise: "If you have wide and keen interests and activities in which you can still be effective, you will have no reason to think about the *merely statistical* fact of the number of years you have already lived, still less of the probable brevity of your future."[12] Russell says to push the thought of death out of your mind so you'll be able to shrug off the number of days you have left as "merely statistical." In other words, think purple elephants.

Carpe Diem, Bucket Lists, and YOLO

There are countless ways to distract yourself. The phrases "carpe diem" and "seize the day" form the names of a Broadway musical, albums, songs, bands, a novel, and a film. They were popularized by the movie *Dead Poet's Society* (1989), in which English teacher John Keating (Robin Williams, 1951–2014) tells the young men in his charge, "Carpe diem. Seize the day, boys. Make your lives extraordinary." "Be wise," counsels the poet Horace (65 BCE–7 CE), "life is so brief: cut short far-reaching hopes. Even as we speak, envious Time is fleeting. *Seize the day*: entrusting as little as possible to tomorrow."[13] We first find this concept of seizing the day in *The Epic of Gilgamesh*.

King Gilgamesh, desperate to find eternal life, is counseled by the goddess and winemaker Siduri, "Gilgamesh, where are you hurrying to? You will never find the life for which you are looking. When the gods created man they allotted to him death, but life they retained in their own keeping." Instead, Siduri says, "Fill your belly with good things; day and night, night and day, dance and be merry, feast and rejoice. Let your clothes be fresh, bathe yourself in water, cherish the little child that holds your hand, and make your wife happy in your embrace; for this too is the lot of man."[14]

Most people "seize the day" by working on their secular salvation strategies. Horace sought to make a name for himself and apparently thought he succeeded: "I have built a monument more lasting than bronze and set higher than the pyramids of kings...I shall not wholly die. A great part of me will escape Libitina [the goddess of funerals]. My fame will grow, ever-renewed in time to come."[15] "Higher than the pyramids"? I'd be surprised if even one adult doesn't know about the pyramids, but if you told some people you were reading Horace, they might offer you a throat lozenge.

When I was in grade school, my parents took me to Disneyland every year for my birthday, and the challenge was to go on all the "big rides" before the park closed. I certainly didn't focus on closing time, but in the back of my mind, I knew it was coming, so I needed to move quickly to do what was most fun. Bucket lists are like that; they allow you to keep busy—to live it up until the end. Once you've checked something off, you can move immediately to the next accomplishment—or in the case of Disneyland, the next line. Thus we can busy ourselves with planning our next trip to Paris or Machu Picchu, skydiving, running a marathon, climbing a mountain, starting a business, seeing the northern lights, or playing a new instrument. Similarly, when people are buying something expensive or engaging in something adventurous or even dangerous, they'll often say "You only live once," which is now popularized as YOLO. When I hear that, I think, "Yeah, but we can live forever."

The major problem with denial and distraction is that it leads to dissipation. "Dissipation" means "the squandering of money, energy, or resources."[16] The fear of death can encourage us to waste our time and money on what doesn't matter. We waste our resources in a variety of ways.

Workaholism

Anderson Cooper, the CNN anchor and *60 Minutes* correspondent, tells Marisa Guthrie in the *Hollywood Reporter*, "I don't really have a life off-air." Cooper happily works every day, even weekends. He says, "I am not good at, like, sitting on a beach...I'm not good at decompressing." But as Guthrie puts it, "Lucky for Cooper, he seldom has time to." After all, Cooper has to maintain *Anderson Cooper 360* and his five-nights-a-week newscast on CNN. Then there's "his gig as a *60 Minutes* correspondent (he'll shoot 10 pieces for the CBS newsmagazine this season); and his new Facebook news series, *Full Circle*; not to mention the live road show he does with pal Andy Cohen, *AC²: Deep Talk and Shallow Tales*." To keep from having to spend time eating, he drinks a liquid meal, coffee-flavored Soylent. "I don't care about food," says Cooper. What drives Cooper's workaholism? As son of heiress Gloria Vanderbilt, it's not the money. When he was 10, his father died during open-heart surgery, and his older brother, Carter, committed suicide when he was 23 years old by jumping from the terrace of Vanderbilt's penthouse. "Those tragedies," writes Guthrie, "are the reason he started roaming the globe as a young freelance journalist to war-torn places like Rwanda and Somalia."[17] Keep yourself busy and you can ignore your fear of death...kind of.

Russian novelist Leo Tolstoy (1828–1910) wrote a novella entitled The Death of Ivan Ilyich. He said that Ivan was a workaholic, and that helped him screen out thoughts of death. But when Ivan is injured, he realizes he is going to die. Tolstoy writes that Ivan "called up a series of other thoughts in place of this thought, in hopes of finding support in them. He tried to go back to his former ways of thinking, which had screened him formerly from the thought of death. But—strange thing—all that had formerly screened, hidden, wiped out the consciousness of death now could no longer produce that effect." Ivan would say, "I'll busy myself with work—why, I used to live by it." But suddenly, that "pain in his side...would begin its own gnawing work." He tries to drive his thoughts of death away, but "it would go on, and it would come and stand directly in front of him and look at him, and he would be dumbstruck, the light would go out in his eyes, and he would again begin asking himself: 'Can it alone be true?'" Ivan comes to a "sad awareness that his work in court could no longer, as before, conceal from him what he wanted concealed." In short, Ivan Ilyich "looked for consolation, for other screens, and other screens appeared and for a short time seemed to save him, but at once they were again not so much destroyed as made transparent, as if it penetrated everything and there was no screening it out."[18]

Although many people rightly recognize workaholism as a bad thing, it's for the most part socially acceptable. Thus when you're being interviewed for a job and they inevitably ask what you consider to be your biggest weakness, the joke answer is, "Well, people say I'm a workaholic, but I don't think that's so bad." But workaholics are famous for ignoring their families, and when Ivan's wife nags him to spend more time with her, it just drives him further into his work. Although work is important (we need to pay the bills, after all), as Ivan's life ends, he realizes that he had ignored other truly important things.

Amusement

Somebody once told me that "amuse" means "to stop thinking." They reasoned that "muse" means "to think," and when you put an "a" in front of "muse," it means "to not think." Well, I wish I could find that etymology, but that's not the word's origin. Nevertheless, that's what it means. "Amuse" means "to entertain or occupy in a light, playful, or pleasant manner." It's interesting that it used to mean "to divert the attention of so as to deceive," because often, that's what it does.[19] Our attention is diverted from what truly matters. And do we love to be amused! We love to get out minds off the seriousness of the human condition—our lost and dying future.

Kevin Feige, president and producer of the Marvel Cinematic Universe, says, "I fell in love with the notion of movies being a thing that can help us escape."[20] Indeed, we all know what Feige means by "escape." Maybe you don't enjoy superhero movies (I do), but it's no accident that successful entertainers—singers, actors, athletes—receive some of the highest salaries in the world. They help with what we need most—to escape thoughts of death! Now, I'm not opposed to watching some television, movies, and sporting contests or engaging in social media, computer games, and so on, but how easy is it for us to waste our lives on these things? And our money! This is why movie stars and professional athletes are paid a hundred times (or much, much more) what we pay teachers. Amusing us—keeping our minds off of our deaths—is the most valuable thing a person can do.

The Neilson Corporation reports that on average, people spent about 10 hours and 24 minutes interacting with media each day (e.g., radio, television, and/or social media). If that seems high, it's because "about 81 percent across all age groups use a digital device while watching TV."[21] In other words, while watching TV, people check social media, look up things they heard on TV, and send emails, texts, or messages about the content. This distracts us from the human condition. But it also wastes our lives here. I'm not saying that no one should ever do those things in moderation—I do—but consider how many more meaningful things we could be doing in service to the Lord and His people.

When Jerusalem was under siege, the Lord told them in Isaiah 22 that their destruction for their sin was coming and that this "called for weeping and mourning, for baldness and wearing sackcloth" (verse 12). But what the Lord found instead was that Judah was saying, "Let us eat and drink, for tomorrow we die" (verse 13). So we read, "The LORD Almighty has revealed this in my hearing: 'Till your dying day this sin will not be atoned for,' says the Lord, the LORD Almighty" (verse 14 NIV). Again, I'm not suggesting we can't watch a clean movie or a sporting event or interact on social media, but as Dallas Willard told us in class, those most useful for the kingdom of God are those who spend the least amount of time doing what doesn't matter.

Sexual Addiction

We've seen that sexual seduction can be an immortality project, but as probably every reader already knows, it's also an escape. If you're feeling trapped in a dead-end job, in chores, or in an unhappy relationship, then lust is motion. In other words, when you're lusting, you're going somewhere pleasurable even if it is only in your mind. You can close your eyes or stare at a monitor and enter a world where you imagine being the seducer or the seduced. As the seducer, you fantasize about persuading people to want you; as the seduced, you fantasize about being desirable to the seducer. Either way, you are wanted, desirable, and don't have to face your meaningless, dead-end existence. Of course, fantasy escape often leads to wanting to seduce or be seduced "for real," which has led to countless affairs, divorces, and molestations. Also well known is that resorting to sexual fantasy damages the possibility of a mature, loving, and healthy sexual relationship with the opposite sex. No one looks barely 18 for long.

Giving yourself to sex is exemplified by the Laura Branigan (1952–2004) song "Self Control," which topped the music chart in six countries. She sang that her seducers took her self-control, and so she lived only for the night. Her seducers helped her forget her daily obligations, and so to feel okay, she sang that she'll just believe "tomorrow never comes." Now, this song may have been no more to Branigan than a catchy moneymaker, but her life is a caution that exemplifies how hard it is to deny death. Branigan spent two and a half years nursing her husband, who died of colon cancer when she was 39, and then, says Branigan, she "had to go through the mourning stage, you know, you can't get around that, you have to go through the fire." Then after years of being away from the spotlight, she returned to music but fell off a ladder at her home, breaking both femurs, which resulted in six months of physical therapy. She returned to music in 2001, but in 2004, she died of a brain aneurysm at 52.[22] Tomorrow came.

Unless you die suddenly, denial and distraction employed to keep you from thinking about death will sooner or later fail. As we've seen, Ivan had denied his own mortality, but there came a time when

> Ivan Ilyich saw that he was dying, and he was in continual despair. In the depths of his soul Ivan Ilyich knew

that he was dying, but not only was he not accustomed to it, he simply did not, he could not possibly understand it. The example of a syllogism he had studied in Kiesewetter's logic—Caius is a man, men are mortal, therefore Caius is mortal—had seemed to him all his life to be correct only in relation to Caius, but by no means to himself. For the man Caius, man in general, it was perfectly correct; but he was not Caius and not man in general, he had always been quite, quite separate from all other beings...And Caius is indeed mortal, and it's right that he die, but for me, Vanya, Ivan Ilyich, with all my feelings and thoughts—for me it's another matter. And it cannot be that I should die.

It would be too terrible.

So it felt to him.[23]

The bubble of denial and distraction is always in danger of being popped by suffering.

This enjoyment of the present is found in sayings such as "Wine, women, and song" and the current "Sex, drugs, and rock and roll." In other words, "Let's party!" Paul clearly references this hedonism in 1 Corinthians 15:32: "Let us eat and drink, for tomorrow we die," but he prefaces it with "If the dead are not raised."[24] However, the dead will rise, and thankfully, in Christ you don't have to deny and distract yourself from the end of life here. As Peter puts it in 1 Peter 1:13, "Therefore, preparing your minds for action, and being sober-minded, set your hope fully on the grace that will be brought to you at the revelation of Jesus Christ." You can, and should, focus on living forever!

Meaninglessness

Another problem for those who have no hope beyond this life is that it is hard, if not impossible, to find any meaning in their lives. Every six months after my cancer operation, I went to the hospital imaging center for an MRI. Most of those in the waiting room were tense. After all, many of them were there to find out whether they had a dreaded disease or their dreaded disease had returned. One day I was sitting in this room with eight or nine others, and some how-to show was on TV. Well, in response to how to baste eggs (or whatever it was), suddenly a 40-something-year-old fellow violated the primary law of waiting room decorum when he wailed, "What does that matter if I'm going to die?" Indeed, what does anything matter if you and everyone you know and the entire universe will be extinct?

If you Google around, you'll find atheists telling you that we make or create our own meaning. But how important is the creation of my own meaning if it's nothing more than something I concocted on a Sunday afternoon? I might have just said something like, "I know! I'll decide that this or that is very important, and I'll dedicate my life to making it happen." Earlier we saw that Stephen Cave falsely concludes that the point of Ecclesiastes is to live in the moment. Rather, Duane A. Garrett writes that Ecclesiastes examines "the vain attempts to gain genuine personal worth through wealth and pleasure, through accomplishments and power, and through knowledge. The Teacher tells his readers how to live in the world as it really is instead of living in a world of false hope." Garrett writes that "*Ecclesiastes urges its readers to recognize that they are mortal.* They must abandon all illusions of self-importance, face death and life squarely, and accept with fear and trembling their dependence on God."[25]

Exactly.

Anxiety

Psychiatrist Irving D. Yalom writes, "Despite the staunchest, most venerable defenses, we can never completely subdue death anxiety: it is always there, lurking in some hidden ravine of the mind."[26] Yes, and these anxieties manifest themselves in a multitude of ways.

One type of anxiety was added as an entry in the *Oxford English Dictionary* in 2013. FOMO (fear of missing out) is the uneasy and sometimes all-consuming feeling that you're missing out. FOMO drives a lot of social media usage. Although for teens and young adults, FOMO is especially prevalent, studies show that at one time or another, most people have been FOMO affected.[27] After all, who hasn't feared that they are missing out on something? I have. But surely those who have rejected the belief in an afterlife will have FOMO more than those who haven't. After all, if this life is all you have, then at the end of your life, you're not going to want to think "A good time was had by all but me!"

Clinical psychologist Jordan Peterson gets it right: "I've often treated people with anxiety and people wonder practically, individually, clinically, 'why are people anxious?' And I think, that's a completely ridiculous question. The reasons for anxiety are starkly self-evident. What I wonder is why aren't people terrified out of their skulls so badly every second of their life that they can't even move?" Peterson continues, "Yeah, and you all laugh because you understand that. It's like, anxiety, that's no mystery, it's like, brief spells of calm, that's a mystery."[28] Although Peterson doesn't specify that the fear of death drives much of our anxiety, he certainly thinks it is a part of it.[29] Of course, the reason secularists are "able to move" in the face of death is because they employ literal or symbolic immortality projects or mortality-mitigation projects. However, in our truthful moments, especially lying awake at night and staring at a dark ceiling, we realize our projects fail. The good—better yet, great—news is that eternal life awaits. It is also comforting to understand what's most important for us while we're in the body: we must love God and love our neighbor! If we're doing that, then missing out on Machu Picchu or skydiving isn't missing anything more valuable than the pennies that fall between the car seats because these things won't bring eternal reward, but loving God and neighbor will.

Depression

Philosopher William James sums up the human condition in his book *The Varieties of Religious Experience*:

> The pride of life and the glory of the world will shrivel. It is after all but the standing quarrel of hot youth and hoary eld. Old age has the last word: the purely naturalistic look at life, however enthusiastically it may begin, is sure to end in sadness. This sadness lies at the

> heart of every merely positivistic, agnostic, or naturalistic scheme of philosophy. Let sanguine healthy-mindedness do its best with its strange power of living in the moment and ignoring and forgetting, still the evil background is really there to be thought of, and the skull will grin in at the banquet.[30]

James continues, "The fact that we *can* die, that we *can* be ill at all, is what perplexes us; the fact that we now, for a moment live and are well is irrelevant to that perplexity. We need a life not correlated with death…a kind of good that will not perish, a good in fact that flies beyond the Goods of nature."[31] Proverbs 14:12-13 (nrsv) reads, "There is a way that seems right to a person, but its end is the way to death. Even in laughter the heart is sad, and the end of joy is grief."[32] Even when things are going well, the thought of death lurks in the background.

I wrote a blog entitled "If You're Honest, You're Depressed (or You're a Christian)." I point out in the blog that there are things other than the fear of death that depress us (like a hormonal imbalance), but the prospect of our deaths, and the deaths of those we love, is *the* major reason for depression. After all, only one thing will prevent you from watching every person you know die from murder, accident, or disease, and that will be your own death from murder, accident, or disease. Unless you have a robust belief that you will live forever with your Christian loved ones, then how can you admit the truth about death and not be depressed? If you are honest—in other words, if you aren't in denial or keeping yourself distracted from the horror of the human condition—then how could you not be depressed? Bertrand Russell writes that we must build our lives on the "firm foundation of unyielding despair."[33] He says, "Brief and powerless is Man's life; on him and all his race the slow, sure doom falls pitiless and dark."[34] Astronomer and science popularizer Carl Sagan's wife, Ann Druyan, talks about being with Carl while he was dying. She says, "As we looked deeply into each other's eyes, it was with a shared conviction that our wondrous life together was ending forever."[35] How depressing!

To make it through the day, *everyone* except the *robust* believer in eternal life through Jesus has to—must—lie to themselves about reality. Let me say that again: outside of Jesus, everyone has to lie to themselves. They have to lie to themselves that advances in medical science might just do what they're supposed to and enable them to live—if not forever, then at least for a very long time. If science isn't fast enough, then they might delude themselves that freezing their brains will work until science figures it out. Then as we saw, most people convince themselves that their symbolic immortality projects will give them some immortality, but deep down, they know they'll still be dead—their consciousnesses will cease.

Finally, we saw how naturalists deceive themselves by saying things like "I don't want to live forever anyway" and "Individual existence is a delusion." How well we convince ourselves that these lies aren't lies is how well we keep from becoming "twitching blobs of biological protoplasm completely perfused with anxiety and unable to effectively respond to the demands of their immediate surroundings."[36] Everyone does these things except (and often including) sincere Christians. It is "normal" to lie to yourself, but with the eternal life in Jesus, you can tell yourself the truth, and the truth is this: you are going to live forever.

Now, I realize that many Christians are suspicious of *secular* psychology—and I'm one of them! Secular psychology is fatally flawed because, as it says in Proverbs 9:10, "The fear of the Lord is the beginning of wisdom." Philosophies that reject biblical truth don't have the beginning of wisdom. That being said, even the old, blind sow gets an acorn once in a while, and since secular psychology's conclusions coincide with Scripture about the fear of death, it's worth pointing out that many psychologists think the fear of death influences much mental illness. Now, I'm *not* arguing that people's fear of death explains all mental illness, but many psychologists say that people's fear of death plays a huge role.

Ernest Becker puts it well: "We can say that the essence of normality is the *refusal of reality*. What we call neurosis enters precisely at this point: Some people have more trouble with their lies than others...This is neurosis in a nutshell: the miscarriage of clumsy lies about reality."[37] Becker writes that things become "more complex" when someone sees "how the lies about reality begin to miscarry." That's when we "apply the label 'neurotic.'"[38] Becker says psychologist Otto Rank "used the term 'neurotic' for the one type of person who was without illusion, who saw things as they were."[39] Similarly, philosopher William James says, "The deadly horror which an agitated melancholiac feels is the literally *right reaction* on the situation."[40]

Becker asks, "Is man an animal who fears death, who seeks self-perpetuation and heroic transcendence of his fate? Then, failure for such an animal is failure to achieve heroic transcendence...mental illness is a way of talking about people who have lost courage, which is the same as saying that it reflects the failure of heroism."[41] Indeed, Yalom argues persuasively that Freud was wrong to say the fear of death is really about something else. Yalom says that when it comes to death, Freud "had a persistent blind spot which obscured for him some patently obvious aspects of man's inner world."[42] Rather, the fear of death is, indeed, fear about death. "Death," writes Yalom, "itches all the time; it is always with us, scratching at some inner door, whirring softly, barely audibly, just under the membrane of consciousness. Hidden and disguised, leaking out in a variety of symptoms, it is the wellspring of many of our worries, stresses, and conflicts."[43] Yalom continues, "The neurotic patient" may "not be out of contact with the reality" of death, "but instead, through failing to erect 'normal' defenses, it may be too close to the truth."[44]

What is a mid-life crisis, after all, if not the realization that you're half-way to being dead? The mid-life crisis is worse for those who judge their immortality projects to be a failure. Twenty to 30 years ago, I worked in a secular corporation and for each person's birthday (most of us were in the 30 to 40 age range) the office was decorated with tombstones, black balloons, and here and there a large RIP. When it was my birthday co-workers would tease me, as they teased everyone, about getting old and I'd always employ a verbal jujitsu. For example, once I said: "Yes, I'm 38 which is halfway to being 76 years old and 76 is when the average American male dies so I'm halfway to being dead!" I'd pause and then add, "But thankfully because I'm a Christian I'm going to live forever!" Yes, I often said that kind of thing. One year, a fellow exclaimed, "It doesn't do any good to kid Clay about this because he always ruins it."

Of course, skeptics will tell us that believing in eternal life in Jesus is also a lie, but Christians have solid evidence for the resurrection of Jesus, which is the guarantee of our having eternal life. I'll present this evidence in the next chapter.

Psychosis

When the lies we tell ourselves, when the denials and distractions completely fail—that's when the wheels come off our emotional freight trains. As Becker puts it, "People have psychotic breaks when repression no longer works, when the forward momentum of activity is no longer possible."[45] The reality of death can become extreme, and when people's immortality projects fail and they see no way to transcend their deaths, they may start to believe they have special knowledge or are special people—like Jesus or Gandhi—or that they are being persecuted by a government agency. When I worked for an insurance company, I reviewed a claim where the insured said the FBI was shooting lasers into his house. (No surprise, there wasn't any laser damage.)

When I was a 25-year-old associate pastor, a tall, good-looking fellow came to see me. When I asked him if anything was wrong, he smiled and said everything was great. I kept asking in different ways what was bothering him to no avail. He kept smiling and saying everything was fine! Well, after this had gone on for some time, it became increasingly strange because I was the pastor on call that day, and he must have come in for some reason, so I finally asked, "Then why are you here?" At that, he leaned forward and whispered, "There's a conspiracy and you can't even tell the President of the United States about it." Frankly—and I'm sincerely embarrassed about this—I couldn't hold back my laughter, and he left in a huff (I probably wasn't going to be able to help him anyway).

I think the social scientists are right that if your normal defenses against mortality fail, you might resort to delusions of grandeur. Psychiatrist Harold Searles (1918–2015) treated deeply psychotic patients for many years, and Yalom calls Searles's work "deeply insightful" and "heroic."[46] In *Psychiatry Quarterly*, Searles writes an article entitled "Schizophrenia and the Inevitability of Death," in which he claims, "Defense-mechanisms of psychiatric illness" are "designed to keep out of the individual's awareness" the "simple fact of life's finitude."[47] He continues, "The patient's having become, and having long remained, schizophrenic" was "*in order to avoid facing*" the "fact that life is finite."[48]

"The paranoid patient," Yalom writes, manifests "delusions of grandeur and omnipotence, one of the primary modes of evading death—a belief in one's own specialness and immortality." He continues, "The patient's primary shield against death, then, is a sense of omnipotence, a key feature in any schizophrenic illness."[49] As Sheldon Solomon, Jeff Greenberg, and Tom Pyszczynski put it, "If you are schizophrenic and think that ninjas are after you, or that you are the president, being routinely rebuffed by others' skeptical disbelief...would surely intensify your already daunting psychological difficulties."[50] Thus, writes Yalom, "Nothing would so completely destroy the sense of personal omnipotence than the acceptance of the inevitability of death, and the schizophrenic patient clings to his or her denial of death with fierce desperation."[51] In the journal *Diseases of the Nervous System*, psychiatrist Karel Planansky and psychologist Roy Johnston penned an article entitled "Preoccupation with Death in Schizophrenic Men." They conclude that "a systemic review of psychiatric histories of 205 hospitalized, schizophrenic men (veterans) revealed that 80 had expressed fear of dying, being killed, of no longer existing, or other evidence of preoccupation with death."[52]

Drugs

That people's lies fail them is why so many numb their fears through alcohol and drugs. Studies show a strong correlation between alcohol and drug use and attempts to numb the fear of death. In 2014, a study was conducted where half the participants were given flyers offering to help them with their fear of death, and the other half of the participants were given flyers offering to help them with their back pain. A few yards away, a friendly student offered the participants a choice between a refreshing nonalcoholic beverage and a strongly alcoholic beverage. The result? Of the people who received the flyer about death, 37 percent purchased the alcoholic beverage compared to 9 percent of the people who received the flyer about back pain.[53] And that was just a flyer! Imagine how many people would belly up to the bar if they were confronted with their deaths in earnest!

Earlier we saw that Barbara Ehrenreich thinks magic mushrooms might just be the answer for coping with the fear of death. Here's what Joe Klein of *Time* magazine thinks:

> For the past several years, I've been harboring a fantasy, a last political crusade for the baby-boom generation. We, who started on the path of righteousness, marching for civil rights and against the war in Vietnam, need to find an appropriately high-minded approach to life's exit ramp. In this case, I mean the high-minded part literally. And so, a deal: give us drugs, after a certain age—say, 80—all drugs, any drugs we want. In return, we will give you our driver's licenses. (I mean, can you imagine how terrifying a nation of decrepit, solipsistic 90-year-old boomers behind the wheel would be?) We'll let you proceed with your lives—much of which will be spent paying for our retirement, in any case—without having to hear us complain about our every ache and reflux. We'll be too busy exploring altered states of consciousness. I even have a slogan for the campaign: "Tune in, turn on, drop dead."[54]

Honestly, if I wasn't a Christian, I'd be cheering this on!

Here's the last paragraph of the last page of Duke University philosopher Alex Rosenberg's book *The Atheist's Guide to Reality: Enjoying Life Without Illusions*: "Epicurus wasn't right when he argued that understanding the nature of reality is by itself enough to make a person happy. Alas, some people do get everything right about the universe and our place in it and remain dissatisfied...they are still troubled." So what's Rosenberg's answer? Here's the last sentence: "Take a Prozac or your favorite serotonin reuptake inhibitor, and keep taking them till they kick in."[55] So Rosenberg's presumably sober advice for dealing with death fears is "Get high!"

Klein, Ehrenreich, and Rosenberg aren't dropouts who never lived responsible lives. Instead, they are intelligent and successful, and they presumably were sober when they argued that drugs are the answer to combatting our fear of death. How much more, then, should we expect people to use drugs to escape perceiving themselves as failures? I don't need to spend time here explaining that the misuse of alcohol and drugs leads not only to heartache and crime but to illness and premature death.

Suicide

According to the Centers for Disease Control and Prevention, the rate of suicide in the United States increased 28 percent from 1999 to 2016. In 2016 alone, 45,000 Americans took their own lives.[56] Some may think that linking suicide to the fear of death is counterintuitive because suicide actually results in death, but those who attempt suicide realize that suicide only hastens the inevitable. For many, the fear of death is so present, so severe, and so unrelenting that they take their mortality into their own hands by ending their own lives. Many people don't want to live with the knowledge that they are going to die. Indeed, Yalom writes that suicide "is an active act; it permits one to control that which controls one."[57] In fact, if the depressed believed they would never die, then surely that would lighten their emotional load. Indeed, we should expect an increase in suicide as more people lose confidence in an afterlife.[58]

"I want to commit suicide," explains Pyotr Stepanovich in Fyodor Dostoyevsky's (1821–81) *The Possessed*, "because I don't like the fear of death."[59] Alfred Lord Tennyson (1809–92) writes, "If there is no immortality, I shall hurl myself into the sea."[60] Indeed, "the majority of suicides," writes the Spanish philosopher Miguel de Unamuno, "would not take their lives if they had assurance that they would never die on this earth. The self-slayer kills himself because he will not wait for his death."[61] As Epicurus's disciple Lucretius says, "And often, on account of the fear of death, such a hatred of life and of seeing the light seizes human beings that, in their state of agony, they commit suicide."[62] Although Epicureans write this off as anti-Epicurean propaganda, the only record we have of Lucretius's death tells us he had bouts of insanity and committed suicide at age 44.[63]

Staks Rosch admits in the *Huffington Post,* "Depression is a serious problem in the greater atheist community and far too often, that depression has led to suicide. This is something many of my fellow atheists often don't like to admit, but it is true."[64] Indeed, a study in the *American Journal of Psychiatry* reports, "Religiously unaffiliated subjects had significantly more lifetime suicide attempts and more first-degree relatives who committed suicide than subjects who endorsed a religious affiliation...Furthermore, subjects with no religious affiliation perceived fewer reasons for living."[65] I doubt, dear reader, that you're surprised by this. And sadly, disbelief is increasing. A recent Gallup poll reported the following: "U.S. church membership was 70% or higher from 1937 through 1976, falling modestly to an average of 68% in the 1970s through the 1990s. The past 20 years have seen an acceleration in the drop-off, with a 20-percentage-point decline since 1999 and more than half of that change occurring since the start of the current decade."[66] People talk about a suicide epidemic, but the real epidemic is an increasing rejection of a robust belief in an afterlife, which renders people's lives hopeless.[67]

Anarchy

We should not be surprised that as people cast off God—and also confidence in an afterlife where we will all come into judgment—anarchy ensues and societies collapse. When I was a child, we never saw anything bad on television, ever. Growing up, I'd watch reruns of the comedy *I Love Lucy* (1951–57), and the worst thing that ever happened was that Lucy (Lucille Ball, 1911–89) would tell a lie, and then the remainder of the episode would be about how Lucy tries to cover up her lie and how, eventually, the lie is exposed. Moral: honesty is the best policy. There was never cursing or nudity. In fact, Jeannie (Barbara Eden), in the television series *I Dream of Jeannie* (1965–70), wasn't allowed to show her belly button. I became a Christian in intermediate school in 1969, and in the late 1960s, I began to see a shift. I was shocked to see a man on top of a woman on *Rowan & Martin's Laugh In* (1968–73), and they were fully clothed! In the 1950s through the early 1970s, even if they weren't actually Christian, Americans had an inherent sense of Christian morality and a belief in the afterlife. I'm not waxing nostalgic; I'm just pointing out how times have changed. Now with rampant violence and pornography on TV and the Internet, we are seeing the Canaanization of American culture.[68] All this encourages anarchy—disorder due to the lack of recognized authority.

This was predictable. Martin Luther (1483–1546) writes, "If you believe in no future life, I would not give a mushroom for your God! Do then as you like. For if no God, so no devil, no hell: as with a fallen tree, all is over when you die. Then plunge into treachery, rascality, robbery, and murder."[69] Duke University psychologist William McDougall (1871–1938) says he has no "religious convictions," but he writes about the afterlife, "It seems to me highly probable that the passing away of this belief would be highly calamitous for our civilization."[70] And why not? As Fyodor Dostoyevsky puts it in *The Brothers Karamazov*, if "God and immortality do not exist," then "man is allowed to become a man-god," and "then everything is permitted."[71]

François-René de Chateaubriand (1768–1848), who founded Romanticism in French literature, writes, "There can be no morality if there be no future state."[72] The bishop of Clermont, Jean Baptiste Massillon (1663–1742), states, "If we wholly perish with the body, what an imposture is this whole system of laws, manners, and usages, on which human society is founded!" He asks, "Why should we heed them, if in this life only we have hope? Speak not of duty. What can we owe the dead, to the living, to ourselves, if all *are*, or *will be*, nothing? Who shall dictate our duty if not our own pleasures—if not our own passions? Speak not of morality. It is a mere chimera, a bugbear of human invention, if retribution terminate with the grave." Massillon points out that "if we must wholly perish, then is obedience to the laws but an insensate servitude; rulers and magistrates are but the phantoms which popular imbecility has raised up; justice is an unwarrantable infringement upon the liberty of men,—an imposition, an usurpation." Indeed, he

writes that "the law of marriage" is "a vain scruple; modesty, a preju-
dice; honor and probity, such stuff as dreams are made of; and incests,
murders, parricides, the most heartless cruelties and blackest crimes,
are but the legitimate sports of man's irresponsible nature; while the
harsh epithets attached to them are merely such as the policy of legisla-
tors has invented, and imposed on the credulity of people."[73] I couldn't
agree more. Without God, morality cannot be objectively established,
and therefore lawmakers will do little more than legislate their whims.
Indeed, Aleksandr Solzhenitsyn (1918–2008), the author of *The Gulag
Archipelago*, who himself spent eight years in a Soviet gulag, sums up
the reason for the horrors and ultimate collapse of the Soviet Union:

> I have spent well-nigh 50 years working on the history
> of our Revolution; in the process I have read hundreds
> of books, collected hundreds of personal testimonies,
> and have already contributed eight volumes of my own
> toward the effort of clearing away the rubble left by that
> upheaval. But if I were asked today to formulate as con-
> cisely as possible the main cause of the ruinous Revolu-
> tion that swallowed up some 60 million of our people,
> I could not put it more accurately than to repeat: "Men
> have forgotten God; that's why all this has happened."[74]

But as the old quip goes, "History teaches us we learn nothing from history." If there's no God and therefore no afterlife or hope, then many
gulags are in our future.

But help comes! As Jesus says in Revelation 22:12, "Behold, I am
coming soon, bringing my recompense with me, to repay each one for
what he has done." Come quickly, Lord Jesus!

Debris

National Review founder and commentator William F. Buckley
(1925–2008) tells a joke about a ten-year-old boy at an astronomy
lecture. At one point, the speaker tells the audience that our sun will
go dark in five billion years. At that, the boy faints and falls out of his

chair. When he comes to, the audience members ask, "What happened? When the speaker said our sun would go dark in five billion
years, you fainted." The boy replies, "Five billion! Oh, I thought he
said five million!"[75] But what difference does it make to a ten-year-old
whether the sun will go dark in five million years or five billion years?
Neither will affect the boy in his lifetime, but there is something omi-
nous about knowing our universe will die, and five billion years does
sound better than five million.

Either way, this is bad news for the naturalist, the environmental-
ist, the animal rights activist, and those who think utopia is possible.
Now, I'm not suggesting we shouldn't protect the environment and
animals—we should. But even if science was able to cure every disease
and we established utopia, one day our sun will die, and as all the stars
die, everything in the entire universe will go dark and reach absolute
zero, a chilly –459.67°F below freezing! Again, I'm reminded of Bertrand Russell's admission: "All the labours of the ages, all the devotion,
all the inspiration, all the noonday brightness of human genius, are destined to extinction in the vast death of the solar system, and that the
whole temple of Man's achievement must inevitably be buried beneath
the debris of a universe in ruins."[76] All our symbolic immortality projects, regardless how successful, are mortal. How sad. If there's no God,
then I'll meet you behind the strip mall for some fentanyl...or whatever you've got!

But "whoever does the will of God abides forever" (1 John 2:17)!

Death

Of course, none of us will be around when our sun dies, and that's
because we'll all be long dead, and everyone inside and outside of
Christ knows this. Bauman puts it well: "Death blatantly defies the
power of reason: reason's power is to be a guide to good choice, but
death is not a matter of choice." Bauman calls mortality the "ultimate
offence against human omnipotence," and that's certainly what the
Lord wants.[77] As Job puts it in Job 14:5 (NIV), "A person's days are determined; you have decreed the number of his months and have set limits he cannot exceed." Consider how arrogant some people are even

though they know that one day, they will die. Imagine these same people's arrogance if they lived to 1,000 years old or if they never died! Death humiliates us and frightens us, and hopefully, prayerfully, it forces many to give up their secular salvation strategies and turn to Him who gives eternal life.

But death is a triumphal graduation for the saved! For the Christian, death is an upgrade. In Jesus, you can live forever and ever. As it says in Revelation 2:7, "He who has an ear, let him hear what the Spirit says to the churches. To the one who conquers I will grant to eat of the tree of life, which is in the paradise of God." Do you hear what the Spirit is saying? Remain in Jesus, and you will live forever!

Eternal Punishment

Although physical death ends every literal immortality attempt, physical death, not eternal punishment, humiliates all symbolic immortality attempts and reveals the hopelessness of coping with death without Christ. As Hebrew 9:27 says, "People are destined to die once, and after that to face judgment." Ecclesiastes 12:14 tells us that "God will bring every deed into judgment, with every secret thing, whether good or evil."

Eternal Punishment and Symbolic Immortality Projects

Eternal punishment shames all symbolic immortality projects because if rebels against God remain in hell forever—and everyone knows they are in hell forever—then their personal "accomplishments," their towering achievements, will forever be viewed, from the perspective of their ongoing fate, as so much babble. Perhaps the eternality of the rebel's punishment is precisely what's needed to offset any hint of their symbolic immortality. What I mean is that when bad men are killed or executed, it sometimes results in their being considered heroes or martyrs. This is captured in the Jon Bon Jovi song "Blaze of Glory" (1990), which reached number one on the Billboard Hot 100 Chart, number one on the Billboard Album Rock Tracks chart, and (for six weeks) number one on the Australian ARIA music chart.[78] Bon Jovi sings about a young six-gun western outlaw, a "devil on the run," who recognizes that he was what "Cain was to Abel," who has "lived life to the fullest," and his hope is to stare down a bullet and go out in a blaze of glory. This sentiment is familiar, right? All too often people glorify even those who do evil. I'll give three examples of beings that achieved symbolic immortality through doing evil.

Billy the Kid

The outlaw gunfighter Billy the Kid (aka William H. Bonney, 1859–81) killed eight men before he was gunned down at age 21. There have been at least ten movies with "Billy the Kid" or "Kid" in the title and many other movies where Billy the Kid is a large part of the plotline. This includes the 3.2 out of 10-star movie *Billy the Kid Versus Dracula* (1966; to be fair, critics did give it the edge over *Jesse James Meets Frankenstein's Daughter*, also 1966). There have been at least ten songs with "Billy the Kid" in the title by artists such as Tom Petty and Billy Joel. Bob Dylan recorded an album entitled *Pat Barrett and Billy the Kid* (1973) as a soundtrack for the Sam Peckinpah film by that name. There have been several poems and several books written on Billy the Kid, including the science fiction novel *The Illegal Rebirth of Billy the Kid* (1991). There have been at least four plays about Billy the Kid, and one of those was a ballet (maybe I could learn to love ballet after all?). Notice that Billy the Kid is dead, and from a human perspective, he has been all but annihilated, yet his bad-boy reputation lives on. But the Judgment, where everyone will see the horror of his evil acts, and his eternal punishment will forever reveal him to be the cruel fool that he was (in my book *Why Does God Allow Evil?*, I argue that the occupants of hell remain eternally unrepentant).

Bonnie and Clyde

Bonnie Parker (1910–34) and Clyde Barrow (1909–34) robbed at least 12 banks and killed 15 people. But one Bonnie and Clyde site refers to them as "Romeo and Juliet in a getaway car" who "continues to captivate today, and they remain *immortal* through their photographs as well as the Academy Award-winning movie depicting their life."[79] Notice the word "immortal"? There have been at least half a dozen movies, dozens of books, a Broadway show, and many songs about Bonnie and Clyde—for example, Merle Haggard's "Legend of Bonnie & Clyde." But the Judgment will reveal them for who they really are—cold-blooded killers who robbed families of loved ones—and their continued unrepentance in hell will forever remove any perceived shine from their misdeeds.

Satan

Then there's the biggest, baddest bad boy, Satan. Consider that many worship Satan (or at least the symbol of what Satan stands for). There are dozens of "black metal," formerly known as "Satanic metal," groups that glorify everything anti-Christian. These bands sport Satanic symbols. The group Von has albums such as *Satanic Blood* (2012) and *Dark Gods: Seven Billion Slaves* (2013). The band Goatwhore has albums such as *Carving Out the Eyes of God* (2009) and *Vengeful Ascension* (2013). The band Belphegor (i.e., a prince of hell) chose as its logo inverted crosses dripping with blood. Then there's the Australian band Deströyer 666 (need I say more?) and Deicide (as in the killing of God), who has albums like *To Hell with God* (2011) and *Overtures of Blasphemy* (2018). Some of their songs include "Kill the Christian," "When Satan Rules His World," "Bible Basher," and "Homage for Satan." Ad infinitum, ad nauseam, ad absurdum.[80]

Then there's Marilyn Manson, who has millions of fans and has produced ten albums—his most recent being *Heaven Upside Down* (2017). Manson has engaged in onstage cutting and has worn fake breasts. In his first album, *Portrait of an American Family*, he introduced himself to the world in his song "Cake and Sodomy." He once chopped up human bones and smoked them in a pipe with some friends: "It was terrible. It smelled like burnt hair" (who knew that wouldn't be a good idea?). Church of Satan founder Anton LeVey appointed Manson as a minister in the church, and Manson wrote the foreword to LeVey's last book, *Satan Speaks*.[81] My point in mentioning these demented bands (I'm convinced after watching a smidge of some performances that many band members are demon possessed) is that they consider Satan to be the ultimate cosmic bad boy.

Consider that rebels often idolize the wicked. Many people admire Adolf Hitler (1889–1945), many admire Osama bin Laden (1957–2011), and some admire even Charles Manson (1934–2017).[82] One otherwise attractive woman even married Manson while he was serving a life sentence. Since this is the case, how does the Lord keep anyone from admiring the wicked throughout eternity? Well, I certainly don't know all of our Lord's reasons for punishment being eternal, but one reason might be that eternal punishment will forever keep anyone from ever admiring Satan, or Hitler, or bin Laden, or Manson again. No one will consider their eternal punishment and think "Wow, that Satan was a real renegade." Eternal punishment in this regard succeeds where annihilation fails. When a wicked person is killed, he often becomes a martyr, and our Lord's simply annihilating Satan and other wicked individuals might have led some to think, "There was once that fellow Satan. Boy, he was one tough hombre." But if you really want to show Satan for who he truly is, then Satan's suffering in hell *forever* will do it.

Maybe it's even possible that those who wanted to could look in on those in hell and see who they really are. Now, I don't know whether this could happen, but remember that Jesus portrays Abraham and Lazarus as looking in on the rich man who was "in anguish" (Luke 16:19-31). They witness the rich man's selfishness when he asks Abraham to send Lazarus to bring him some water—presumably through the flames! They witness the rich man's unrepentance—he doesn't apologize to Lazarus for ignoring his suffering. They witness the rich man's veiled self-justification that he himself is being punished because he wasn't given sufficient warning (he argued that Moses and the prophets were insufficient warning to his brothers, which implies that Moses and the prophets were insufficient warning to him). C.S. Lewis's fictional portrayal of hell in *The Great Divorce* is brilliant in its depiction of the lost making excuses for their lost condition. Imagine the kinds of things Hitler would say in hell. Or Osama bin Laden. Or Satan. Now, as I said, I don't know whether this will happen, and taking a position either way would be speculating. But if it does, then that would be an eternal lesson of symbolic immortality's folly.[83]

Eternal Punishment and Mortality Mitigating Projects

Obviously, eternal punishment also humiliates all atheists' attempts at mitigating the horror of their mortality. Sadly, Christians who say the rebel will be only annihilated rather than eternally punished give the overwhelming majority of atheists exactly what they say they most desire: a belief that their deaths will end in their annihilation rather than judgment.[84] As philosopher Thomas Nagel writes, "If one thinks about it logically, it seems as though death should be something to be afraid of only if we *will* survive it, and perhaps undergo some terrifying transformation." And that's the problem for those without Jesus: "the sting of death is sin" (1 Corinthians 15:56), "after that comes Judgment" (Hebrews 9:27), and after the Judgment comes "eternal punishment" (Matthew 25:46). This haunts even the most ardent anti-Christian crusaders—just Google "fear of hell" and "atheist" or things like that to see what I mean. Critic of Christianity Bart D. Ehrman admits he "still wonder[s], deep down inside...Will I burn in hell forever?" He says, "The fear gripped me for years and there are still moments when I wake up at night in a cold sweat."[85]

Paul tells us in Romans 2:6, "He will render to each one according to his works," and for "those who are self-seeking and do not obey the truth, but obey unrighteousness, there will be wrath and fury" (verse 8). But for the Christian "who by patience in well-doing seek for glory and honor and immortality, he will give eternal life" (verse 7). Let us then through well-doing "seek for glory and honor and immortality," and He will give us eternal life. As the Spirit proclaims in Revelation 2:11, "He who has an ear, let him hear what the Spirit says to the churches. The one who conquers will not be hurt by the second death." Do you hear what the Spirit is saying? Stay faithful to Jesus, dear Christian, and eternal life in God's kingdom awaits! We can have confidence about that because Jesus was raised from the dead. It's a fact of history. We'll talk about that next.

I'll close this chapter will a pastoral thought. Even among Christians, "carpe diem," "seize the day," and "YOLO" are popular sayings, but if Christianity is true and our every thought and deed will be

examined at the Judgment, and then we will be ushered into eternal
life where our deeds will follow us (Revelation 14:13), then let us live
every day for God and our neighbor. When we stand before the Judgment, whether we ate dinner atop the Eiffel Tower or saw the northern
lights, not only do these things not matter, but they can count against
us because we've wasted much of our lives pursuing what doesn't matter. Let me be clear: if Christianity is true and you're striving to love
the Lord with all your heart, soul, mind, and strength, then you cannot miss out. You. Can. Not. Miss. Out. At the Father's right hand are
"pleasures forevermore" (Psalm 16:11). Let us make that our focus.

Happy forever!

6

The Evidence for the Resurrection of Jesus

One thing that surprises me is how often skeptics write that if Christianity were true, then it would fulfill our longing to escape death. As I mentioned in the introduction, philosopher Stephen Cave says reconciling the fact that we know we will die with our desire to live forever is something "Christianity achieved spectacularly well, with enormous consequences for the development of Western civilization."[1] And Sam Harris tells an atheist convention, "There's no other story you can tell somebody who has just lost her daughter to cancer, say, to make her feel good. You know it is consoling to believe that the daughter was just taken up with Jesus and everyone is going to be reunited in a few short years. There's no replacement for that."[2] Of course, Harris rejects Christianity, but he agrees that if Christianity were true, then it does fulfill our deepest need.

Parisian philosopher Luc Ferry comes to the same conclusion about the wonder of Christianity's promise: "What we would like above all is to be reunited with our loved ones, and, if possible, with their voices, their faces—not in the form of undifferentiated cosmic fragments, such as pebbles or vegetables. In this arena Christianity might be said to have used its big guns. It promises us no less than everything that we would wish for: personal immortality *and* the salvation of our loved ones."[3] Later Ferry writes that "the Christian response to mortality, for believers at least, is without question the *most 'effective' of all responses*:

it would seem to be the only version of salvation that enables us not only to transcend the fear of death, but also to beat death itself."[4] In fact, Ferry states that Christianity's doctrine of salvation "turns out to be 'stronger than death.'"[5]

It always amazes me when an atheist can get Christianity so right—and that's what anthropologist Ernest Becker does in his appraisal of the Christian worldview:

> When man lived securely under the canopy of the Judeo-Christian world picture he was part of a great whole; to put it in our terms, his cosmic heroism was completely mapped out, it was unmistakable. He came from the invisible world into the visible one by the act of God, did his duty to God by living out his life with dignity and faith...offering his whole life—as Christ had—to the Father. In turn he was justified by the Father and rewarded with eternal life in the invisible dimension. Little did it matter that earth was a vale of tears, of horrid sufferings of incommensurateness, of torturous and humiliating daily pettiness, of sickness and death, a place where man felt he did not belong, "the wrong place," as Chesterton said...In a word, man's cosmic heroism was assured, even if he was as nothing. This was the most remarkable achievement of the Christian world picture: that it could take slaves, cripples, imbeciles, the simple and the mighty, and make them all secure heroes, simply by taking a step back from the world into another dimension of things, the dimension called heaven. Or we might better say that Christianity took creature consciousness—the thing man most wanted to deny—and made it the very condition for his cosmic heroism.[6]

That's right! Christians don't need to be heroes or search for or invent a sense of meaning for their lives. As Jesus says in John 4:14, "Whoever drinks of the water that I will give him will never be thirsty again. The water that I will give him will become in him a spring of water welling up to eternal life."[7] It's simple and direct: the Christian lives a life honoring to God in the face of sickness, suffering, persecution, and death, and because of the work of Jesus, they are rewarded with eternal life!

But for centuries, skeptics have argued that Christianity is no more than a man-made belief to help the fearful and weak-minded cope with their fear of death. As comparative religion author Karen Armstrong puts it, "From the very earliest times, men and women devised religions to help them cultivate a sense that our existence has some ultimate meaning and value, despite the dispiriting evidence to the contrary."[8] But we've now reviewed the intellectual contortions skeptics contrive to make them feel good about their demise—namely, you wouldn't want to live forever anyway, individual existence is unreal, your dust continues on, ad absurdum. As we've seen, these contortions don't succeed. We've also seen how literal and symbolic attempts to live forever fail. But is the Christian hope a similarly *man*ufactured belief? No, there are compelling reasons to believe there is a God and historical evidence for the resurrection of Jesus Christ from the dead.

There Is a God

The first thing we need to acknowledge is that there is a God. The design we find in the universe is obvious to anyone except for those who don't *want* there to be a God. Even skeptics agree the universe appears designed. As Richard Dawkins puts it, "Biology is the study of complicated things that give the appearance of having been designed for a purpose." Dawkins then points out that physics books may be "complicated," but "the objects and phenomena that a physics book describes are simpler than a single cell in the body of its author. And the author consists of trillions of those cells, many of them different from each other, organized with intricate architecture and precision-engineering into a working machine capable of writing a book." But, skeptics tell us, these things only "appear" designed, and this apparent design is really the result of luck.

Atheists are okay with appealing to luck as long as there's not too much luck. As Dawkins puts it in *The Blind Watchmaker*, "We can accept a certain amount of luck in our explanations, but not too much...We can allow ourselves the luxury of an extravagant theory [regarding the origin of life on our planet], provided that the odds of coincidence do not exceed 100 billion billion to one [10^{20}]."[9] 100 billion billion to one! But atheist Fred Hoyle (1915–2001), who Dawkins calls a "brilliant physicist and cosmologist,"[10] likens the probability of life originating on earth as "no greater than the chance that a hurricane, sweeping through a scrapyard, would have the luck to assemble a Boeing 747."[11] If you read his book, you'll find that Dawkins does not disagree with Hoyle about his 747 analogy! But we can't force our imaginations to conjure up how that 747 assembly would occur by luck, right? In fact, I can't imagine (I've tried) how a hurricane could screw a single nut onto a bolt and tighten it to the necessary degree, can you?

Similarly, atheist and Nobel Prize winner Francis Crick reports that the pure luck involved in the assembly of one polypeptide chain "of rather modest length" is 10^{260}. To explain the immensity of this luck, Crick points out that all the atoms in the visible universe only come to 10^{80}.[12] As Joseph E. Gorra and I write in the *Christian Research Journal* in an article entitled "The Folly of Answering Distracting Atheistic Arguments," "What does belief in this supercalifragilisticexpialidocious kind of luck tell us about those who argue for it?"[13] It tells us they don't *want* to believe there is a God. Thus Paul writes in Romans 1:18, "The wrath of God is revealed" against the "unrighteousness of men, who by their unrighteousness suppress the truth." They suppress the truth! God's wrath is justified because "what can be known about God is plain to them, because God has shown it to them. For his invisible attributes, namely, his eternal power and divine nature, have been clearly perceived, ever since the creation of the world, in the things that have been made" (verses 19-20). Thus Paul's next words are, "So they are without excuse."[14]

Now, I could go on and on presenting arguments for God's existence, but many books have been written on this, and in our Lord's considered opinion, an unbiased look at creation will suffice.[15]

Reliable Primary Sources

The second thing we need to establish is that the primary source documents that tell us of the resurrection of Jesus—the Gospel of Matthew, the Gospel of Mark, the Gospel of Luke, the Gospel of John, the Acts of the Apostles, and 1 Corinthians—record that eyewitnesses testify that Jesus was raised from the dead. Although some skeptics object that these primary source documents haven't been accurately transmitted to us, they are mistaken. The bibliographical test demonstrates that we can have confidence that the Gospels, Acts, and 1 Corinthians have been reliably transmitted. The bibliographical test compares the closeness of the New Testament's oldest extant (surviving) manuscripts to the date of its autographs (the original handwritten documents) and the sheer number of the New Testament's extant manuscripts with the number and earliness of extant manuscripts of other ancient documents such as Homer, Aristotle, and Herodotus. In the *Christian Research Journal*, I wrote an article entitled "The Bibliographical Test Updated" that reads: "Since the New Testament manuscripts outstrip every other ancient manuscript in sheer number and proximity to the autographs, the New Testament should be regarded as having been accurately transmitted." In other words, the overwhelming majority of skeptics accept as accurately transmitted most other ancient works, which have much less manuscript tradition to establish their reliability.

When comparing the manuscript evidence of other ancient documents to the New Testament, the New Testament wins the race when others have barely left the starting gate. As perhaps the greatest New Testament manuscript expert of the twentieth century, Bruce M. Metzger (1914–2007), and Bart D. Ehrman put it,

> In contrast with these figures [of other ancient works], the textual critic of the New Testament is embarrassed by a wealth of material. Furthermore, the work of many ancient authors has been preserved only in manuscripts that date from the Middle Ages (sometimes the late Middle Ages), far removed from the time at which they lived and wrote. On the contrary, the time between the composition of the books of the New Testament and the earliest extant copies is relatively brief. Instead of a lapse of a millennium or more, as is the case of not a few

classical authors, several papyrus manuscripts of por-
tions of the New Testament are extant that were copied
within a century or so after the composition of the original documents.[16]

Much more could be said about this. I encourage anyone who
wants more to see my article "The Bibliographical Test Updated" or
the many excellent resources that defend the reliability of the New
Testament.[17] Now that we've seen that the primary source documents,
which testify to Jesus's resurrection, have been accurately transmitted,
we can examine the evidence for the resurrection of Jesus. Every year I
teach a two-unit course to our master's students entitled "In Defense
of the Resurrection"—that's 24 hours of lecture! Here I will sum up
the argument for the resurrection of Jesus.

Jesus Himself said that His resurrection was *the* sign to the world. In
Matthew 12:38, the scribes and Pharisees tell Jesus, "Teacher, we wish
to see a sign from you." But Jesus replies, "An evil and adulterous generation seeks for a sign, but no sign will be given to it except the sign
of the prophet Jonah. For just as Jonah was three days and three nights
in the belly of the great fish, so will the Son of Man be three days and
three nights in the heart of the earth" (verses 39-40). Here Jesus proclaims that an "evil and adulterous generation" always seeks more evidence, another "sign," but Jesus is only going to give them one sign:
His resurrection from the dead. Later in Matthew 16, the Pharisees and
Sadducees again demand more evidence—"a sign"—but again Jesus
replies, "An evil and adulterous generation seeks for a sign, but no sign
will be given to it except the sign of the prophet Jonah" (verse 4). So
let's now look at the four key pieces of evidence for this sign—the resurrection of Jesus.

Jesus Died of Roman Crucifixion

The first evidence that Jesus was raised from the dead is that Jesus
died from Roman crucifixion, and about this, even most skeptical scholars agree. For example, Jesus Seminar cochair John Dominic Crossan writes in *Jesus: A Revolutionary Biography*, "That he was

crucified is as sure as anything historical can ever be."[18] Understand that Crossan does not believe that Jesus was raised from the dead, but he considers Jesus's crucifixion "as sure as anything historical can ever be." Another example comes from atheist Gerd Lüdemann, who is the chair of history and literature of early Christianity at the University of Göttingen. In his book *What Really Happened to Jesus?*, Lüdemann writes, "It is *certain* that Jesus was crucified around the year 30."[19] Also, in *Resurrection of Jesus: History, Experience, Theology*, Lüdemann says, "The fact of Jesus' death as the consequence of crucifixion is *indisputable*."[20]

Why is it that these men consider Jesus's crucifixion to be "certain," "indisputable," and "as sure as anything historical can ever be"? Crossan explains the evidence: "I take it absolutely for granted that Jesus was crucified under Pontius Pilate. Security about the *fact* of the Crucifixion derives not only from the unlikelyhood that Christians would have invented it but also from the existence of two early and independent non-Christian witnesses to it, a Jewish one from 93–94 C.E. and a Roman one from the 110s or 120s C.E."[21] Here Crossan mentions three things. First, *if* the early Christians were going to invent a religion, then Crossan considers it unlikely they would invent a religion where its leader was branded a criminal, stripped naked, and tortured to death. Remember that the Jews at the time were looking for a messiah/deliverer, not a humiliated, tortured, and executed criminal. Why would they make a story up like that? Then Crossan mentions two early non-Christian sources.

The Jewish source to which Crossan refers is Flavius Josephus (37/38–100) in what is called his *Testimonium*. Although the Western version has obviously suffered from some Christians adding material to it, an Arabic version has been discovered that says,

> At this time there was a wise man who was called Jesus. His conduct was good, and [he] was known to be virtuous. And many people from among the Jews and the other nations became his disciples. Pilate condemned him to be crucified and to die. But those who had become his disciples did not abandon his discipleship.

They reported that he had appeared to them three days after his crucifixion, and that he was alive; accordingly he was perhaps the Messiah, concerning whom the prophets have recounted wonders.[22]

Some skeptics challenge the authenticity of the *Testimonium*, but Crossan and a *majority* of skeptical scholars think that most of the *Testimonium* is original to Josephus.[23]

The Roman source to which Crossan refers is the historian Publius Cornelius Tacitus (56–120), who writes, "Nero fastened the guilt and inflicted the most exquisite tortures on a class hated for their abominations, called Christians by the populace. Christus, from whom the name had its origin, suffered the extreme penalty during the reign of Tiberius at the hands of one of our procurators, Pontius Pilatus."[24] In my studies on human evil, I've learned a lot of different ways to torture a person to death, and I don't know of a more torturous death than crucifixion because those crucified were often on the cross for days until they died.

It was easy to tell when a crucified man was dead because he no longer lifted himself up to breathe. As William D. Edwards, Wesley J. Gabel, and Floyd E. Hosmer explain in the *Journal of the American Medical Association*, "The major pathophysiologic effect of crucifixion was an interference with normal respirations." This is because when the victim is hanging from his wrists, it is difficult for him to exhale. Thus to exhale, the victim must regularly lift himself by pushing on his pierced feet and pivoting on his pierced wrists (not hands, as often depicted in art). Of course, that would be excruciatingly painful and, in time, physically exhausting. Once the victim could no longer lift himself to breathe, he quickly suffocated and died. Crucifixion is indeed the "extreme penalty." In fact, "excruciating" comes from the Latin *ex crucis*, for "out of the cross."

This is why in John 19 we read that when the Jews didn't want victims hanging on the cross on the Sabbath, they "asked Pilate that their legs might be broken and that they might be taken away" (verse 31). Once you broke a crucified victim's legs, he would no longer be able to push himself up to breathe. Thus John reports that the soldiers broke the legs of the other two, but when they came to Jesus "and saw that he was already dead, they did not break his legs" (verse 33). Just to make sure, however, "one of the soldiers pierced his side with a spear, and at once there came out blood and water" (verse 34). Then John adds in verse 35, "He who saw it has borne witness—his testimony is true, and he knows that he is telling the truth—that you also may believe." So John in essence writes, "Hey, everyone, listen up: I didn't learn this through hearsay, I personally witnessed this happening." Thus Edwards, Gabel, and Hosmer conclude, "Accordingly, death resulted primarily from hypovolemic shock [blood or fluid loss] and exhaustion asphyxia. Jesus' death was ensured by a thrust of a soldiers spear into his side. Modern medical interpretation of the historical evidence indicates that Jesus was dead when taken down from the cross."[25] That Jesus died sooner than usual is probably due to the severity of the scourging He endured: Jesus bled to death.

Jesus Was Buried, but Later His Tomb Was Found Empty

After Jesus was crucified and died, He was buried, but three days later, His tomb was found empty. After Jesus died, all four Gospels record that Jesus was taken down from the cross and then wrapped in a linen cloth, all four Gospels record that Joseph of Arimathea asked Pilate for Jesus's body so he could bury Him, and all four Gospels record that Jesus was then buried in a tomb. It would be hard to invent a character like Joseph of Arimathea and place him on the Sanhedrin if he never existed. Professor James D.G. Dunn writes, "Joseph of Arimathea is a very plausible historical character" because "he is attested in all four Gospels" and in "*the Gospel of Peter*."[26] Similarly, professor Raymond E. Brown (1928–98) thinks this is highly probable because "Christian fictional creation from nothing of a Jewish Sanhedrist who does what is right is almost inexplicable," since the early Christians held the "Jewish authorities responsible for the death of Jesus." Further, that Joseph was "'from Arimathea,' a town very difficult to identify and reminiscent of no scriptural symbolism, makes a thesis of invention even more implausible."[27] This kind of argument is why even the cofounder and president emeritus of Internet Infidels, Jeffery Jay Lowder, writes, "Finally, like [William Lane] Craig, I think the role of Joseph of Arimathea in the story of Jesus' burial is much more likely on the assumption of a historical burial than on the non-burial hypothesis. Therefore, the burial of Jesus by Joseph of Arimathea has a high final probability."[28]

Then all four Gospels report that it was women who first discovered that the tomb was empty. Ehrman agrees that we "have solid traditions to indicate that women found this tomb empty three days later."[29] This is significant because in first-century Palestine, a woman's testimony wasn't considered trustworthy. I could give many examples, but I'll just quote one. Josephus writes, "But let not the testimony of women be admitted, on account of the levity and boldness of their sex."[30] There-fore, that the Gospels record women as being the first to discover the empty tomb makes it likely because of what is called the "criterion of embarrassment." The criterion of embarrassment is a type of criti-cal analysis where authors are presumed to be telling the truth if they record something that might be embarrassing to them or their cause. In short, no one in first-century Palestine would concoct a story with women taking the lead in the most vital discovery of Christianity![31]

But there's one last argument that Jesus's tomb was found empty: if it wasn't empty, then Christianity could never have begun! After all, if the tomb wasn't empty, then all the enemies of Christ had to do was produce Jesus's body and Christianity was over, done, *fini, finito, ter-minado*, kaput! Certainly the Romans who crucified Jesus and those Jews who wanted Jesus crucified had the motive and the opportunity to end this upstart religion once and for all by producing Jesus's body! Instead, Matthew 28:11-15 reports about the soldiers who were guard-ing the tomb:

> Some of the guard went into the city and told the chief priests all that had taken place. And when they had assembled with the elders and taken counsel, they gave a sufficient sum of money to the soldiers and said, "Tell

people, 'His disciples came by night and stole him away while we were asleep.' And if this comes to the governor's ears, we will satisfy him and keep you out of trouble." So they took the money and did as they were directed. And this story has been spread among the Jews to this day.

Consider that if this theft story wasn't actually being circulated, why would Matthew put it in people's heads? That wouldn't make sense.

Further, Justin Martyr (100–165) mentions the theft story in his *Dialog with Trypho* the Jew:

> You have sent chosen and ordained men throughout all the world to proclaim that a godless and lawless heresy had sprung from one Jesus, a Galilaean deceiver, whom we crucified, but his disciples stole him by night from the tomb, where he was laid when unfastened from the cross, and now deceive men by asserting that he has risen from the dead and ascended to heaven.[32]

Why would Justin write this if this story wasn't being circulated? This is another example of the criterion of embarrassment. And notice, the theft story affirms that the tomb was empty![33]

Jesus's Disciples Proclaimed That Jesus Was Raised

After Jesus died on the cross and His tomb was found empty, the disciples began to proclaim that Jesus had been raised from the dead. Acts 17:31 (NIV) reports that Paul preached in Athens that the Lord "has set a day when he will judge the world with justice by the man he has appointed. He has given *proof* of this to everyone by raising him from the dead." One of the most important passages on Jesus's resurrection is found in 1 Corinthians 15:3-8:

> For I delivered to you as of first importance what I also received: that Christ died for our sins in accordance with the Scriptures, that he was buried, that he was raised on the third day in accordance with the Scriptures, and

> that he appeared to Cephas, then to the twelve. Then
> he appeared to more than five hundred brothers at
> one time, most of whom are still alive, though some
> have fallen asleep. Then he appeared to James, then to
> all the apostles. Last of all, as to one untimely born, he
> appeared also to me.

Notice Paul writes that he is delivering what he has "received." In other words, this statement originated earlier. Since Crossan says 1 Corinthians was "written from Ephesus in the winter of 53–54 C.E.," then this statement is earlier than that.[34] Further, Gerd Lüdemann says of this particular passage, "We can assume that all the elements in the tradition are to be dated to the first two years after the crucifixion of Jesus."[35] Atheist Michael Goulder writes that Paul's testimony "goes back at least to what Paul was taught when he was converted, a couple of years after the crucifixion."[36]

It's no wonder, then, why the overwhelming majority of studied skeptics accept as fact that the disciples soon proclaimed Jesus's resurrection. Notice, I didn't say skeptics agree that Jesus was raised from the dead, but a large majority of them agree the disciples soon began to proclaim that Jesus was raised from the dead. For example, in his book *The Case Against Christianity*, Michael Martin writes that it "is correct that the Resurrection was proclaimed by the early Christians."[37] Similarly, Bart D. Ehrman writes, "Historians, of course, have no difficulty whatsoever speaking about the belief in Jesus' resurrection, since this is *a matter of public record*. For it is *a historical fact* that some of Jesus' followers came to believe that he had been raised from the dead soon after his execution. We know some of these believers by name; one of them, the apostle Paul, claims quite plainly to have seen Jesus alive after his death."[38]

Thus Lüdemann writes, "It is *certain* that something must have happened after Jesus' death which led his followers to speak of Jesus as the risen Christ."[39] Later, Lüdemann writes, "It may be taken as *historically certain* that Peter and the disciples had experiences after Jesus' death in which Jesus appeared to them as the risen Christ...The only thing that we can *certainly* say to be historical is that there were resurrection appearances in Galilee (and in Jerusalem) soon after Jesus death."[40] Now again, Lüdemann does not believe they actually saw the risen Jesus, but he does believe the disciples thought they saw the risen Jesus.

Consider the words of skeptic Keith Parsons: "Jesus' crucifixion marked the bitter end of a failed mission. He had come to Jerusalem full of messianic fervor and gripped by an apocalyptic vision. Yet the predicted apocalypse did not occur. Instead Jesus was seized...beaten, humiliated, and subjected to a painful and shameful death. His disciples, despondent and fearful for their own lives, scattered and hid."[41] Notice that Parsons agrees that Jesus was crucified and then His disciples scattered and hid. That is what the Gospels tell us. Parsons continues, "Then something extraordinary happened. The former followers of a failed and disgraced prophet became convinced that their executed leader had risen from the grave. Soon they were back in Jerusalem, fearlessly proclaiming Jesus' resurrection to all that would hear. What happened? From the earliest days, the best argument for the historical veracity of the Resurrection has focused on these *facts.*" Parson agrees that the frightened disciples soon began to proclaim having seen the risen Jesus. He calls Jesus's crucifixion, the disciples' despondency, and then their proclaiming the risen Jesus "facts." "Facts"!

Parsons continues, "What other than the actual appearance of the risen Jesus to his disciples could account for their radical transformation from terrified and dejected fugitives to evangelists and missionaries quite willing to risk their lives to preach their gospel? Obviously, the disciples were convinced that Jesus had risen." Again, a *majority* of studied skeptics agree that Jesus died of Roman crucifixion, that He was buried, that His tomb was found empty, and that His disciples began to proclaim they saw Him raised from the dead. These are historical facts.

You may wonder how Parsons could remain a skeptic, since he grants all these things as "facts." Parsons explains, "But is actual resurrection the best explanation for the *fact* that the disciples believed it? Skeptics have always had an alternative explanation, namely, that some of the disciples experienced visions or hallucinations that convinced them that Jesus had arisen."[42] Similarly, atheist Richard Carrier writes, "I believe the best explanation, consistent with both scientific findings and the surviving evidence (particular to Christianity *and* the general cultural milieu in which it rose), is that the first Christians experienced hallucinations of the risen Christ, of one form or another."[43] So here is the most popular skeptical explanation: the disciples only hallucinated what they believed were actual appearances of the resurrected Jesus![44]

This hallucination theory, however, is plagued. First, many of the appearance testimonies involved more than one individual, but hallucinations are individual, subjective experiences that cannot be shared. As clinical psychologist and professor Gary Collins puts it, "Hallucinations are individual occurrences. By their very nature only one person can see a given hallucination at a time. They certainly are not something which can be seen by a group of people. Neither is it possible that one person could somehow induce an hallucination in somebody else. Since an hallucination exists only in this subjective, personal sense, it is obvious that others cannot witness it."[45] I can't be dreaming of swimming with giant sea turtles in Barbados and then wake up my wife and say, "Honey, I just had a dream that I was in Barbados. Go back to sleep and join me so we can enjoy it together."[46] As clinical psychologist Gary A. Sibcy reports, "I have surveyed the professional literature (peer-reviewed journal articles and books) written by psychologists, psychiatrists, and other relevant healthcare professionals during the past two decades and have yet to find a single documented case of a group hallucination, that is, an event for which more than one person purportedly shared in a visual or other sensory perception where there was clearly no external referent."[47] That's no surprise, right? How could one share a hallucination?

Second, the disciples would have had to have interlocking hallucinations. For just one example, while Thomas was hallucinating Jesus telling him to touch the wounds on His hands and side, the other ten disciples would have to have had hallucinations of Jesus telling Thomas to do that (John 20:24-29; for another, see 21:1-9). Third, as theologian and lawyer John Warwick Montgomery points out, "Had anything, even a deluded state of mind, caused the disciples to distort Jesus' biography, the hostile witnesses would surely have used that against them."[48] Fourth, the hallucination theory cannot explain the empty tomb or missing body. All they had to do was present Jesus's body to prove the hallucinations false. Fifth, there were many witnesses in very different moods. As theologian John Stott (1921–2011) points out, "Mary Magdalene was weeping; the women were afraid and astonished; Peter was full of remorse, and Thomas of incredulity. The Emmaus pair were distracted by the events of the week and the disciples in Galilee by their fishing."[49] Jesus's brother, James, questioned Jesus's mental state, and Paul was trying to stamp out Christianity. Yet all these people hallucinated Jesus's resurrection? Finally, hallucinations rarely transform lives. Gary Habermas points out that "studies indicate that even those who do hallucinate often disavow the experiences when others present have not seen the same thing...It is highly unlikely that this quality of conviction came about through false sensory perceptions without anyone rejecting it later."[50] And indeed, this leads me to the last piece of evidence.

Jesus's Disciples Were Willing to Suffer and Die for This Belief

So convinced were the disciples of Jesus's resurrection that, as we heard from Parsons, the disciples were transformed "from terrified and dejected fugitives to evangelists and missionaries quite willing to risk their lives to preach their gospel." In reading the Acts of the Apostles and church history, we find that the disciples boldly proclaimed the resurrection of Jesus and often suffered for their proclamations. As Paul puts it in Acts 24:21, "I shouted as I stood in their presence: 'It is concerning the resurrection of the dead that I am on trial before you today'" (NIV). We read in Acts 4 that disciples were arrested and imprisoned. In Acts 5, the disciples were again arrested, imprisoned, and flogged. In Acts 7, Stephen the deacon is stoned to death. In Acts 12, James, the brother of John, is martyred, and Peter is imprisoned. And so on.

Tertullian (155/160–after 200) writes about James, Paul, and Peter: "That James is slain as a victim at the altar, that Paul is beheaded has been written in their own blood. And if a heretic wishes his confidence to rest upon a public record, *the archives of the empire will speak*, as would the stones of Jerusalem. We read the lives of the Cæsars: At Rome Nero was the first who stained with blood the rising faith. Then is Peter girt by another, when he is made fast to the cross."[51] Notice regarding Paul's beheading that Tertullian essentially says, "If you don't believe me, go check it out for yourself!"[52]

Similarly, the church historian Eusebius (236–339) points to additional evidence: "Thus [Nero] publicly announcing himself as the first among God's chief enemies, he was led on to the slaughter of the apostles. It is, therefore, *recorded* that Paul was beheaded in Rome itself, and that Peter likewise was crucified under Nero. This account of Peter and Paul is substantiated by the fact that their names are preserved in the cemeteries of that place even to the present day."[53] Like Tertullian, Eusebius writes, go check it out for yourself—check the records and even check the cemetery!

We know that after Jesus appears to His brother, James, he becomes a leader in the Christian church. Josephus (37/38–100), in his *Antiquities of the Jews* (93 CE), writes that the high priest Ananus "assembled the Sanhedrin of judges, and brought before them the brother of Jesus, who was called Christ, whose name was James, and some others, and when he had formed an accusation against them as breakers of the law, he delivered them to be stoned."[54] Consider how much evidence it would take for you to so believe that your brother was raised from the dead, you'd be willing to die for Him. This isn't the place to present further evidence for the martyrdom of Peter, Paul, and James, but anyone who wishes for more can see Sean McDowell's book *The Fate of the Apostles: Examining the Martyrdom Accounts of the Closest Followers of Jesus*.

So I ask, Who dies for what they know is a lie? Sometimes people respond that people die for lies all the time. While it's true that people die for what they think is true, which might turn out to be false, no one dies for what they know is false! Christianity is based on the resurrection of Jesus from the dead, and in Acts you'll find that in every major sermon, Peter and Paul proclaim the resurrection of Jesus. But if they didn't actually see Jesus alive again after His crucifixion, then they would be risking their lives—not to mention betraying their Jewish religion—for something they knew was false! Why would they do that? Thus Paul writes in 1 Corinthians 15:14-15, "If Christ has not been raised, our preaching is useless and so is your faith. More than that, we are then found to be false witnesses about God, for we have testified about God that he raised Christ from the dead" (NIV). But as Paul puts it in verse 54, "Death is swallowed up in victory" (ESV).

So convinced were the early Christians of the disciples' testimony that large numbers were willing to die for Jesus. The second-century satirist Lucian (ca. 125–after 180) writes about these Christians: "These misguided creatures start with the general conviction that they are immortal for all time, which explains the contempt of death and voluntary self-devotion which are so common among them."[55] W.E.H. Lecky (1838–1903), in his *History of European Morals: From Augustus to Charlemagne*, sums up the early Christians' boldness in the face of death:

> Those hateful games, which made the spectacle of human suffering and death the delight of all classes, had spread their brutalizing influence wherever the Roman name was known, had rendered millions absolutely indifferent to the sight of human suffering, had produced in many, in the very centre of an advanced civilization, a relish and a passion for torture, a rapture and an exultation in watching the spasms of extreme agony...The most horrible recorded instances of torture were usually inflicted, either by the populace, or in their presence, in the arena. We read of Christians bound in chains of red-hot iron, while the stench of their half-consumed flesh rose in a suffocating cloud to heaven; of others who were torn to the very bone by shells, or hooks of iron; of holy virgins given over to the lust of gladiator or to the mercies of the pander; of two hundred and twenty-seven converts sent on one occasion to the mines, each with the sinews

of one leg severed by a red-hot iron, and with an eye scooped from its socket; of fires so slow that the victims writhed for hours in their agonies; of bodies torn limb from limb, or sprinkled with burning lead; or mingled salt and vinegar poured over the flesh that was bleeding from the rack; of tortures prolonged and varied through entire days. For the love of their Divine Master, for the cause they believed to be true, men, and even weak girls, endured these things without flinching, when one word would have freed them from their sufferings.[56]

The early Christians' willingness to suffer torture and death can only be because they were convinced by the first disciples' testimony of having seen the resurrected Jesus!

Jesus died on the cross for our sins, and He was raised from the dead! Thus as Paul says in 1 Corinthians 15:54, "Death is swallowed up in victory." We can have eternal life in Jesus. You can be truly immortal.

7

Living the High Life—
Enjoying True Immortality

If you're in Jesus, then you will live forever, and you can revel in that based on Jesus's resurrection from the dead. In this chapter, I will talk about how you might prepare yourself for the only earthly thing you know about your future *absolutely for sure*—that you will die. Christians don't need to live in mortal fear about the prospect of their deaths. In fact, Christians can enjoy the prospect of their living forever in God's kingdom, where "'He will wipe every tear from their eyes. There will be no more death' or mourning or crying or pain, for the old order of things has passed away" (Revelation 21:4 NIV). But there are several things you need to do, and not do, to enjoy the Christian promise that is stronger than death.

The Reason You Might Wish to Stay Alive

But before we examine how you can be peaceful, even joyful, about your death, we need to note that there is a legitimate reason you might not want to die. In short, it's not wrong to want to stay alive to be a blessing to others in the Lord.[1] Paul provides this perspective in Philippians 1, where he writes from a Roman prison, "For to me to live is Christ, and to die is gain" (verse 21). Paul sees his death as a grand improvement—his death is a plus, an upgrade! But he continues, "If I am to live in the flesh, that means fruitful labor for me" (verse 22). Paul says he is "hard pressed between the two. My desire is to depart and be with Christ, for that is far better. But to remain in the flesh is more necessary on your account" (verses 23-24). This is important because it shows that even the devout Christian who believes that dying is "far better" because they will enter the eternal kingdom can still be conflicted about dying. In other words, there's a legitimate reason to want to stay in our bodies on this earth, and it is to bless others.

That's how I felt 15 years ago when I got the news that I had bone cancer. You can believe this or not, but the prospect of my physical death didn't trouble me. Now, people question me about saying that the prospect of my physical death didn't trouble me. Surely, they say, it must have troubled me a little. All I can say is that I don't remember being troubled by the thought of my *body* being dead. Rather, I felt incredibly close to God during that time—as close as any time in my life.

But there were two things that did trouble me, and that's why when we got the news that I had a severe form of bone cancer that would probably kill me within two years, Jean E. and I both had tears streaming down our faces. The first thing that troubled me was the prospect of leaving my darling wife, Jean E., alone. That hurt. I wanted to stay for her sake! For her sake, I thought it was better that I remain. Now, we both knew that if God were to call me away, He knew better than I did what Jean E. needed and He would take care of her, but I wanted to be there for her. I want to emphasize that if I were to pass, we knew God would care for Jean E. We also realize that unless we die at the same time, one of us will leave the other to be cared for by our Father in heaven. But that didn't eliminate the sadness of thinking that I would leave my wife, causing her to have sorrow upon sorrow.

Paul tells us something similar in Philippians 2, where he writes about Epaphroditus, his "brother and fellow worker and fellow soldier," who was "ill, near to death" (verses 25,27). Even though Paul and Epaphroditus both know they will see each other in heaven, Paul writes that "God had mercy on him, and not only on him but on me also, lest I should have sorrow upon sorrow" (verse 27). Notice three things. One, in the great apostle's mind, it wasn't a given that Epaphroditus would be healed. Healing isn't a given—everyone will sooner or later die of something. Two, the apostle said that sparing Epaphroditus's life was merciful toward Epaphroditus. We don't know what Epaphroditus had going on, but apparently he had things he wanted to see through or people he didn't want to leave. Three, the apostle isn't embarrassed to say that if Epaphroditus dies, Paul will have "sorrow upon sorrow." Thus Paul tells us in Romans 12:15 to "weep with those who weep." When someone is bereaved, we are not to give them bromides like the lost loved one "is in a better place" (Christians already know that, and that's not why they're weeping), that "all things together work for good" (Romans 8:28; most Christians already know that too, but they're sad to lose a loved one), or other insensitive, nonweeping responses.

The knowledge that loved ones who will die will immediately enjoy the kingdom helps greatly, but it still hurts to lose them. As I wrote in *Why Does God Allow Evil?*, when Jean E. and I got the news that I had cancer, and then later when we got the news that I had terminal cancer (that turned out to be mistaken, but we didn't know that for several weeks), on both occasions, tears streamed down our faces. I'm in no way embarrassed to tell you about the tears. This is real! You can honor the Lord even while you're crying your eyes out! After all, you don't see Jesus rebuking everyone for crying at Lazarus's funeral and blithely telling them "Be happy; Lazarus is in a better place." On the contrary, we read, "Jesus wept" (John 11:35) even though He knew His friend Lazarus would be enjoying the kingdom (I wonder if some today would have told Jesus not to cry because Lazarus was "in a better place").

But it wasn't just losing Jean E. The second thing that troubled me at the prospect of my death was that there were many ministry opportunities I wanted to pursue before I passed away (I wanted to publish my book *Why Does God Allow Evil?*, and I had just begun teaching for Biola the month of my operation). Well, for whatever reason, the Lord in His mercy spared Jean E. and me much sorrow and has enabled me to keep ministering, but if He hadn't, then, yes, the Lord would have worked it out for our good. If I were to die, then we would have tearfully rejoiced, as we knew we would soon be reunited forever in heaven.[2] But aside from honorable opportunities for service, we need not fear our own deaths. In fact, as Paul did, we can look forward to death because we recognize the glory that awaits us for eternity.

I want to digress here because I know that some reading this have lost a spouse. The week after I wrote the above paragraph, Jean E. and I went to Kentucky for me to speak at a camp.[3] The first person we met as we arrived at the camp was Kim Warren. Kim told me the story of losing her husband, Bob, who for many years had been the camp director. Bob, by all accounts, had been a beloved teacher and administrator (many people praised his teaching and service to me). Kim said that five years ago, Bob went out on a three-mile run and apparently came back into the house and had a severe heart arrhythmia. He had not answered her calls that morning, and when she returned to the house, she found Bob lying on the dining room floor, clearly past the point of resuscitation. Later she told me that when she found Bob, she fell down next to him and sobbed. She soon got up and, shaking so badly she could barely hold the phone, called some friends for help. They arrived quickly to comfort her, and she found herself repeating out loud to the Lord, "You are faithful, You are worthy." She said his loss was "excruciating" and that sometimes she was "a puddle on the floor," but she looked at me intently and said repeatedly, "God will sustain you!" Their ministry carries on, and she looks forward to being united with Bob again in heaven for eternity. She said Bob would often say things like "Why do we fight so hard to stay alive; why don't we think more about our continuation into heaven?" I couldn't agree more!

Why did God spare my life but not Bob's? Of course, I don't know. But except for the Lord's return, I know two things absolutely for sure. First, unless we die at the same time, sooner or later either Jean E. or I will die, leaving the other in God's hands and knowing, as Kim said, God will be faithful. Second, the day will come when Jean E. and I and Kim and Bob will enjoy each other's company in heaven forever. Forever. For sure! And we also look forward to being with you, dear Christian! Sooner or later, you are going to lose loved ones, but if you trust in the Lord, God will be faithful.

Staring Down Death

In speaking with Christians about the fact that literal immortality awaits them in Jesus, it saddens me that many, even most, find the prospect of their spending eternity in heaven of little comfort. Many who call themselves Christians (I'm not saying they are or not) are almost as afraid of dying as anyone else! The reason for this is obvious: unless you are at peace with God and have a robust view of a glorious eternity awaiting you, then you're going to fear death. Thankfully, there are specific things you can do, must do, if you're going to be confident in facing your death. Now we will examine how Christians—in concert with the work of the Holy Spirit in our lives—can eliminate our fear of death by looking forward to eternity in Jesus.

First, if we're not going to fear death, we must love the Lord with all our hearts, souls, minds, and strength and not love this present world. After all, if we love this present world, if this world consumes our hearts, then we're certainly going to dread leaving it. In 1 John 2:15-17, we are commanded, "Do not love the world or the things in the world. If anyone loves the world, the love of the Father is not in him. For all that is in the world—the desires of the flesh and the desires of the eyes and pride of life—is not from the Father but is from the world. And the world is passing away along with its desires, but whoever does the will of God abides forever." Notice that this world is dying—it is "passing away" (even atheists agree with that!)—and if you love the world, then you won't love the Father, and when the world dies, you will die with it. Instead, John tells us, "Do not love the world." If you can do this, you will abide forever!

We have a Red Barron peach tree, and its peaches are delicious. Sadly, in this fallen world, pests harm it. So I went to Home Depot to find a solution. The warning label of one fungicide that I suspect does the job very well says it might be fatal if swallowed or inhaled and might cause "permanent, irreversible eye damage." Really? I'm not going to wear a hazmat suit! I don't need peaches that badly (thankfully, our tree survived without it)! Well, the Bible is the world's warning label: "Love this world, and you will die." The trouble is that most of us would be much more careful with something that causes permanent, irreversible eye damage and was fatal if inhaled than something that, if misused, causes not only our physical deaths but also our spiritual deaths. Let us be alarmed, dear reader—do not love this world or the things of this world. The converse of loving the world is found in Matthew 22:37: "You shall love the Lord your God with all your heart and with all your soul and with all your mind." Of course, the second greatest command is found in verse 39: "You shall love your neighbor as yourself." You're either going to love God and His people or you're going to love the world, but you're going to be madly in love with something.

You can choose what you love. Except for a chemical/hormonal imbalance, the cliché "Feelings aren't right or wrong; they just are" is nonsense. You can choose where you set your affections, and if you don't want to fear death, then you need to choose to not love this world or the things of this world. Decades ago when I was a college and career pastor, a girl named Kathy told me about how attractive a certain boy was, and then she added, "But I know he's not good for me, so I'm not going to let myself love him." I was surprised. Wow, this 19-year-old girl understood something that so many don't—you can choose upon what you set your heart. The best way to not love this world is to do what this 19-year-old did: she reminded herself of this guy's flaws. Similarly, we must remind ourselves that the world is deeply flawed. In fact, even naturalists agree that this world is heading toward a grisly death! Don't love this dying, decaying, polluted, lust-filled world, which will sooner or later break your heart. Instead, love that which will never die! As Solomon says in Proverbs 4:23 (NIV), "Above all else, guard your heart, for everything you do flows from it." But if you love that which will never die—and this takes determination—then you will abide "forever"!

The first time I'd ever skied, some married friends took Jean E. and me. My wife went with him, and I went with her. Again, I had never been on skis before. Well, she told me that if I wanted to turn or slow down, I needed to "snowplow" (also known as a wedge turn)—I needed to turn my feet in such a way that I formed a plow with my skis.

I thought, "Okay, I get it." The next thing I know, we were getting on the "intermediate" ski lift, and then we were off. No kidding, I must have fallen 50 times that first time down the mountain. Really. Every few feet, I fell. What I didn't understand is that you don't just turn your feet into a V shape and hope for the best; you have to dig in! You have to make a plow with your feet—that's why they call it a snowplow—but I was just forming an awkward and tragic V that caused me to fall face first again and again. Skiing was no fun. Well, once I understood that I needed to apply pressure, I dug in—and voilà, less tumbling! Following Jesus is like that—we need to work at it. We need to force our minds off this present world and onto Him who lives forever.

Jean E. and I enjoy gardening, and of course, intellectually we have always acknowledged that plants need fertilizer. Duh. You didn't need to convince us of the truth that plants need fertilizer. We moved into a house and planted many flowering plants, especially roses, and we would sporadically—sometimes, once in a while (or not)—fertilize them. Many of them started looking sickly, and some died. Well, after some years of replacing dying plants, a novel, brilliant thought came to me: we need to be more diligent about fertilizing! Shocking—"Plants actually need fertilizer! Who knew?" (that's a joke between Jean E. and me). It wasn't enough for us to assent to the belief that plants needed fertilizer. I had to make it happen! Regularly. You already see where I'm going: when it comes to not loving this world but loving God, we actually have to work at it. It isn't enough for you to assent to not loving this world and setting your mind on eternity—you have to work at it.

Second, we must drink in, bathe in, swim in, and revel in the word of God. Psalm 1:2-3 tells us that the "blessed" person's "delight is in the law of the Lord, and on his law he meditates day and night. He is like a tree planted by streams of water that yields its fruit in its season, and its leaf does not wither. In all that he does, he prospers." I love those verses! If you want to bear fruit and not wither like everything else is withering, then meditate on the word of God.

Similarly, Jesus says in John 8:31-32, "If you abide in my word, you are truly my disciples, and you will know the truth, and the truth will set you free." Notice that Jesus says the sign of your "truly" being His disciple is abiding in His word. Sadly, many who call themselves Christians do not abide in Jesus's word, and so many of them aren't actually Jesus's disciples. Also, if we don't abide in God's word, we fail to comprehend the truth about reality, and then the truth about reality doesn't set us free from sin or from the fear of death. Again, this takes effort. Jean E. and I were talking with a woman who told us that she didn't feel as close to God as she used to. It turns out she wasn't reading the Bible, so we told her she needed regular study of God's word. She replied, "That's not it; I need God to do it!" That sounds spiritual, but it's lazy—that's like a person saying he wants to lose weight, but when you tell him he needs to eat fewer calories than he burns, he says, "That's not it; I need it to just happen on its own." News flash: the words "disciple" and "discipline" have more in common than their spelling. If we're going to be Jesus's disciples, then we need to discipline ourselves. If we're going to live a buoyant Christian life in the face of death, then we need to abide in—hang out in—God's word. It should flow through our minds.

Jesus says in Matthew 10:28, "Do not fear those who kill the body but cannot kill the soul. Rather fear him who can destroy both soul and body in hell." Here Jesus says not to fear those who can murder you! And if we shouldn't fear being murdered, then we don't need to fear dying in other ways (I'm not suggesting there isn't a legitimate fear of the pain of dying in a particular way). Why not? Because in Jesus's considered opinion, your physical death isn't very important! Now, you might be thinking, "Well, my physical death is important to me!" I get that, but the eternal life of your soul is *infinitely* more important than living on earth for a few more miserable years. As I write this, I realize that if you're in love with this world, then this is just so much crazy talk because you haven't been "transformed by the renewal of your mind" (Romans 12:2). But if you are abiding in God's word, then you will resonate with this. Take this in. Revolve it in your mind. Now when Jean E. and I get on a plane, I think, "Well, we're together, and if a terrorist were to blow up our plane, then this is as good a day to die as any." I mean it. I kid that there may be a white-knuckle minute or two as we plunge to the ground—after all, not fearing being dead isn't the same thing as not wanting to suffer—but then it's life everlasting! These thoughts are only possible if we're abiding in God's word.

Third, we must have a robust appreciation of the glory that awaits us in heaven forever! For too many Christians, eternal life is the P.S. to the Christian life. Eternal life is an "also ran" doctrine. For many, eternal life earns only a "participation trophy" in the contest for things that are important to us. Most Christians crave to achieve the American Dream and take small solace in the fact that, yes, when they die, they will inherit that live-forever thingy. Too often, we concentrate on the few decades (or not!) we have on earth and ignore that we're going to live forever. But eternal life in Jesus isn't the encore, it's the main event, and it is precisely upon what we must set our hope.

Even worse, there's this blather that you can be "so heavenly-minded you're no earthly good." I like to tell my classes that I've never met that person! And I mean it. I've never met a person so heavenly minded that they were no earthly good. In fact, sadly, I've rarely met a heavenly minded person! Now, I have met some mystically minded people who seemed to be of no earthly good, but not a heavenly minded person. C.S. Lewis was absolutely right in *Mere Christianity*:

> If you read history you will find that the Christians who did most for the present world were precisely those who thought most of the next. It is since Christians have largely ceased to think of the other world that they have become so ineffective in this. The Apostles themselves, who set on foot the conversion of the Roman Empire, the great men who built up the Middle Ages, the English Evangelicals who abolished the Slave Trade, all left their mark on Earth, precisely because their minds were occupied with Heaven. It is since Christians have largely ceased to think of the other world that they have become so ineffective in this.[4]

So where did this too-heavenly-minded idea come from? Well, Satan, of course, and he's disseminated it as a talking point to his minions ever since.

First Peter 1:13 tells us, "Therefore, preparing your minds for action, and being sober-minded, set your hope fully on the grace that will be brought to you at the revelation of Jesus Christ." That isn't three separate commands. We are told to prepare our minds for action and to be ready for the specific purpose that we can "set" our "hope fully" on the grace that will be given us at the return of Jesus. This is the exact opposite of the worldly goals related to living in the present and pursuing a bucket list. We are commanded to do God's will here while focusing on the future.

The New Testament often compares our Christian life to a race. First Corinthians 9:24 tells us, "Do you not know that in a race all the runners run, but only one receives the prize? So run that you may obtain it." In other words, get off your idle derrière (I resisted using the popular phrase) and run for the glories of eternal life. When Paul anticipates his death (he was beheaded by Nero), he writes in 2 Timothy 4:6-8, "The time of my departure has come. I have fought the good fight, I have finished the *race*, I have kept the faith. Henceforth there is laid up for me the crown of righteousness, which the Lord, the righteous judge, will award to me on that day, and not only to me but also to all who have loved his appearing." Paul looks to the future crown of righteousness. Similarly, Hebrews 12:1-2 tells us, "Let us also lay aside every weight, and sin which clings so closely, and let us run with endurance the race that is set before us, looking to Jesus, the founder and perfecter of our faith, who for the joy that was set before him endured the cross, despising the shame, and is seated at the right hand of the throne of God." Jesus is able to despise the pain and shame of the cross precisely because of "the joy that was set before him"—for eternal glory. Notice the future, heavenly, eternal orientation of these passages!

I often look at audiences and say, "There's something I know absolutely for sure about every single one of you! Every one of you! There are no exceptions!" Then after a pause, I say, "You are all full of lust! Every one of you is full of lust!" When I say that, I'm not kidding or exaggerating. You see, the Lord created us as beings with strong desires, or lusts (both English terms used in the New Testament are from the Greek word *epithumeo*).[5] He could have made us beings with weak desires. He could have made us so that if someone told us our house was on fire, we'd reply, "Oh, so it is." But He made us with strong desires. He made us to lust, and we're either going to lust after people, possessions, positions, and pleasures or we're going to lust after God and His kingdom—but either way, we are going to lust. You need to choose what you're lusting after.

In mythology, there's the story of the Sirens, creatures (think mermaids but part bird instead of part fish) that care "only for the destruction of men."[6] The Sirens live on an island, and when ships pass by, they come out and sing to the men on the ship. Bewitched by their song, sailors turn the ship toward the island—only to have the boat dashed on the rocks, and everyone dies. We are told that around the Sirens "lie great heaps of men, flesh rotting from their bones, their skin all shriveled up."[7] One ship's captain wants to hear the music of the Sirens, so he puts wax in his men's ears and has himself securely tied to the ship's mast. As expected, the Sirens call out, "Odysseus! Come here! You are well-known from many stories! Glory of the Greeks! Now stop your ship and listen to our voices. All those who pass this way hear honeyed song, poured from our mouths. The music brings them joy." Odysseus writes, "Their song was so melodious, I longed to listen more. I told my men to free me. I scowled at them, but they kept rowing on."[8] In fact, as instructed, when he begs them to stop, they only add more ropes and tie the knots tighter. Finally, the island is out of earshot, so the men untie him.

Many Christians live their entire lives like Odysseus. They listen to the music of this world and struggle against their Christian commitment. So many Christians lust after this world but manage—sort of—to not go headlong into sin. But too many escape their bonds, and their lives are destroyed. I'm reminded of Solomon's counsel to his sons about avoiding the adulterous woman. In Proverbs 7:21-23, we read about the foolish man: "With much seductive speech she persuades him; with her smooth talk she compels him. All at once he follows her, as an ox goes to the slaughter, or as a stag is caught fast till an arrow pierces its liver; as a bird rushes into a snare; he does not know that it will cost him his life." We've all heard the Siren's song. I've certainly heard the

Siren's song countless times and have felt like I'm tied to a mast by my commitments (and accountability!). But we don't have to live like that!

There's another story about the Sirens, this one more hopeful. One day, a ship called the Argo comes near, and the Sirens, "ever on the watch to draw mariners to their destruction...sang all together their lulling song." The "Sirens sang a clear, piercing song that called to each of the voyagers. Each man thought that his own name was in that song. 'O how well it is that you have come near,' each one sang, 'how well it is that you have come near where I have awaited you, having all delight prepared for you!'" Enticed, the wearied voyagers let their oars go with the waves and drift toward the Sirens.[9] But on board was Orpheus, who "knew all the stories of the gods," and "when he sang to his lyre the trees would listen and the beasts would follow him."[10] Knowing the danger, Orpheus takes up his lyre and sings, and "his voice and the music of his lyre prevailed above the Sirens' voices" and the men were saved.[11] Orpheus plays a more alluring song. He sings to them that they were "men who were the strength of Greece, men who had been fostered by the love and hope of their country. They were the winners of the Golden Fleece and their story would be told forever." He sings that "they who were born for great labors and to face dangers that other men might not face," and "soon hands would be stretched out to them—the welcoming hands of the men and women of their own land."[12]

Similarly, the world plays a piercing song, and if you follow its song throughout your life, then it will draw you to your death and destruction. But there is a better music!

In the mid-1980s, I worked for a large corporation, and my territory consisted of the San Francisco Bay area. While watching TV one night in a Burlingame hotel, on came a commercial for porn that would begin in just 20 minutes on the station I was watching. I was torn! I wanted to see it, but I turned off the TV and, feeling desperate, got out my Bible and turned to a passage I'd memorized because I'd read it so many times:

> Praise be to the God and Father of our Lord Jesus Christ!
> In his great mercy he has given us new birth into a living

hope through the resurrection of Jesus Christ from the
dead, and into an inheritance that can never perish,
spoil or fade. This inheritance is kept in heaven for you,
who through faith are shielded by God's power until
the coming of the salvation that is ready to be revealed
in the last time. In this you greatly rejoice, though now
for a little while you may have had to suffer grief in
all kinds of trials. These have come so that the proven
genuineness of your faith—of greater worth than gold,
which perishes even though refined by fire—may result
in praise, glory and honor when Jesus Christ is revealed
(1 Peter 1:3-7 NIV).

I read this passage quickly, urgently. When I finished, I read it again.
And again. And again. I don't know how many times. But as I kept
reading it, a calm came over me. I never turned the TV back on, and
I went to sleep. I had refocused my desires onto something glorious:
"An inheritance that can never perish, spoil, or fade—kept in heaven
for you." I was enamored of the better music.

Quoting verses like this doesn't work like magic: if I hadn't focused
regularly on eternity (I was also accountable to my wife), then my
quoting this would have had little effect. Our hearts must be fixed not
on this world but on God and His eternal kingdom. When we do this,
it will transform our lives. As Paul says in Colossians 1:4-5, "We heard
of your faith in Christ Jesus and of the love that you have for all the
saints, because of the hope laid up for you in heaven." Notice that you
have love for the saints because of the hope laid up for you in heaven.
As Richard R. Melick Jr. puts it, "About these verses Paul believed that
the hope offered in Christ inspires assurance and, as a result, produces
spiritual fruit. The basis of believing Christ (faith) and serving others
(love) is that this world is not the end."[13] That's right, an eternal focus
not only frees you from the lusts of this world; it helps you love your
neighbor.

In 1982, I began to get a glimpse of the glorious eternity that awaited
us and that became my favorite subject to teach on. In my research

on that topic, I came across some verses I memorized and have since prayed daily. In Ephesians 1:16-19, Paul tells us he prays "that the God of our Lord Jesus Christ, the Father of glory, may give you the Spirit of wisdom and of revelation in the knowledge of him, having the eyes of your hearts enlightened, that you may know what is the hope to which he has called you, what are the riches of his glorious inheritance in the saints, and what is the immeasurable greatness of his power toward us who believe." Paul says he does not cease to pray this, so I've been praying this prayer regularly for all the saints ever since. I find seven hopes in Scripture: the hope of adoption, the hope of Christ's return, the hope of resurrection, the hope of bodily redemption, the hope of salvation, the hope of eternal life, and the hope of glory. It's the hope of glory that I will focus on in the next chapter. Please join me in praying Ephesians 1:16-19.

It's important to note Peter's words: "now," in this very *mean*time, we have to "suffer grief in all kinds of trials" (1 Peter 1:6 NIV). I wish it were just that through sheer force of will, we could cause our minds and hearts to reject this world and focus ourselves on the glory to be revealed in us. But the world's seductive song is everywhere, and it is so easy to love this present world. Thus the Lord in His kindness allows us often to suffer specifically so that we will not cling to this present world and that our faith will be purified of all the literal and symbolic immortality projects—otherwise known as gods or idols—upon which we so easily depend.

As Corrie ten Boom and as a host of others have said, "You don't know that Jesus is all you need until Jesus is all you have." We need that knowledge, but it comes through suffering. Thus I've been telling my classes for years, "God's Plan A for your life is to take you through regular periods of suffering, and there is no Plan B!" Our Lord actually does us a favor by allowing suffering to come into our lives. Just as human glory almost always comes through the suffering of hard work, eternal glory also comes through suffering. In fact, the word "glory" in the New Testament is regularly related to suffering (Luke 24:26; Romans 5:2, 8:17-18; 2 Corinthians 4:17; Ephesians 3:13; 2 Timothy 2:10; Hebrews 2:10; 1 Peter 1:6-7, 5:1,10). In 2 Corinthians 4:16-18,

Paul writes that there is a direct relationship between suffering and glory: "So we do not lose heart. Though our outer self is wasting away, our inner self is being renewed day by day. For *this light momentary affliction is preparing for us an eternal weight of glory beyond all comparison*, as we look not to the things that are seen but to the things that are unseen. For the things that are seen are transient, but the things that are unseen are eternal."

That others we love die, and that our own deaths regularly threaten us, teaches us to not love this present world, it teaches us to ignore the Siren's song, and it teaches us (often forces us) to focus on eternal life in Jesus. God uses suffering to teach us to shun this world and to focus on what really matters: eternal life in His kingdom. Thus the Lord allows us to be surrounded by—sometimes swamped by—suffering and death to keep us from loving this present world.

I want to encourage you, dear reader, on a practical note. When this world's suffering saddens me, I take comfort in the salvation available in Jesus and in relationship with Jesus. Although I'm not often sad, on those occasions when I am, I go off alone and ask the Lord for help in dealing with what troubles me. Then I sing praises to our Lord, thank Him for loving me, and thank Him for working everything out for our good and giving us eternal life. I tell Him that I love Him. In other words, I enter into worship, and that *always* uplifts and emboldens me. Learn to worship Jesus. Sometimes I think this life is perfectly designed to lead Christians into this worship relationship. As we age, as we struggle with our weakening bodies and the suffering of those around us, increasingly we can learn (we are pushed, really) to find joy in worshiping Jesus. If you haven't done this, then the next time you're down, seek comfort through worshiping the Lord.

I took spiritual formation as a doctoral course from Dallas Willard, and Dallas (that's what he went by) encouraged us to memorize what is now one of my favorite passages, Colossians 3:1-4: "If then you have been raised with Christ, seek the things that are above, where Christ is, seated at the right hand of God. Set your minds on things that are above, not on things that are on earth. For you have died, and your life is hidden with Christ in God. When Christ who is your life appears, then you also will appear with him in glory." This is the other music, the music that leads to eternal life.

In the next chapter, we will examine what it means for us to appear with Him in glory. We need to do this because, as we have seen, skeptics often portray eternal life as a cosmic bummer.

8

Our Heart's Desire—
Glorious Immortality

What happens to you the moment your body dies? Notice I said the moment your *body* dies. I say this because the essential you—your soul, your consciousness—will absolutely, positively not experience death. Remember, you're not a body that has a soul; you're a soul that has a body. Your body enables your soul to interact with the physical world. So even though your body dies, your soul will not be harmed. Jesus said some amazing things about death. In John 8:51, Jesus says, "Truly, truly, I say to you, if anyone keeps my word, he will never see death." Notice the "truly, truly." Jesus is telling us to listen up. He's emphasizing that what He says next are words we can count on. And He says, you "will never see death." Now, of course, Jesus isn't talking about the death of your body. Jesus wasn't in denial. Your body will die. But the most essential you will never die.

In Luke 21:16-18, Jesus tells His disciples, "You will be delivered up even by parents and brothers and relatives and friends, and some of you they will put to death. You will be hated by all for my name's sake. But not a hair of your head will perish." So here Jesus says some of His disciples will actually be put to death (that's happening around the world right now), but then He says something amazing: "Not a hair of your head will perish." Well, wait a minute. Many Christians have been burned to death, others have been beheaded (many in the last few years), and we would typically say that having our heads set on fire or removed from our torsos would harm at least some, if not all, of our hairs. But Jesus said if they kill you, they will not harm even a hair on your head. What Jesus means is that they can kill your body, but they cannot touch *you*—your conscious soul will be unharmed. Therefore, as Jesus says next in verse 19, "By your endurance you will gain your lives." After Bob Warren's passing, his wife Kim told people, "This is where the rubber meets the road in my faith, this is it." She said she needed to say out loud something she knew to be true. This is an example of the faith, which results in endurance, by which you will gain your life (Matthew 10:22, 24:13: "The one who endures to the end will be saved"). Continue to honor God in suffering and persecution, Christian, and—metaphorically speaking—no one can harm a hair on your head. Your soul, your consciousness, will live on, and one day we will all be reunited with our spiritual bodies (more about that shortly).

So what happens to your soul when you die? The answer is that your soul will be immediately transferred into the spiritual realm—"to the city of the living God, the heavenly Jerusalem, and to innumerable angels in festal gathering, and to the assembly of the firstborn who are enrolled in heaven, and to God, the judge of all, and to the spirits of the righteous made perfect, and to Jesus, the mediator of a new covenant" (Hebrews 12:22-24). As Jesus says to the thief being crucified next to Him, "Truly, I say to you, *today* you will be with me in paradise" (Luke 23:43), and "paradise" is one of the biblical names for heaven.[1] There will be no delay. In fact, your transition into the unseen realm will be so smooth, so seamless, and so natural, it may take you a while to realize you've died. If you happen to turn and see your body lying on the floor, or in a mangled car, or on an operating table, then you can take that as evidence of your passing.[2]

You will have entered what is called the "intermediate state" (the state of your disembodiment but before you possess your glorified, resurrected body). In this state, you'll be, as Alan Gomes puts it, in "direct and glorious communion with Christ and an immediate apprehension of God's presence—far more so than anything enjoyed in this life."[3] Thus Paul encourages us in 2 Corinthians 5:1-2, "For we know that if the tent that is our earthly home is destroyed, we have a building from

God, a house not made with hands, eternal in the heavens. For in this tent we groan, longing to put on our heavenly dwelling." And boy, do we groan in this tent of our body, with all the aches, pains, colds, flus, fevers, cancers, and dementias. We long "that what is mortal may be swallowed up by life" (verse 4). Recognizing this, says Paul, "we are of good courage, and we would rather be away from the body and at home with the Lord" (verse 8). Notice that when you are away from the body, you are at home with the Lord. As with the thief on the cross, when you die, you will be with Jesus in paradise. Are you of good courage, dear Christian? If not, remember this world's corruption and coming destruction and then focus on the glory that awaits you for eternity, which you can never lose (we'll talk more about this in a moment).

Earlier we discussed Philippians 1:23, where Paul says his desire is to "depart and be with Christ," but he says at this time, he will "remain in the flesh." It's clear Paul believes his death will bring him into the glorious kingdom. Above I referenced Hebrews 12:23, where it says we have come to "the spirits of the righteous made perfect." Similarly, in Revelation 6:9, John tells us that he saw "the souls of those who had been slain for the word of God and for the witness they had borne." Notice that John sees the "souls" of those who had been slain. John could have just said, "I saw those who had been slain," but he doesn't; he says he saw their souls. Being a disembodied spirit won't be a problem for us, because until the creation of a new heavens and a new earth, we won't need a body to interact with the physical world. The more I think about this, the more exciting it becomes, as my present body increasingly has more aches and pains. Remember, John 4:24 tells us that "God is spirit," and so in that way, we will be like Him and with Him and each other. But we're not going to stay that way! Let's now examine our ultimate glorification.

In Colossians 1:25-26, Paul writes that he was sent "to make the word of God fully known, the mystery hidden for ages and generations but now revealed to his saints." In verse 27, we read, "God chose to make known how great...are the riches of the glory of this mystery, which is Christ in you, the hope of glory." Dear saints of God, do you hear that? The glorious riches of the mystery of the ages is "Christ in you, the hope of glory"! Paul writes in Romans 5:2, "We rejoice in the hope of the glory of God." Douglas Moo translates this as "We *boast* in the hope of the glory of God."[4] We revel in the hope of the glory of God!

Sadly, few Christians talk much about our glorification. As the famous preacher of Westminster Chapel D. Martyn Lloyd-Jones puts it, "For some remarkable reason it is something that is tragically neglected by us all, and by the Church in general. We talk much about our sanctification, but how little do we talk about our glorification. When did you last hear emphasis placed upon it?"[5] Indeed, dear reader, when did you last hear or talk about your glorification except, perhaps, in passing? No wonder so many Christians are so this-world focused. We don't hear enough or think enough about kingdom come and our glorious place in it. So let's talk about it now.

"Glory" is an odd word. It is the strongest word to communicate that something is magnificent, courageous, resplendent, beautiful, worthy, honorable, and renowned. Americans call their flag "Old Glory." We use "glory" to describe our army's victory in battle. We say that mountains and sunsets are glorious. Sometimes people will attribute glory to themselves or something they've done (computer gamers sometimes talk about their glorious victories), but humans *rarely* refer to other humans as glorious except sarcastically: "There he is in all his glory."

We've seen that humans outside of Christ strive to transcend their puniness and their mortality—in other words, to obtain some sense of immortal glory—through symbolic immortality projects. Indeed, the self-esteem advocates get one thing exactly right: we humans really do need to feel good about ourselves. But the self-esteem advocates get it insanely wrong when they try to base self-esteem on human uniqueness.

Uniqueness in and of itself never imparts any value whatsoever. Every dog dropping is unique, but we don't attribute any value to them for that. And as we've seen, human accomplishment—secular salvation strategies—are all doomed to destruction. But eternal glory satisfies our innermost longings. We want to be glorious. "Glorious" means "having, worthy of, or bringing fame or admiration" or "having a striking beauty or splendor that evokes feelings of delighted admiration."[6] This is a good definition, and it is what God has planned for our eternity. Paul writes something almost too wonderful in Romans 8:30: "Those whom he justified he also glorified." God intends to glorify us! But what does it mean for us to be glorified? Before we discuss *our* glorification, let's see what Scripture says about the glory of God.

"Glory" in its various forms occurs more than 400 times in Scripture, and the vast majority of the time, it refers to God. We are told that the "heavens declare the glory of God" (Psalm 19:1). Before Jesus raises Lazarus from the dead, He tells those at the funeral, "You will see the glory of God" (John 11:40 NIV). Just before he was stoned to death, Stephen, "full of the Holy Spirit, gazed into heaven and saw the glory of God, and Jesus standing at the right hand of God" (Acts 7:55). We are told that one day, every tongue will acknowledge "that Jesus Christ is Lord, to the glory of God the Father" (Philippians 2:11). We are told the New Jerusalem shone with "the glory of God, its radiance like a most rare jewel, like a jasper, clear as crystal" and that the city doesn't need the sun or the moon to shine on it, "for the glory of God gives it light, and its lamp is the Lamb" (Revelation 21:11,23). Jesus says that one day, everyone "will see the Son of Man coming on the clouds of heaven with power and great glory" (Matthew 24:30).

Probably the most dramatic portrayal of the glory of God is found in Revelation 4. There John tells us that he beheld a throne in heaven, and the one seated on the throne had the appearance of jasper and carnelian, and around the throne was a rainbow that had the appearance of an emerald. From the throne came flashes of lightning and rumblings and peals of thunder, and before the throne were burning seven torches of fire, which are the seven spirits of God. Before the throne, there was a sea of glass *like* crystal.

Around the throne are 24 elders dressed in white with crowns on their heads and seated on 24 thrones. We are told that four living creatures "full of eyes in front and behind" surround the throne. The first living creature is "*like* a lion, the second living creature *like* an ox, the third living creature with the face of a man, and the fourth living creature *like* an eagle in flight. And the four living creatures, each of them with six wings, are full of eyes all around and within" (verses 6-8 emphasis added). Notice that John uses the word "like" to describe the wonders of what he saw. This is because John isn't seeing a lion or an eagle or an ox; John is approximating. He's doing his best to describe what he sees.

About these creatures, John says they never cease to say, "Holy, holy, holy, is the Lord God Almighty, who was and is and is to come!" (verse 8). When these creatures "give *glory* and honor and thanks to him who is seated on the throne, who lives forever and ever, the twenty-four elders fall down before him who is seated on the throne and worship him who lives forever and ever" (verses 9-10). Then "they cast their crowns before the throne, saying, 'Worthy are you, our Lord and God, to receive *glory* and honor and power, for you created all things, and by your will they existed and were created'" (verse 11).

So now that we've glimpsed what it means for God to be glorious, let's see what it means for God to glorify us. The Lord God is doing and will do—this is known as "the already, not yet"—four major things to and through us: we will be resurrected, perfected, resplendent, and renowned. Let's enjoy each of these in turn.

Resurrected

The first facet of our glorification is that we will be resurrected with a spiritual body.[7] One of the worst distortions about our future is that we'll be less than we are here. As I discuss in *Why Does God Allow Evil?*, this is promoted by the movie *City of Angels* (1998), which is a riff of "the sons of God" having sex with "the daughters of man" (Genesis 6:2). In that movie, angel Seth (Nicholas Cage) has no sense of taste, touch, or smell. As the plot develops, he falls in love with human Maggie (Meg Ryan), gives up his angelic status ("falls"), and becomes a human so that he can make love to Maggie, which he does. The next morning, however, a truck kills Maggie as she is out riding her bike. When another angel asks Seth if it was worth giving up his immortality to become human, Seth replies, "I would rather have had one breath of her hair, one kiss from her mouth, one touch of her hand, than eternity without it. One."[8] Seth would give up eternity for just one chance to smell her hair? In other words, for Seth, eternal life was a cosmic bummer. This is *not* what the Bible tells us.

As Paul puts it in Romans 8:11, "If the Spirit of him who raised Jesus from the dead dwells in you, he who raised Christ Jesus from the dead will also give life to your *mortal bodies* through his Spirit who dwells in you." We are told that we will be resurrected in "spiritual bodies": "It is sown a perishable *body*," says Paul. "It is raised an imperishable *body*; it is sown in dishonor, it is raised in *glory*; it is sown in weakness, it is raised in power; it is sown a natural body, it is raised a spiritual body. If there is a natural body, there is also a spiritual *body*" (1 Corinthians 15:42-44 NASB).

Our bodies will be like Jesus's glorious postresurrection body. So Paul says in Philippians 3:20-21, "But our citizenship is in heaven. And we eagerly await a Savior from there, the Lord Jesus Christ, who, by the power that enables him to bring everything under his control, will transform our lowly bodies so that they will be like his *glorious* body" (NIV). Similarly, we are told in 1 Corinthians 15:49, "Just as we have borne the image of the man of dust, we shall also bear the image of the man of heaven." Alan Gomes is right: "What this means is that when we examine the biblical descriptions of Christ's postresurrection body, we may take them as specifying what our own bodies will be like."[9] That Jesus had a body of flesh is clear when He tells His disciples in Luke 24:39, "See my hands and my feet, that it is I myself. Touch me, and see. For a spirit does not have flesh and bones as you see that I have." Similarly, Jesus invited Thomas to touch His crucifixion wounds to demonstrate that it really was Him (John 20:27).[10] That Jesus had a body of flesh is also evidenced by the fact that the women hugged Jesus (Matthew 28:9). Further, Jesus ate fish (Luke 24:41-43) and even cooked and served His disciples a breakfast of bread and fish (John 21:9-13).[11]

In addition, we are invited to a banquet, to "a feast of rich food, a feast of well-aged wine, of rich food full of marrow, of aged wine well refined" (Isaiah 25:6-7). In other words, we'll be eating the best! Imagine eating without health concerns or the fear of gaining weight. In fact, we are invited to the wedding banquet (Matthew 22:1-10; Revelation

19:6-9)! In Jesus's day, a wedding banquet ideally lasted seven days and was designed to be a time of joy and celebration.[12] Imagine attending the wedding banquet of Jesus!

But Jesus's body wasn't standard-issue flesh and bones. As we've read, it was a "spiritual body." Jesus could be touched, even hugged, but His body was also supernatural. Jesus passed through His grave clothes without disturbing them. In John 20:6-7, the apostle John thinks it noteworthy that when he and Peter enter the tomb, they find "the linen cloths lying there, and the face cloth, which had been on Jesus' head, not lying with the linen cloths but folded up in a place by itself." D.A. Carson contrasts that with the resurrection of Lazarus in John 11:44, where Lazarus "came from the tomb wearing his grave-clothes, the additional burial cloth still wrapped around his head. Jesus' resurrection body apparently passed through his grave-clothes, spices and all."[13]

Then in John 20:19 we read, "On the evening of that day, the first day of the week, *the doors being locked* where the disciples were for fear of the Jews, Jesus came and stood among them and said to them, 'Peace be with you.'" John thinks it is important to emphasize that "doors being locked" doesn't hinder Jesus. About this, Carson comments, "As his resurrection body passed through the grave-clothes (verses 6-8), so it passed through the locked doors and simply 'materialized.'"[14] Similarly, in Luke 24:30-31 we read, "When he was at table with them, he took the bread and blessed and broke it and gave it to them. And their eyes were opened, and they recognized him. And he vanished from their sight."[15] Now, we don't know exactly how Jesus's body did these things. As Gomes suggests, "Perhaps the resurrection body has special properties that allow it to violate the normal laws of physics as we know them, enabling it to appear and disappear at will. Perhaps it can pass through solid objects."[16] Indeed, we know Jesus could do these things, but it's not important to understand how He did them. Whatever the case, our hope is to have a body like Jesus's postresurrection body—one that is indestructible but can receive and give hugs, enjoy the best of foods, and apparently, go anywhere instantly! This is our hope based on the fact of the resurrection of Jesus!

Perfected

The second facet of our glorification is that we will be perfected.[17] But perfection gets a bad rap. We tend to associate perfection with a legalistic adherence to a code of conduct. We mostly relate perfection to the utterly unobtainable, to perfectionists who desperately try to measure up, or to the cold, dispassionate, unfeeling sterility of something like a doctor's office. Most of us, if asked, would not want to spend time with someone perfect. If Christianity is true, then we would expect Satan to confuse our language, and he has done that with the concept of something being "perfect."

Jesus was perfect, yet He got angry with hypocrites, and contrary to Hollywood's image of stern or hypocritical preachers, sinners surrounded Him (Luke 15:1). He spent the day with a thief (Luke 19:1-10). A sinful woman washed His feet with her hair (Luke 7:44). He cared for the sick and spent time with children. He cried with Mary and Martha over Lazarus's death (John 11:33).

Jesus was perfect, but He publicly rejected legalistic, man-made holiness codes that sounded spiritual but were not. Although the Pharisees complained, Jesus allowed His hungry disciples to pick and eat grain on the Sabbath (Matthew 12:1-2). When the Pharisees and the Scribes complained that Jesus and His disciples didn't wash their hands before they ate, Jesus rebuked them for "teaching as doctrines the commandments of men" (Mark 7:7). The Pharisees told Jesus it was unlawful to heal on the Sabbath, but He did anyway, and they responded by plotting to kill Him (Mark 3:1-6). In short, Jesus rejects the moral maxims of men.

Jesus was perfect, but He ate and drank so often with sinners that the Pharisees said, "Here is a glutton and a drunkard, a friend of tax collectors and 'sinners'" (Matthew 11:19 NIV). Jesus was perfect, but when they ran out of wine at the wedding at Cana, Jesus's first miracle was to turn water into wine, and He made a lot of it—estimates range from 120 to 150 gallons.[18] And it was very good wine because the guests exclaimed that the host had saved the best wine for last (verse 10). Jesus could have had His first miracle be to heal the blind or the deaf, thus announcing Himself as the one who would enable people to see or hear. Or He could have raised someone from the dead, demonstrating that He came to conquer death. But Jesus made wine. My point isn't that anyone should start drinking wine—many shouldn't—or that if someone does drink wine, they shouldn't be cautious not to stumble into others. My point is that we need to be careful not to present Christianity as antipleasure. After all, it was the Lord who made orgasms possible. Since nothing was made that wasn't made through Him, then Jesus created all the pleasures! My point is that our perfect Lord does not oppose pleasure; He opposes pleasure's misuse.

This is perfection, and we will have it. Jesus demands perfection: "Be perfect, therefore, as your heavenly Father is perfect" (Matthew 5:48 NIV). But then He supplies what He demands, "for by one sacrifice he has made perfect forever those who are being made holy" (Hebrews 10:14 NIV). And so we read that those in heaven are "the spirits of the righteous made perfect" (Hebrews 12:23).[19] I long for the day when I will no longer feel guilty for eating too much, for saying the wrong thing, for wasting money on something that once seemed smart, ad infinitum, don't you? Can you imagine no guilt forever? That eternal life comes!

Resplendent

The third facet of our glorification is that the Lord intends to make us resplendent—beautiful and shining in splendor. We often describe beautiful people in resplendent terms: her eyes sparkled, her hair shined, her smile beamed, her skin was radiant. We also call the most successful athletes and actors "sports stars" and "movie stars." Sometimes we say that a beautiful star "lights up the room." Well, consider that the Creator of blazing stars intends to make us beautiful and resplendent as we behold His glory.

Most people seek worldly resplendence in tanning beds or with Botox, breast implants, waxings, tattoos, facelifts, and on and on. People seek to beautify themselves—and if not that, to at least get attention. The American Society of Plastic Surgeons reports that "there were 17.5 million surgical and minimally invasive cosmetic procedures performed in the United States in 2017, a 2 percent increase over 2016." Although 7.23 million of these were Botox treatments, there were more than 300,000 breast augmentations, about 246,000 liposuctions, 219,000 nose reshapings, 210,000 eyelid surgeries, and 130,000 tummy tucks—and this was all in one year.[20] Although some of these were medically beneficial, many of the more than 12,000 labiaplasties (a 39 percent increase from 2016) were for cosmetic reasons.[21] Labiaplasties, sadly, are *largely* due to the proliferation of porn. After all, if it wasn't for porn, how would a woman (or a man) know what it means to look "normal" down there?

Then consider cosmetics and jewelry. Globally, people spent $532 billion in 2017 on cosmetics and $316 billion in 2016 on jewelry (costume and fine).[22] Combined, that's closing in on $1 trillion a year.

We do these things because we want not only to see beauty but to be beautiful. As C.S. Lewis puts it, "We do not want merely to see beauty, though, God knows, even that is bounty enough. We want something else which can hardly be put into words—to be united with the beauty we see, to pass into it, to receive it into ourselves, to bathe in it, to become part of it."[23] These are all attempts at being beautiful, glorious, but none of them is more than a delay of the inevitable: our death and decay. All these are failed attempts to be beautiful, even resplendent, without Jesus.

Well, the Lord intends to make you glorious. When it comes to humans, consider that in Exodus 28, Moses is commanded to employ the most skilled craftsmen to make "holy garments" for the priests "for glory and for beauty" (verse 2). Notice that Old Testament priests were to be clothed so they would look glorious and beautiful! Their garments were to be made of "blue and purple and scarlet yarns" and adorned with precious stones, including emeralds, sapphires, and diamonds, and these jewels were to be set in gold. Jewels sparkle because they reflect light, and the priests were to be adorned in jewels.

Then consider that after Moses stood before the Lord, his face would become so radiant, so bright, that the Israelites "were afraid to come near him" (Exodus 34:30). In fact, Moses's face was so bright, "the Israelites could not look steadily" at his face "because of its glory"

(2 Corinthians 3:7 NIV). His face was too bright to even look at! It hurt their eyes! Also consider that this light wasn't a normal reflection of light that ceased as soon as the source was removed. Moses was still bright even when the Lord was no longer visibly present. This is significant because, as Paul asks, "If the ministry of death, carved in letters on stone, came with such glory that the Israelites could not gaze at Moses' face because of its glory, which was being brought to an end, will not the ministry of the Spirit have even more glory?" (2 Corinthians 3:7-8). What will our persons be like when we regularly behold the glory of God?[24]

In Colossians 3:4, Paul tells us, "When Christ who is your life appears, then you also will appear with him in glory." Daniel 12:3 tells us that "those who are wise will shine like the brightness of the heavens, and those who lead many to righteousness, like the stars for ever and ever" (NIV). As the Lord says about his people in Zechariah 9:16, "They will sparkle in his land like jewels in a crown" (NIV). Jesus reaffirms this when He says, "The righteous will shine like the sun in the kingdom of their Father" (Matthew 13:43).[25] Above in Matthew 17:2, we read that at the transfiguration, Jesus's face "shone like the sun." But it wasn't just Jesus. Luke 9:31 says Moses and Elijah also "appeared in glory." As professor Vern Poythress posits it in his book *Theophany: A Biblical Theology of God's Appearing*, "In the consummation, we ourselves will reflect the glory associated with glory theophanies, such as the appearance of glory on the Mount of Transfiguration."[26] Alan Gomes asks, "What exactly do the biblical writers mean when they describe the resurrection body in such 'luminous language' or 'glowing terms'? Do they have in mind a literal, physical brightness similar to when Jesus stood transfigured before Peter, James, and John (Matt. 17:2)? Perhaps."[27]

As the bride of Christ, Revelation 19:7-8 tells us that at the wedding supper of the Lamb, "fine linen, bright and clean, was given her to wear" (NIV). Later in Revelation 21:9-11, we read, "'Come, I will show you the bride, the wife of the Lamb.' And he carried me away in the Spirit to a mountain great and high, and showed me the Holy City, Jerusalem, coming down out of heaven from God. It shone with the glory of God, and its brilliance was like that of a very precious jewel, like a jasper, clear as crystal" (NIV). Just as the priests were adorned with jewels, so in Revelation 21 the New Jerusalem, the bride of Christ, is similarly adorned "with every kind of jewel" (verse 19 ESV). About this jewel-toned brilliance, Grant R. Osborne writes, "It is best to see this list as a general depiction of the glory of the people of God."[28] Finally, in Revelation 22:5, we are told that the saints "will not need the light of a lamp or the light of the sun, for the Lord God will give them light. And they will reign for ever and ever" (NIV).[29]

Now, I don't know exactly what all this will mean for our persons, and we shouldn't get too precise in what we will be like—maybe we'll be luminous or maybe we won't (or maybe we'll have a choice, depending on the situation). As John writes in 1 John 3:2, "Dear friends, now we are children of God, and what we will be has not yet been made known. But we know that when Christ appears, we shall be like him, for we shall see him as he is" (NIV). In other words, we don't know exactly what we will be like, but whatever we become, it will be glorious.

Renowned

The fourth facet of our glorification is that the Lord intends to honor us—we will be renowned. Although I've heard many people proclaim they don't care what others think about them, we've seen that the lost desperately seek renown and employ all kinds of symbolic immortality projects in an attempt to transcend their deaths. But at the Judgment, where all our thoughts and deeds will be revealed to everyone (but not the Christian's sins; Isaiah 1:18; 1 John 1:9), all symbolic immortality projects fail, and only those things done for Him in love are eternally valuable. Paul tells us in 1 Corinthians 4:5 that the Lord "will bring to light what is hidden in darkness and will expose the motives of the heart. At that time each will receive their praise from God" (NIV). Our praise won't be based on the gold standard—that's nothing! Gold is the asphalt of heaven. Nor will our praise be based on how we succeeded—or not—in relationship to others. There will be no "I did better than them!" Instead, our praise is based on the opinion of the Creator of the universe. When the motives for our deeds are exposed, then the Lord God Almighty will praise us.

I briefly considered analogizing the significance of God's opinion compared to the opinions of others by writing something like "Who cares if fellow employees don't like you if your boss thinks you're doing a great job?" But it immediately occurred to me (and I'm sure to you) that sometimes, the boss really is a dolt (a major theme of Dilbert comics). That also goes for some military commanders, sports team managers, politicians, and so on. On the one hand, leaders are often mistaken, and a person's fellows are often the better judges. On the other hand, sometimes the boss sees more clearly than fellow employees who have agendas of their own.

God's opinion, however, is sui generis: not just unique but in a category all by itself. There's nothing like it. The Lord's opinion eclipses all other opinions. In fact, if we seek the renown of men, then we will fail to obtain the renown of God and will ultimately and inevitably find that human praise is worthless. As Jesus says in John 5:44, "How can you believe, when you receive glory from one another and do not seek the glory that comes from the only God?" Only God's opinion counts. In fact, Christians who embrace that only God's opinion counts often turn down worldly honors—not because these Christians are unworthy of worldly honors but because worldly honors are unworthy of them.[30]

The Lord commands us to keep our focus on praise from Him, and He warns that we must expect men's scorn. So suffering occurs in this facet of glory. Sometimes righteous living will result in our disparagement, demotion, and even destruction. Paul writes from prison in 2 Timothy 3:12 that "*all* who desire to live a godly life in Christ Jesus will be persecuted." Jesus says in Luke 6:22-23, "Blessed are you when people hate you and when they exclude you and revile you and spurn your name as evil, on account of the Son of Man! Rejoice in that day, and leap for joy, for behold, your reward is great in heaven; for so their fathers did to the prophets." Next time someone slanders you for righteousness's sake, leap for joy (you can do that literally, but I wouldn't do it in front of them). Why would your reward be great when people think you're gross? Because you're not living for the praise of men but for the praise of God—eternal renown! We read in Revelation 14:13, "I heard a voice from heaven saying, 'Write this: Blessed are the dead who die in the Lord from now on.' 'Blessed indeed,' says the Spirit, 'that they may rest from their labors, for their deeds follow them!'" Notice that your faithfulness to Jesus here on earth and your faithfully enduring persecution and suffering will follow you into the eternal kingdom.

So in Christ, we long to hear what will be said in front of all created beings: "Well done, good and faithful servant. You have been faithful over a little; I will set you over much. Enter into the joy of your master" (Matthew 25:21). After an interview for a Talbot Seminary podcast, Sean McDowell asks apologist Os Guinness what he thinks his legacy might be. Guinness replies that "legacy" is a secular idea and that Christians should only desire to hear God say, "Well done, my good and faithful servant."[31]

I'm going to digress for a moment because many Christians worry that they haven't accomplished very much, at least from an outward perspective. But we need to realize that the *size* of our ministry is irrelevant to God's judgment of us, and if it is irrelevant to God's judgment of us, then it is irrelevant. It doesn't matter. I ask my classes who they think is going to be greater in the kingdom of God. Will it be _____ [insert the name of the Christian leader you most respect] or will it be the woman who was abused as a child, who couldn't go to college, who isn't brilliant, who isn't particularly good looking, and who works in a convalescent home? But in that convalescent home, she loves the people in her care. She cares for them like she was caring for Christ Himself. She cares for them because she loves them, and she shares Christ with them as she has the opportunity. Then I ask, "Who's going be greater in the kingdom of God?" There's always silence. Then I pronounce, "There is only one possible answer." Students laugh, but I'm not kidding. There is *only one possible answer*. The only possible answer is, "I don't know!" But I know *for sure* that the answer isn't *necessarily* this or that famous Christian leader. It might be the famous Christian leader, but that's not a given. Motives will be exposed, and if ministry isn't done out of love, it's worthless (1 Corinthians 4:1-5, 13:1-3); teachers will be "judged with greater strictness" (James 3:1); and "everyone who has been given much, much will be demanded" (Luke 12:48 NIV). We are going to be judged solely on how far we got with what God has given us.

In Matthew 20:21, we read that Jesus was asked if two of His disciples could sit at Jesus's right hand and left hand in His kingdom. Jesus could have replied a lot of things. One thing He could have replied was, "It doesn't work like that! Everyone is going to be equal in the kingdom. You'll all get to take turns sitting at my right and left hands."

But Jesus doesn't say that.

Instead, Jesus says in verse 23, "To sit at my right hand and at my left is not mine to grant, but it is for those for whom it has been prepared by my Father." In other words, some will have honors that others won't. Does this make you want to get more Twitter followers? That's not the criterion. Then in verses 26-28, Jesus tells us the criterion for who will be great in His kingdom: "Whoever would be great among you must be your servant, and whoever would be first among you must be your slave, even as the Son of Man came not to be served but to serve, and to give his life as a ransom for many."

So there it is! Who will be greatest in God's kingdom isn't dependent on academic accolades, audience size, book sales, blog visitors, Twitter followers, Facebook friends, and so on. Rather, if you want to be great in God's kingdom, then be a loving servant! Let's get off the fool's gold standard of ministry success.

Knowing this humbles and alarms me because I know I've often done things for the wrong motives, and I'm frequently aware that I didn't use my gifting as well as I should have. But more than that, knowing that I won't be judged in comparison to others frees me. If we base our perceived success on others' success, then we will be frustrated and jealous. This will make us lustful and crazy. But thankfully, when we work to please the Audience of One, then how successful we are in comparison to others is irrelevant.[32]

Paul writes in Romans 9:22-24 that God patiently endures those who have rebelled against Him "in order to make known the riches of his glory for vessels of mercy, which he has prepared beforehand for glory—even us whom he has called." He demonstrates His patience and the riches of His glory by glorifying us! We've been prepared for glory. We are told that even creation "waits in eager expectation for the children of God to be revealed" (Romans 8:19 NIV). Robert H. Mounce comments that this "personification of nature would not sound strange to those who were at home with rivers that 'clap their hands' and mountains that 'sing together for joy' (Ps 98:8; cf. Isa 55:12)."[33] All this is possible because we've been "filled with the fruit of righteousness that comes through Jesus Christ, to the glory and praise of God" (Philippians 1:11). In other words, bearing the fruit of the Holy Spirit in our lives and continuing to honor God through persecution and suffering purifies and proves our faith, which results in God being praised and glorified. Don't we desire that people glorify God because they see in us the glorious work of God?

We learn from 1 Peter 1:7 that "the tested genuineness of your faith—more precious than gold that perishes though it is tested by fire—may be found to result in praise and glory and honor at the revelation of Jesus Christ." If our faith is real, if we reject the gods of symbolic immortality and trust only in Him who gives true, literal immortality, then we will receive "praise, glory and honor." Thomas R. Schreiner writes, "The eschatological reward will be given to them because of the genuineness of their faith, which is proved by the sufferings they endure. God brings sufferings into the lives of believers to purify their faith and to demonstrate its genuineness." He continues, "The eschatological reward reveals that believers have been transformed by God's grace, inasmuch as they rejoice in God so much they are willing to undergo pain."[34] Let us continue to honor God through suffering, and "praise, glory and honor" await.

Paul tells us in Ephesians 2:6, "God raised us up with Christ and seated us with him in the heavenly realms in Christ Jesus" (NIV). How are we presently seated with Christ even while we live here on earth? It's because we, right now, have an organic union with Jesus—He lives in us, and we live in Him (John 17:21-23). So because of our organic union with Jesus, we are already seated with Jesus in the heavenly realms, and in the coming ages, this will be fully realized. Thus in Revelation 3:21, we are told, "The one who conquers, I will grant him to sit with me on my throne, as I also conquered and sat down with my Father on his throne." Allen P. Ross writes that "sitting...is a sign of honor and majesty (1 Kings 2:19). Kings (Deut. 17:18; Isa. 10:13) or judges (Exod. 18:14; Mal. 3:3) sit, and their attendants and servants stand to wait upon them or do their will."[35] But it says we are *seated* with Him.

So if we conquer ("conquer," or "overcome," is from the Greek word *nike*) the pains and persecutions of this life by patiently and faithfully honoring God through them, we will sit with Him on His throne. Then in the next sentence (verse 22), John gives what I call a divine "listen up!": "He who has an ear, let him hear what the Spirit says to the churches." If you have the Spirit in you, then with this, you will resonate. That God intends to glorify you for eternity is clearly taught. If these things aren't true, then Christianity is a false religion, and we should all be doing something else with our time. But if these things are true, then a glorious eternity awaits you and all those who trust in Jesus. Death is defeated, and you're going to live forever and ever!

Conclusion

In his lecture "The Weight of Glory," C.S. Lewis imparts one of his most quoted passages:

> It is a serious thing to live in a society of possible gods and goddesses, to remember that the dullest most uninteresting person you can talk to may one day be a creature which, if you saw it now, you would be strongly tempted to worship, or else a horror and a corruption such as you now meet, if at all, only in a nightmare. All day long we are, in some degree helping each other to one or the other of these destinations. It is in the light of these overwhelming possibilities, it is with the awe and the circumspection proper to them, that we should conduct all of our dealings with one another, all friendships, all loves, all play, all politics. There are no ordinary people. You have never talked to a mere mortal. Nations, cultures, arts, civilizations—these are mortal, and their life

is to ours as the life of a gnat. But it is immortals whom we joke with, work with, marry, snub, and exploit— immortal horrors or everlasting splendors.[36]

Indeed! If you're in Christ, then God intends to glorify you for eternity. Let us "seek the things that are above" (Colossians 3:1) and "set your hope fully on the grace that will be brought to you at the revelation of Jesus Christ" (1 Peter 1:13). I encourage you to pray, dear Christian, for God to give you a revelation of the seriousness and the wonder of these things.

As Paul says in 1 Corinthians 3:21, for all of eternity, "all things are yours." Enjoy!

APPENDIX

Why Do People Reject Jesus's Offer?

If it's true that glorious immortality is available in Jesus, the question arises: Why do so many people refuse to come to Jesus to enjoy it? The answer is simple: in our lost condition, we don't see it as glorious to have to submit our wills to His will. Most people want to be glorious on their own terms, in their own way. These individuals, and we were all once like that, want to do what they want to do. William Ernest Henley (1849–1903) represents this need to be glorious on our own terms in his poem "Invictus":

> Out of the night that covers me,
> Black as the pit from pole to pole,
> I thank whatever gods may be
> For my unconquerable soul.
> In the fell clutch of circumstance
> I have not winced nor cried aloud.
> Under the bludgeonings of chance
> My head is bloody, but unbowed.
> Beyond this place of wrath and tears
> Looms but the Horror of the shade,
> And yet the menace of the years
> Finds and shall find me unafraid.
> It matters not how strait the gate,
> How charged with punishments the scroll,
> I am the master of my fate,
> I am the captain of my soul.

Although few are as outspoken as Henley, most people, nonetheless, want to pursue life on their own terms—unbowed and in charge. A life of their own making. As Frank Sinatra puts it in his song, "I did it my way."

Luc Ferry writes, "The most powerful and profound lesson of Greek mythology" is that "the ultimate end of human existence is not, as the Christians (further down the line) would come to believe, to secure eternal salvation by all available means, including the most morally submissive and tedious, to attain immortality. On the contrary, a mortal life well lived is worth far more than a wasted immortality!"[1] Notice that Ferry believes that gaining immortality through Christianity is "the most morally submissive and tedious." This is precisely the problem with those who reject the Gospel of Jesus—they don't *want* to submit their will to His. Those who reject the Gospel of Jesus don't want to be "morally submissive" to the Lord, who they would regard as "tedious."

As paltry as it is, we are intoxicated by our *selves* and by our *self*-created salvation. By being individuals in our own not-so-glorious right. Only those individuals who have come to an end of themselves—those who realize that without Jesus, they are coming to a horrible end—who see their immortality projects as failures, are ready to relinquish whatever puny salvation they might think they have eked out on their own. Thus Jesus says in Matthew 10:37, "Whoever loves son or daughter more than me is not worthy of me." Certainly, then, you cannot view—whether consciously or not—your children as your immortality. Then He says, "Whoever finds his life will lose it, and whoever loses his life for my sake will find it" (verse 39). That's clear, right? To have the life that is life indeed, you need to be willing to lose those things that you think might give you life on your own terms. We must abandon our immortality projects, but that's not something people want to do.

Philosopher Thomas Nagel is right that many have a "fear of religion." "I speak from experience, being strongly subject to this fear myself," writes Nagel. "I want atheism to be true and am made uneasy by the fact that some of the most intelligent and well-informed people I know are religious believers. It isn't just that I don't believe in God and, naturally, hope that I'm right in my belief. It's that I hope there is no God! I don't want there to be a God; I don't want the universe to be like that."[2] An atheist friend told me, "I'd love it if there was a god!" But by that, he does not mean that he'd love it if Christianity were true. Far from it! He does not want Christianity to be true. What he would love is that a god of his own making would exist, a god that let him do his own thing. As C.S. Lewis puts it in the *Problem of Pain*, "What would really satisfy us would be a God who said of anything we happened to like doing, 'What does it matter so long as they are contented?'" Rather, Lewis writes, "we want, in fact, not so much a Father in Heaven as a grandfather in heaven—a senile benevolence who, as they say, 'liked to see young people enjoying themselves,' and whose plan for the universe was simply that it might be truly said at the end of each day, 'a good time was had by all.'"[3] That's what my friend wants. People want a god who will not stand in the way of them glorifying themselves. Satan sought to glorify himself, and all the sickness and death in the universe resulted from his rebellion.

In Matthew 9, we read that the Pharisees ask why Jesus spends time with "tax collectors and sinners" (verse 11). Jesus replies, "Those who are well have no need of a physician, but those who are sick. Go and learn what this means: 'I desire mercy, and not sacrifice.' For I came not to call the righteous, but sinners" (verses 12-13). It's important to note that Jesus doesn't think there are any healthy, righteous persons. Everyone, in Jesus's mind, is a sick sinner. What Jesus means is that only those people who realized they are sick sinners are capable of having a relationship with Him. To put it in our terms, only those people who realize that they cannot save themselves—that their immortality projects are bankrupt—are in a position to receive the eternal life that Jesus gives. Knowing this is what has given me a greater compassion for the lost.

There may be a cautionary analogy in the death of Apple cofounder Steve Jobs. In October 2003, Jobs got a CT scan of his kidneys that turned out to be normal, but the scan revealed a "shadow" on his pancreas. A biopsy confirmed that he had a slow-growing type of pancreatic cancer, and because it was discovered early, it could be surgically removed before it spread. In other words, it's possible that Jobs could have been cured. But "to the horror of his friends and wife, Jobs decided not to have the surgery to remove the tumor, which was the only accepted medical approach." Jobs said he didn't "want them to open up my body." Instead, "he kept to a strict vegan diet with large quantities of fresh carrot and fruit juices," used acupuncture, and even consulted a psychic. His wife and his friends urged him to have the surgery. One of his board members, Art Levinson, said that he "pleaded every day" with Jobs to get the surgery. But for nine months, Jobs refused. His biographer, Walter Isaacson, writes about his obstinacy—that part of it was "the dark side of his reality distortion field. 'I think Steve has such a strong desire for the world to be a certain way that he wills it to be that way,' Levinson speculated. 'Sometimes it doesn't work. Reality is unforgiving.'"[4] Unfortunately for Jobs, by the time he took the advised course of medical treatment, the cancer had spread, and it ultimately took his life—he was 56. Yes, reality is unforgiving. Similarly, countless people demand that reality be as they wish it to be, and what they wish for is that they can save themselves, that they won't have to open themselves up to God. As I said, realizing this has increased my compassion for the unbeliever. The lost strive to cobble together a salvation without submitting themselves to Jesus who would give them eternal life.

ACKNOWLEDGMENTS

I thank God for my friend Craig Hazen's immense support over these many years, for his suggestions and encouragement regarding this book, and for his giving me the opportunity to teach in our master of arts in Christian apologetics program at Talbot Seminary. I thank God for the many suggestions of Mitch Stokes regarding my section on mortality mitigation projects (if I got something wrong, the fault is mine). I thank God for Julie Miller, who guided me regarding transhumanism. I thank God for Harvest House's Terry Glaspey's encouragement and many suggestions and for Betty Fletcher's excellent communication. And I thank God for my darling wife, Jean E. Jones, who has encouraged me, given me many helpful suggestions, and has been a supportive partner in our quest to honor Jesus as we await the glorious eternity where we will enjoy each other and all the saints forever. Ultimately, I thank God, who has saved us from our sins and delivered us from the fear of death through the promise of life eternal. Thank You, Jesus!

ABOUT THE AUTHOR

Clay Jones (DMin) is an associate professor of Christian apologetics at Biola University and the chairman of the board for Ratio Christi, an international university apologetics ministry. Previously he hosted the nationally syndicated talk radio program *Contend for Truth* and served on the pastoral staff of two large churches. Clay and his wife, Jean E., live in Southern California.

NOTES

Introduction

1. Luc Ferry, *A Brief History of Thought: A Philosophical Guide to Living*, trans. Theo Cuffe (New York: Harper, 2010), 2–3.
2. Ibid., 12.
3. Plato, *Phaedo*, 67.4–6., trans. David Gallop (Oxford: Oxford University Press, 2009), 14.
4. Ibid., 81e–82e; G.M.A. Grube, trans., *Plato: Five Dialogues:* Euthyphro, Apology, Crito, Meno, Phaedo, 2nd ed., rev. John M. Cooper (Indianapolis: Hackett, 2002), 119.
5. Stephen Cave, *Immortality: The Quest to Live Forever and How It Drives Civilization* (New York: Crown, 2012), 100.
6. "Sam Harris: Death and the Present Moment," YouTube video uploaded by Atheist Foundation of Australia Inc., June 2, 2012, https://www.youtube.com/watch?v=ITTxTCz4Ums (accessed June 29, 2018).
7. Carl Sagan, *Cosmos* (New York: Ballantine, 2013), 1.

Chapter 1

1. Blaise Pascal, *Pensées*, 199, trans. W.F. Trotter (Mineola, NY: Dover, 2018), 60.
2. Albert N. Wells, *Pascal's Recovery of Man's Wholeness* (Richmond, VA: John Knox, 1965), 92, see also 94–95.
3. After Gilgamesh's friend dies, Gilgamesh says, "How can I rest, how can I be at peace? Despair is in my heart. What my brother is now, that shall I be when I am dead. Because I am afraid of death." N.K. Sandars, trans., *The Epic of Gilgamesh* (New York: Penguin, 1972), 42.
4. Irvin D. Yalom, *Staring at the Sun: Overcoming the Terror of Death* (San Francisco: Wiley, 2008), 1–2.
5. Sheldon Solomon, Jeff Greenberg, and Tom Pyszczynski, "Tales from the Crypt: On the Role of Death in Life," *Zygon* 33, no. 1 (March 1998): 12, http://plaza.ufl.edu/phallman/terror%20management%20theory/312997.pdf (accessed September 15, 2017).
6. Zygmunt Bauman, *Mortality, Immortality, and Other Life Strategies* (Stanford: Stanford University Press, 1992), 12.
7. Ibid., 13 (emphasis original).
8. Elisabeth Kübler-Ross, *On Death and Dying: What the Dying Have to Teach Doctors, Nurses, Clergy and Their Own Families* (New York: Scribner, 2014), 109–10.
9. *Merriam-Webster*, s.v. "numb," https://www.merriam-webster.com/dictionary/numb (accessed February 5, 2018).
10. Kübler-Ross, *On Death and Dying*, 15.
11. Robert Lindsey, "An Early Leader in Counsel for the Dying Moves into Spiritualism," *New York Times*, September 17, 2019, https://www.nytimes.com/1979/09/17/archives/an-early-leader-in-counsel-for-the-dying-moves-into-spiritualism.html (accessed February 14, 2019).

12. Don Lattin, "Expert on Death Faces Her Own Death: Kübler-Ross Now Questions Her Life's Work," *SFGate*, May 31, 1997, http://www.sfgate.com/news/article/Expert-On-Death-Faces -Her-Own-Death-Kubler-Ross-2837216.php (accessed July 18, 2017).

13. Holcomb B. Nobleaug, "Elisabeth Kübler-Ross, 78, Dies; Psychiatrist Revolutionized Care of the Terminally Ill," *New York Times*, August 26, 2004, https://www.nytimes.com/2004/08/26 /us/elisabeth-kubler-ross-78-dies-psychiatrist-revolutionized-care-terminally-ill.html (accessed January 1, 2019).

14. William James, *The Varieties of Religious Experience: Being the Gifford Lectures on Natural Religion Delivered at Edinburg in 1901–1902* (New York: Longmans, Green, 1903), 139.

15. Ibid., 140.

16. See Deborah Blum, *Ghost Hunters: William James and the Search for Scientific Proof of Life After Death* (New York: Penguin, 2006).

17. Sheldon Solomon, Jeff Greenberg, and Tom Pyszczynski, *The Worm at the Core: On the Role of Death in Life* (New York: Random House, 2015), 10–11.

18. Ibid., 12.

19. Ibid., 14. It's important to point out that some people don't agree, as Michael Shermer puts it in *Heavens on Earth: The Scientific Search for the Afterlife, Immortality, and Utopia* (New York: Henry Holt, 2018), that "civilization is the product not of ambition but of trepidation." Shermer makes several counterarguments: "First, it is not obvious why contemplating death should lead people to experience terror, get defensive about cultural world view, or feel the need to bolster self-esteem. It could just as well lead people to feel more sympathy for others who, after all, are in the same existential boat." But is this really an either or? Can't one be terrified at the thought of one's own death and also terrified at the thought of those they know dying? Is it not "obvious" to Shermer that people want to live very badly and so their deaths scare them? Shermer writes, "Second, why would such despair lead people to just give up building or creating anything, since it is fruitless in the long run, if not the short?" But that's what symbolic immortality is about— it's a way to feel like you live on after you're dead. Also, as for "the long run," the heat death of the universe, very few people think about that eventuality. Then he writes, "Third, TMT scientists admit that much of their theory depends on *unconscious* states of mind that are notoriously difficult to discern and require subtle priming of the brain to elicit" (15). Okay, but the TMT professors say there have been more than 500 studies, so they have an informed idea about this. Also, Shermer is a Humanist, and Humanists believe people can be good without God. Thus the last thing he wants to believe is that most of the accomplishments of the ages are because people fear death and so are engaged in symbolic immortality projects. The American Humanist Society states, "Humanism is a progressive lifestance that, without theism or other supernatural beliefs, affirms our ability and responsibility to lead meaningful, ethical lives capable of adding to the greater good of humanity." "Are You a Humanist?," American Humanist Association, https:// americanhumanist.org/what-is-humanism/ (accessed July 24, 2018).

20. Elisabeth Kübler-Ross and David Kessler, *Life Lessons: Two Experts on Death and Dying Teach Us About the Mysteries of Life* (New York: Scribner, 2000), 137.

21. Ernest Becker, *The Denial of Death* (New York: Free Press, 1973), xvii.

22. Ibid., 32–33 (emphasis mine).

23. Stephen Cave, *Immortality: The Quest to Live Forever and How It Drives Civilization* (New York: Crown, 2012), ix (emphasis mine).

24. Bauman, *Mortality*, 31 (emphasis mine).

25. Solomon, Greenberg, and Pyszczynski, *Worm at the Core*, x.

26. Ibid.

27. Ibid.

28. Duane A. Garrett, *Proverbs, Ecclesiastes, Song of Songs*, New American Commentary 14, ed. E. Ray Clendenen (Nashville: B&H, 1993), Wordsearch e-book (emphasis original).

Chapter 2

1. Jonathan Clements, *The First Emperor* (Stroud, UK: Sutton, 2006), xi.

2. Ibid., 117.

3. Sima Qian, *The First Emperor: Selections from the Historical Records* (Oxford: Oxford University Press, 2009), 69. The second-century BCE record of the Chinese court historian Sima Qian reads, "Next year the First Emperor again travelled along the sea coast, and went as far as Langye. He passed Mount Heng and returned via Shangdang. Three years later he travelled to Jieshi and interrogated the magicians who had gone to sea, and then returned home via Shang province. Five years later the First Emperor went south and reached Mount Xiang, and next he climbed Kuaiji and went along the sea coast, hoping to come across the marvelous elixirs from the three spirit mountains in the sea. He did not obtain them and, when he reached Shaqiu on his return, he passed away" (98–99). See also Clements, *First Emperor*, 118.

4. Clements states, "Before long, the First Emperor ordered the execution of 460 scholars who had been unable to offer any evidence of their supernatural schemes. The precise method is unclear, but the text of the Historian implies that they were buried alive. Since this punishment was not on the Qin statue books, it may have been the ultimate means of testing their abilities. If any of them had magic powers, then they would surely come back to life when they were let out again." Clements, *First Emperor*, 134.

5. Regarding the possibility of mercury poisoning killing the emperor, Clements says, "Lion Television in early 2006 aired a two-hour documentary entitled 'The First Emperor: The Man Who Made China' on the Discovery Channel that summarizes some of the recent work on the tomb. While it reviewed new evidence about the tomb, this documentary also presented as fact much fanciful speculation, ranging from claims that the First Emperor was an illegitimate child—a claim dating at least to Sima Qian's time—to charges that the First Emperor became a madman who lost his grip on reality in his last years due to mercury poisoning" (ibid., 165).

6. Steven Shapin and Christopher Martyn, "How to Live Forever: Lessons of History," National Center for Biotechnology Information, December 23, 2000, https://www.ncbi.nlm.nih.gov/pmc/articles/PMC1119261/ (accessed January 3, 2018).

7. Gaston Tissandier, *Histoire des Ballons: Et des Aéronautes Célèbres 1783–1800* (Paris: Librairie Artistique, 1887), 80. Thanks to Cheryl Hack for translating this for me!

8. Benjamin Franklin, "Letter to Joseph Priestly, February 8, 1780," Papers of Benjamin Franklin, n.d., http://franklinpapers.org/franklin/framedVolumes.jsp?vol=31&page=455a (accessed May 31, 2018).

9. Tanza Loudenback, "Ex-Facebook President and Billionaire Sean Parker Reveals One of the Biggest Advantages Rich People Have over Everyone Else," *Business Insider*, November 10, 2017, http://www.businessinsider.com/ex-facebook-president-sean-parker-billionaire-advantage-better-healthcare-2017-11 (accessed May 31, 2018).

10. "Asprey's Quest for 180," *The Week*, February 15, 2019, 10.

11. Aubrey de Grey, "A Roadman to End Aging," TED talk given at TEDGlobal, July 2005, https://www.ted.com/talks/aubrey_de_grey_says_we_can_avoid_aging (accessed May 31, 2018).

12. Ray Kurzweil and Terry Grossman, *Fantastic Voyage: Live Long Enough to Live Forever* (Emmaus, PA: Rodale, 2004), 3.

13. Zygmunt Bauman, *Mortality, Immortality, and Other Life Strategies* (Stanford: Stanford University Press, 1992), 152.

14. Ibid., 153.

15. Ibid., 155.

16. Jessica E. Brown, "We Fear Death, but What If Dying Isn't as Bad as We Think?," *Guardian*, July 25, 2017, https://www.theguardian.com/science/blog/2017/jul/25/we-fear-death-but-what-if -dying-isnt-as-bad-as-we-think (accessed May 31, 2018).

17. Rebecca Robbins, "Young-Blood Transfusions Are on the Menu at Society Gala," *Scientific American*, March 2, 2018, https://www.scientificamerican.com/article/young-blood-transfusions -are-on-the-menu-at-society-gala/ (accessed February 2, 2019).

18. Obviously, sometimes the disease was a direct result of some negative habit, like heavy smoking and lung cancer.

19. This is called the just-world hypothesis: "The idea that people need to believe one will get what one deserves so strongly that they will rationalize an inexplicable injustice by naming things the victim might have done to deserve it. Also known as *blaming the victim*, the *just-world fallacy*, and the *just-world effect*." Renée Grinnell, "Just-World Hypothesis," *PsychCentral*, 2018, https://psychcentral .com/encyclopedia/just-world-hypothesis/, (accessed April 23, 2019).

20. Stephen Pastis, *Pearls Before Swine*, Go Comics, July 19, 2009, https://www.gocomics.com /pearlsbeforeswine/2009/07/19 (accessed May 31, 2018).

21. "Global Health Observatory (GHO) Data—Life Expectancy," World Health Organization, 2016, http://www.who.int/gho/mortality_burden_disease/life_tables/situation_trends/en/ (accessed June 1, 2018).

22. S. Jay Olshansky and Bruce A. Carnes, *The Quest for Immortality: Science at the Frontiers of Aging* (New York: W.W. Norton, 2001), 85. By the way, for those who might think this 2001 book is dated, they reported that life expectancy in the United States was "about 78 years," but the 2016 World Health Organization's number mentioned previously is 78.5 years—and don't forget that some of that is still from lessened infant mortality.

23. Nathan Keyfitz, "What Difference Would It Make If Cancer Were Eradicated? An Examination of the Taeuber Paradox," *Demography* 14, no. 4 (November 1977): 417. Some might see this was published in 1977 and think the study is dated, but that would be mistaken. Keyfitz's article is about how the demographics of curing cancer would affect mortality tables, and he concludes they will not be affected much without also curing the other diseases that kill us.

24. Stephen Cave, *Immortality: The Quest to Live Forever and How It Drives Civilization* (New York: Crown, 2012), 67.

25. Ibid., 68.

26. Susan Dominus, "The Lives They Lived: Ladies of the Gym Unite!," *New York Times*, December 28, 2003, https://www.nytimes.com/2003/12/28/magazine/the-lives-they-lived-ladies-of-the -gym-unite.html (accessed September 17, 2018).

27. John Kallas, "Euell Gibbons: The Father of Modern Wild Foods," *Wild Food Adventurer Newsletter* 3, no. 4 (November 25, 1998), https://wildfoodadventures.com/about/john-kallas/wild-food -adventurer/wfa-by-volumeyear/euell-gibbons/ (accessed March 9, 2019).

28. Wolfgang Saxon, "Adelle Davis, Nutritionist, Best-Selling Author, Dies," *New York Times*, June 1, 1974, https://www.nytimes.com/1974/06/01/archives/adelle-davis-nutritionist-bestselling-aut hor-dies-an-outspoken.html (accessed March 9, 2019).

29. Jane Gross, "James F. Fixx Dies Jogging; Author on Running Was 52," *New York Times*, July 22, 1984, https://www.nytimes.com/1984/07/22/obituaries/james-f-fixx-dies-jogging-author-on -running-was-52.html (accessed March 9, 2019). It's true that Fixx was a two-pack-a-day smoker until he was 35.

30. Wolfgang Saxon, "Daniel Rudman, 67; Studied Hormones and Aging," *New York Times*, April 20, 1994, https://www.nytimes.com/1994/04/20/obituaries/daniel-rudman-67-studied-hormones -and-aging.html (accessed March 9, 2019).

31. "Remembering Paavo Airola," *Vegetarian Times*, August 1983, https://books.google.com/books?id=oAcAAAAAMBAJ&pg=PA5&lpg=PA5&dq=Paavo+Airola++death&source=bl&ots=mFrBo6cebQ&sig=ACfU3U0IeIpniWwAMiSC4aFVu08W2UkhvA&hl=en&sa=X&ved=2ahUKEwj27cnE2_XgAhVROKwKHQIfCWoQ6AEwCnoECAMQAQ#v=onepage&q=Paavo%20Airola%20%20death&f=false (accessed March 9, 2019).

32. Martin Weil, "Diet Author Pritikin Dies in Apparent Suicide," *Washington Post*, February 23, 1985, https://www.washingtonpost.com/archive/local/1985/02/23/diet-author-pritikin-dies-in-apparent-suicide/80213960-637f-41c8-8c03-694e9d4020c9/?utm_term=.84b0ba7ed2b7 (accessed December 13, 2018).

33. Dennis Hevesiaug, "Michel Montignac, Creator of Trend-Setting Diet, Dies at 66," *New York Times*, August 26, 2010, https://www.nytimes.com/2010/08/27/business/27montignac.html (accessed December 13, 2018).

34. Simone Haber, "Robert E. Kowalski, 1942–2007," *New Hope Network*, April 24, 2008, https://www.newhope.com/news/robert-e-kowalski-1942-2007 (accessed March 9, 2019).

35. Chris Crowley, "Harry Lodge: A Personal Memoir," *Younger Next Year*, March 16, 2017, https://www.youngernextyear.com/harry-lodge-personal-memoir/ (accessed September 17, 2018).

36. "J. I. Rodale Dead; Organic Farmer," *New York Times*, June 8, 1971, https://www.nytimes.com/1971/06/08/archives/j-i-rodale-dead-organic-farmer-espoused-the-avoidance-of-chemical.html (accessed August 9, 2018).

37. John H. Knowles, *Doing Better and Feeling Worse: Health in the United States* (New York: W.W. Norton, 1977), 59.

38. Lawrence K. Altman, "John H. Knowles, Leading Medical Figure, Dies at 52," *New York Times*, March 7, 1979, https://www.nytimes.com/1979/03/07/archives/john-h-knowles-leading-medical-figure-dies-at-52-individual-can.html (accessed March 9, 2019).

39. Douglas Martin, "Futurist Known as FM-2030 Is Dead at 69," *New York Times*, July 11, 2000, https://www.nytimes.com/2000/07/11/us/futurist-known-as-fm-2030-is-dead-at-69.html (accessed June 6, 2018).

40. Ibid.

41. "Larry King Interviews Futurist FM-2030," YouTube video uploaded by FM2030Videos, January 9, 2011, https://www.youtube.com/watch?v=XkMVzEft7Og (accessed June 6, 2018).

42. I write "We *may* live a *little* longer" because there are always those who are like Winston Churchill (1874–1965). Churchill didn't exercise, was overweight, smoked cigars, and drank heavily but was active in public life until just before he died of a stroke at age 90. Again, I'm not suggesting we live like Churchill. Jean E. and I try to eat healthy foods and exercise daily, but I'm pointing out that diet and exercise don't *guarantee* you a healthy or long life, and apparently living what most consider an unhealthy life doesn't necessarily mean a short life. That said, the odds are that living a healthier lifestyle will result in increased longevity.

43. Mary Shelley and Leslie S. Klinger, *The New Annotated Frankenstein* (New York: Liveright, 2017), xliv.

44. "George Foster: Executed at Newgate, 18th of January, 1803, for the Murder of His Wife and Child, by Drowning Them in the Paddington Canal; with a Curious Account of Galvanic Experiments on His Body," *Newgate Calendar*, n.d., http://www.exclassics.com/newgate/ng464.htm (accessed August 29, 2018).

45. Shelley and Klinger, *New Annotated Frankenstein*, 298.

46. Michael Le Page, "Unnatural Selection: How Humans Are Driving Evolution," *New Scientist*, April 27, 2011, https://www.newscientist.com/article/mg21028101-800-unnatural-selection-how-humans-are-driving-evolution/ (accessed August 16, 2018).

47. Ariana Eunjung Cha, "Tech Titans' Latest Project: Defy Death," *Washington Post*, April 4, 2015, https://www.washingtonpost.com/sf/national/2015/04/04/tech-titans-latest-project-defy-death/?noredirect=on&utm_term=.b3fa06073a12 (accessed August 18, 2018).

48. Mike Wilson, *The Difference Between God and Larry Ellison: Inside the Oracle Corporation* (New York: HarperBusiness, 2002), 266. It had been all too clear for some time that Miner would not be returning to Oracle. He would have been happy to have someone pack up his San Francisco office and send his things home, but Ellison would not hear of it. Miner might die, but Ellison was not about to let him resign. "Larry is so funny. He kept my dad on the payroll," Nicola Miner said. "He was like, 'You're coming back to work, you're not quitting.'" Miner's reaction, according to his daughter, was, "It's ridiculous, but I'm so sick I don't care." "Dad and Larry were both into living forever, the fountain of youth kind of stuff," Nicola said. "I think my dad's illness really freaked Larry out…My dad always said that Larry had a hard time facing his own mortality" (265).

49. Ariana Eunjung Cha, "Tech Titans' Latest Project," *Washington Post*, April 4, 2015.

50. Peter Thiel, "The Education of a Libertarian," *Cato Unbound*, April 13, 2019, https://www.cato-unbound.org/2009/04/13/peter-thiel/education-libertarian (accessed February 22, 2019).

51. Ray Kurzweil, *The Singularity Is Near: When Humans Transcend Biology* (New York: Penguin, 2005), 256.

52. Ibid., 256–57.

53. Regarding *Avatar* being the worldwide box office leader, see "All Time Box Office," *Box Office Mojo*, n.d., https://www.boxofficemojo.com/alltime/world/ (accessed January 10, 2019). This is also seen in films such as *Star Trek: The Motion Picture* (1979), *Tron* (1982), *The Lawnmower Man* (1992), *Freejack* (1992), *The 6th Day* (2000), *Captain America: The Winter Soldier* (2014), *Transcendence* (2014), and a host of others.

54. "Days of Future Future," *The Simpsons* episode 548, originally aired April 13, 2014.

55. Kurzweil, *Singularity Is Near*, 199.

56. David Smith, "2050—and Immortality Is Within Our Grasp: Britain's Leading Thinker on the Future Offers an Extraordinary Vision of Life in the Next 45 Years," *Guardian*, May 21, 2005, https://www.theguardian.com/science/2005/may/22/theobserver.technology (accessed August 16, 2018).

57. David Chalmers, "The Singularity: A Philosophical Analysis," in *Science Fiction and Philosophy: From Time Travel to Superintelligence*, 2nd ed., ed. Susan Schneider (West Sussex, UK: Wiley, 2016), 205.

58. Ibid.

59. As philosopher Susan Schneider puts it, "Humans cannot upload *themselves* to the digital universe; they can upload only copies of themselves—copies that may themselves be conscious beings." Schneider, "The Philosophy of 'Her,'" *New York Times*, March 2, 2014, https://opinionator.blogs.nytimes.com/2014/03/02/the-philosophy-of-her/#more-152209 (accessed June 2, 2018).

60. Indeed, this is no more than science fiction, and even if we could upload your consciousness into a computer, it would no longer be your consciousness. Neuroscientist Michael Hendricks writes, "Any suggestion" that through uploading "*you* can come back to life is simply snake oil. Transhumanists have responses to these issues. In my experience, they consist of alternating demands that we trust our intuition about nonexistent technology (uploading *could* work) but deny our intuition about consciousness (it *would not* be me)." Hendricks, "The False Science of Cryonics: What the Nervous System of the Roundworm Tells Us About Freezing Brains and Reanimating Human Minds," *MIT Technology Review*, September 15, 2015, https://www.technologyreview.com/s/541311/the-false-science-of-cryonics/ (accessed June 7, 2018; emphasis original).

61. Mark Walker, "Personal Identity and Uploading," *Journal of Evolution and Technology* 22, no. 1 (November 2011): 37–51, https://jetpress.org/v22/walker.htm (accessed April 6, 2018).

62. Chalmers says there's also "reconstructive uploading," which would involve "reconstruction of the original system from records. Here, the records might include brain scans and other medical data; any available genetic material; audio and video records of the original person; their writings; and the testimony of others about them. These records may seem limited, but it is not out of

the question that a superintelligence could go a long way with them. Given constraints on the structure of a human system, even limited information might make a good amount of reverse engineering possible. And detailed information, as might be available in extensive video recordings and in detailed brain images, might in principle make it possible for a superintelligence to reconstruct something close to a functional isomorph of the original system." Chalmers, "Singularity," 212.

63. Ibid., 208.

64. Ibid., 211 (emphasis mine).

65. Ibid., 200 (emphasis mine).

66. Ibid.

67. Ibid. (emphasis mine).

68. Denise Chow, Shivani Khattar, and Brock Stoneham, "'Westworld' Science Adviser Shares His Vision of Robots and the Future of AI," *Mach*, June 16, 2018, https://www.nbcnews.com/mach /science/westworld-science-adviser-shares-his-vision-robots-future-ai-ncna883321?cid=sm_npd_ nn_tw_ma (accessed January 25, 2019).

69. Hubert L. Dreyfus, *What Computers Still Can't Do: A Critique of Artificial Reason* (Cambridge, MA: MIT Press, 1992), xxvi.

70. John R. Searle, *Expression and Meaning: Studies in the Theory of Speech Acts* (New York: Cambridge University Press, 1979), 95. About these kinds of problems, Searle concludes, "There are…whole classes of metaphors, that function without any underlying principles of similarity. It just seems to be a fact about our mental capacities that we are able to interpret certain sorts of metaphor without the application of any underlying 'rules' or 'principles' other than the sheer ability to make certain associations." John R. Searle, *Intentionality: An Essay in the Philosophy of Mind* (Cambridge: Cambridge University, 1983), 149.

71. Erik J. Larson, "The Limits of Modern AI: A Story," *The Quad*, https://thebestschools.org /magazine/limits-of-modern-ai/ (accessed December 13, 2018).

72. Chow, Khattar, and Stoneham, "'Westworld' Science Adviser."

73. John R. Searle, "What Your Computer Can't Know," *New York Review of Books*, October 9, 2014, http://static.trogu.com/documents/articles/palgrave/references/searle%20What%20Your %20Computer%20Can%E2%80%99t%20Know%20by%20John%20R.%20Searle%20 %7C%20The%20New%20York%20Review%20of%20Books.pdf (accessed August 26, 2018).

74. Hendricks, "False Science of Cryonics" (emphasis mine). Hendricks continues, "Synapses are the physical contacts between neurons where a special form of chemoelectric signaling—neurotransmission—occurs, and they come in many varieties. They are complex molecular machines made of thousands of proteins and specialized lipid structures. It is the precise molecular composition of synapses and the membranes they are embedded in that confers their properties. The presence or absence of a synapse, which is all that current connectomics methods tell us, suggests that a possible functional relationship between two neurons exists, but little or nothing about the nature of this relationship—precisely what you need to know to simulate it.

"Additionally, neurons and other cells in the brain are in constant communication through signaling pathways that do not act through synapses. Many of the signals that regulate fundamental behaviors such as eating, sleeping, mood, mating, and social bonding are mediated by chemical cues acting through networks that are invisible to us anatomically. We know that the same set of synaptic connections can function very differently depending on what mix of these signals is present at a given time. These issues highlight an important distinction: the colossally hard problem of simulating *any* brain as opposed to the stupendously more difficult task of replicating a *particular* brain, which is required for the promised personal immortality of uploading.

"The features of your neurons (and other cells) and synapses that make you 'you' are not generic. The vast array of subtle chemical modifications, states of gene regulation, and subcellular distributions of molecular complexes are all part of the dynamic flux of a living brain. These things are not details that average out in a large nervous system; rather, they are the very things that engrams (the physical constituents of memories) are made of.

"While it might be theoretically possible to preserve these features in dead tissue, that certainly is not happening now. The technology to do so, let alone the ability to read this information back out of such a specimen, does not yet exist even in principle. It is this purposeful conflation of what is *theoretically conceivable* with what is *ever practically possible* that exploits people's vulnerability."

75. Ian Sample, "Interview: Sebastian Seung: You Are Your Connectome," *Guardian*, June 9, 2012, https://www.theguardian.com/technology/2012/jun/10/connectome-neuroscience-brain -sebastian-seung (accessed January 10, 2019).

76. Kurzweil, *Singularity Is Near*, 7.

77. Ibid., 27–28.

78. Ibid., 377 (emphasis mine). Later Kurzweil writes, "I do believe that we humans will come to accept that nonbiological entities are conscious, because ultimately the nonbiological entities [computers and such] will have all the subtle cues that humans currently possess and that we associate with emotional and other subjective experiences. Still, while we will be able to verify the subtle cues, we will have no direct access to the implied consciousness" (385).

79. Ibid., 8.

80. Ray Kurzweil, "Superintelligence and Singularity," in *Science Fiction and Philosophy*, Second ed. Schneider, 148.

81. Irving J. Good, "Speculations Concerning the First Ultraintelligent Machine," *Advances in Computers* 6 (1996): 31–88, http://web.archive.org/web/20010527181244/http://www.aeiveos .com/~bradbury/Authors/Computing/Good-IJ/SCtFUM.html (accessed August 24, 2018). Here's the longer quote: "Let an ultraintelligent machine be defined as a machine that can far surpass all the intellectual activities of any man however clever. Since the design of machines is one of these intellectual activities, an ultra-intelligent machine could design even better machines; there would then unquestionably be an 'intelligence explosion,' and the intelligence of man would be left far behind…Thus the first ultraintelligent machine is the last invention that man need ever make, provided that the machine is docile enough to tell us how to keep it under control."

82. Vernor Vinge, "What Is the Singularity?," 1993, Mindstalk, http://mindstalk.net/vinge /vinge-sing.html (accessed August 23, 2018). He continues, "If the Singularity can not be prevented or confined, just how bad could the Post-Human era be? Well…pretty bad. The physical extinction of the human race is one possibility."

83. Ellie Zolfagharifard and Victoria Woollaston, "Could Robots Turn People into PETS? Elon Musk Claims Artificial Intelligence Will Treat Humans like 'Labradors,'" *Daily Mail*, March 25, 2015, http://www.dailymail.co.uk/sciencetech/article-3011302/Could-robots-turn-people -PETS-Elon-Musk-claims-artificial-intelligence-treat-humans-like-Labradors.html (accessed June 4, 2018).

84. Rory Cellan-Jones, "Stephen Hawking Warns Artificial Intelligence Could End Mankind," *BBC*, December 2, 2014, http://www.bbc.com/news/technology-30290540 (accessed June 4, 2018).

85. Neil Strauss, "Elon Musk: The Architect of Tomorrow," *Rolling Stone*, November 15, 2017, https://www.rollingstone.com/culture/features/elon-musk-inventors-plans-for-outer-space-cars -finding-love-w511747 (accessed June 5, 2018).

86. Nick Bostrom, *Superintelligence: Paths, Dangers, Strategies* (Oxford: Oxford University Press, 2014), 117–18.

87. Ibid., 118. Here's the whole quote: "The final phase begins when the AI has gained sufficient strength to obviate the need for secrecy. The AI can now directly implement its objectives on a full scale. The overt implementation phase might start with a 'strike' in which the AI eliminates the

human species and any automatic systems humans have created that could offer intelligent oppo-
sition to the execution of the AI's plans. This could be achieved through the activation of some
advanced weapons system that the AI has perfected using its technology research superpower and
covertly deployed in the covert preparation phase. If the weapon uses self-replicating biotechnology or nanotechnology, the initial stockpile needed for global coverage could be microscopic:
a single replicating entity would be enough to start the process. In order to ensure a sudden and
uniform effect, the initial stock of the replicator might have been deployed or allowed to diffuse
worldwide at an extremely low, undetectable concentration. At a pre-set time, nanofactories
producing nerve gas or target-seeking mosquito-like robots might then burgeon forth simultaneously from every square meter of the globe (although more effective ways of killing could
probably be devised by a machine with the technology research superpower)."

88. Ibid., 212.

89. Here's a dialog between Elon Musk and Neil deGrasse Tyson:

> Musk: I mean, we won't be like a pet Labrador if we're lucky.
>
> Tyson: A pet Lab.
>
> Musk: I have a pet Labrador by the way.
>
> Tyson: We'll be their pets.
>
> Musk: It's like the friendliest creature.
>
> Tyson: No, they'll domesticate us.
>
> Musk: Yes! Exactly.
>
> Tyson: So we'll be Lab pets to them.
>
> Musk: Yes. Or something strange is going to happen.
>
> Tyson: They'll keep the docile humans and get rid of the violent ones.
>
> Musk: Yeah.
>
> Tyson: And then breed the docile humans.
>
> Zolfagharifard and Woollaston, "People into PETS?"

90. Elon Musk says, "I've had so many simulation conversations it's crazy. The strongest argument
for us…probably being in a simulation, I think, is the following, that 40 years ago we had Pong.
Two rectangles and a dot. That was what games were. Now 40 years later we have photoreal-
istic, 3D simulations with millions of people playing simultaneously and it's getting better every
year. And soon we'll have virtual reality, we'll have augmented reality. If you assume any rate
of improvement at all, then the games will become indistinguishable from reality…The odds
that we are in base reality is one in billions." Jacob Furedi, "Bank of America Analysists Think
There's a 50% Chance We're Living in a Matrix," *Independent*, September 14, 2016, https://
www.independent.co.uk/life-style/gadgets-and-tech/news/bank-of-america-the-matrix-50
-per-cent-virtual-reality-elon-musk-nick-bostrom-a7287471.html (accessed June 4, 2018). I
slightly cleaned Musk's words.

91. "Neil deGrasse Tyson: It's Hard to Argue That We Aren't Living in a Simulated World," YouTube
video uploaded by Larry King, July 3, 2017, https://www.youtube.com/watch?v=SYAG9dAfy8U
(accessed June 4, 2018). Graham Templeton shows the folly of the belief that we are living in
a simulation: "It's not so much that this [simulation] thinking is 'flawed' as it is 'so useless it
invalidates all of human thought and achievement from pre-history to today.' Think about it:
If we are to be convinced by this sort of non-argument, then why not assume that every person
around you is a time traveler? After all, if we imagine that time travel will one-day exist on an
infinite time-line, then we must also assume that time travel has been used to visit every single
time and place in our planet's history—including this one. People will, *in principle*, want to
have fun vacations in the past, putting on period-appropriate clothing and walking around
using slang wrong; how could we be so arrogant as to assume that the people we meet are

part of the real, finite population of our time, and not from the far more numerous ranks of temporal travelers from *any* time?" Templeton, "Neil deGrasse Tyson Says It's 'Very Likely' the Universe Is a Simulation," *Extremetech*, April 22, 2016, https://www.extremetech.com /extreme/227126-neil-degrasse-tyson-says-its-very-likely-the-universe-is-a-simulation (accessed June 4, 2018).

92. Myles Udland, "Bank of America: There's a 20%–50% Chance We're Inside the Matrix and Reality Is Just a Simulation," *Business Insider*, September 8, 2016, https://www.businessinsider .com/bank-of-america-wonders-about-the-matrix-2016-9 (accessed August 24, 2018).

93. David Klinghoffer writes why computer consciousness isn't coming: "Philosopher John Searle offered another reason in his Chinese Room argument. Imagine a room with a little man named Pudge. He receives messages in Chinese slipped through a slot in the door. Pudge looks at the message and goes to a large bank of file cabinets in the room where he looks for an identical or similar message. Each folder in the file cabinet has two sheets of paper. On one is written the message that might match the message slipped through the door slot. The second sheet of paper in the file is the corresponding response to that message. Once Pudge matches the right message, he copies the corresponding response. After refiling the folder and closing the file drawer, Pudge walks back to the slot in the door through which he delivers the response and his job is done." Klinghoffer, "Hype and Fearmongering About Artificial Intelligence Passes Its Sell-By Date," *Evolution News and Science Today*, October 3, 2017, https://evolutionnews.org/2017/10/hype -and-fearmongering-about-artificial-intelligence-passes-its-sell-by-date/ (accessed June 11, 2018).

94. Larson, "Limits of Modern AI" (emphasis mine). This is a long but insightful examination of the limits of AI.

95. Hubert L. Dreyfus, "A History of First Step Fallacies," *Minds and Machines* 22, no. 2 (May 2012): 87.

96. Chalmers, "Singularity," 202. Earlier Chalmers writes, "There is nothing even approaching an orthodox theory of why there is consciousness in the first place" (201).

97. There are many books that debunk the idea of a purely naturalistic account of the universe, and it is out of the scope of this book to engage that topic. I recommend William Lane Craig's *Reasonable Faith: Christian Truth and Apologetics*, 3rd ed. (Wheaton, IL: Crossway, 2008) as an excellent response to naturalism.

98. Thanks to Steven C. Meyer for confirming the accuracy of these five sentences.

99. Eric J. Larson, "Reading David Chalmers on the Coming 'Singularity,'" *Evolution News and Science Today*, April 1, 2015, https://evolutionnews.org/2015/04/reading_david_c/ (accessed June 18, 2018). For another excellent article on how the human brain isn't a computer, see Robert Epstein, "The Empty Brain: Your Brain Does Not Process Information, Retrieve Knowledge or Store Memories. In Short: Your Brain Is Not a Computer," *Aeon*, May 18, 2016, https://aeon .co/essays/your-brain-does-not-process-information-and-it-is-not-a-computer (accessed July 11, 2018). In this article, Epstein sums up one of the major problems: "The information processing (IP) metaphor of human intelligence now dominates human thinking, both on the street and in the sciences. There is virtually no form of discourse about intelligent human behaviour that proceeds without employing this metaphor, just as no form of discourse about intelligent human behaviour could proceed in certain eras and cultures without reference to a spirit or deity. The validity of the IP metaphor in today's world is generally assumed without question.

   "But the IP metaphor is, after all, just another metaphor—a story we tell to make sense of something we don't actually understand. And like all the metaphors that preceded it, it will certainly be cast aside at some point—either replaced by another metaphor or, in the end, replaced by actual knowledge.

   "Just over a year ago, on a visit to one of the world's most prestigious research institutes, I challenged researchers there to account for intelligent human behaviour without reference to any aspect of the IP metaphor. *They couldn't do it*, and when I politely raised the issue in subsequent email communications, they still had nothing to offer months later. They saw the problem. They didn't dismiss the challenge as trivial. But they couldn't offer an alternative. In other words, the IP metaphor is 'sticky.' It encumbers our thinking with language and ideas that are so powerful we have trouble thinking around them.

"The faulty logic of the IP metaphor is easy enough to state. It is based on a faulty syllogism—one with two reasonable premises and a faulty conclusion. *Reasonable premise #1:* all computers are capable of behaving intelligently. *Reasonable premise #2:* all computers are information processors. *Faulty conclusion:* all entities that are capable of behaving intelligently are information processors.

"Setting aside the formal language, the idea that humans must be information processors just because *computers* are information processors is just plain silly, and when, some day, the IP metaphor is finally abandoned, it will almost certainly be seen that way by historians, just as we now view the hydraulic and mechanical metaphors to be silly."

100. C.S. Lewis, *Miracles: A Preliminary Study* (New York: HarperOne, 1996), 17.

101. It's true they will say it's natural selection, but natural selection is working entirely on lucky mutations.

102. For more, see my article with Joseph E. Gorra, "The Folly of Answering Distracting Atheistic Arguments," *Christian Research Journal* 36, no. 4 (2013), http://www.equip.org/article/folly-answering-distracting-atheistic-arguments/ (accessed October 20, 2018).

103. Searle, "What Your Computer Can't Know."

104. Kristen Philipkoski, "Ray Kurzweil's Plan: Never Die," *Wired*, November 18, 2002, https://www.wired.com/2002/11/ray-kurzweils-plan-never-die/ (accessed August 16, 2018).

105. There's also *Forever Young* (1992), *2001: A Space Odyssey* (1968), *The Demolition Man* (1993), and so on.

106. David McCormack, "'We Did It Out of Love': Baseball Legend Ted Williams' Daughter' Finally Speaks Out About Why She and Her Brother Spent $100,000 to Have Their Father's Body Cryogenically Frozen," *Daily Mail*, May 19, 2014, http://www.dailymail.co.uk/news/article-2632809/We-did-love-Baseball-legend-Ted-Williams-daughter-finally-speaks-brother-spent-100-000-fathers-body-cryogenically-frozen.html#ixzz5HCs7Ap5I (accessed June 1, 2018).

107. Jonathan Petre, "Simon Cowell: I'm Going to Freeze My Body When I Die So I Can Be Brought Back to Life," *Daily Mail*, February 21, 2009, http://www.dailymail.co.uk/tvshowbiz/article-1151872/Simon-Cowell-Im-going-freeze-body-I-die-I-brought-life.html#ixzz5Cgz91aDA (accessed April 14, 2018); "Seth MacFarlane on Cryonics: Larry King Now," YouTube video uploaded by Ora TV, July 17, 2012, https://www.youtube.com/watch?v=DdQOoove5Qo (accessed April 1, 2018).

108. See the Larry King Interview with Conan O'Brien, "Larry King Demands Conan Freeze His Corpse," YouTube video uploaded by Team Coco, February 13, 2014, https://www.youtube.com/watch?v=PF7NpKG_S8g (accessed April 1, 2018).

109. See Ben Makuch in "Frozen Faith: Cryonics and the Quest to Cheat Death," YouTube video uploaded by Motherboard, May 5, 2016, https://www.youtube.com/watch?v=m5KuNAeOtJ0 (accessed December 15, 2018).

110. Antonio Regalado, "A Startup Is Pitching a Mind-Uploading Service That Is '100 Percent Fatal,' Nectome Will Preserve Your Brain, but You Have to Be Euthanized First," *MIT Technology Review*, March 13, 2018, https://www.technologyreview.com/s/610456/a-startup-is-pitching-a-mind-uploading-service-that-is-100-percent-fatal/ (accessed June 7, 2018).

111. Chalmers, "Singularity," 216.

112. "Frozen Faith."

113. See "FAQs," Alcor Life Extension Foundation, n.d., https://alcor.org/FAQs/faq02.html#now

(accessed June 6, 2018; emphasis mine). "It should be obvious" sounds like they are annoyed at having to answer this question even on their own site!

114. Howard Witt, "The Cold, Hard Facts on Cryonics: Progress Aside, Don't Hold Your Breath for Immortality," *Chicago Tribune*, August 22, 2005, http://articles.chicagotribune.com/2005-08-22/news/0508220106_1_alcor-life-extension-foundation-american-cryonics-society-preservation-process (accessed June 7, 2018).

115. Ibid. Emphasis mine. Then there's a new company called Nectome: "Nectome is a preserve-your-brain-and-upload-it company. Its chemical solution can keep a body intact for hundreds of years, maybe thousands, as a statue of frozen glass. The idea is that someday in the future scientists will scan your bricked brain and turn it into a computer simulation. That way, someone a lot like you, though not exactly you, will smell the flowers again in a data server somewhere. This story has a grisly twist, though. For Nectome's procedure to work, it's essential that the brain be fresh. The company says its plan is to connect people with terminal illnesses to a heart-lung machine in order to pump its mix of scientific embalming chemicals into the big carotid arteries in their necks while they are still alive (though under general anesthesia)." This may avoid shattering your brain, but "there's no expectation here that the preserved tissue can be actually brought back to life, as is the hope with Alcor-style cryonics. Instead, the idea is to retrieve information that's present in the brain's anatomical layout and molecular details." In other words, your thinking processes might be replicated, but you won't actually be you. Thus you won't be immortal in this method, and they have to kill you in the process! Regalado, "Startup Is Pitching."

116. See "FAQs," Alcor Life Extension Foundation.

117. John Warwick Montgomery, *Christ Our Advocate: Studies in Polemical Theology, Jurisprudence, and Canon Law* (Eugene, OR: Wipf & Stock, 2016), 164.

118. "Frozen Faith."

119. N.R. Kleinfield, "Just What Killed the Diet Doctor, and What Keeps the Issue Alive?," *New York Times*, February 11, 2004, https://www.nytimes.com/2004/02/11/nyregion/just-what-killed-the-diet-doctor-and-what-keeps-the-issue-alive.html (accessed December 16, 2018).

120. Henry Blodget, "Guess How Much Google Futurist Ray Kurzweil Spends on Food That Will Make Him Live Forever?!," *Business Insider*, April 13, 2015, https://www.businessinsider.com/google-futurist-ray-kurzweil-live-forever-2015-4m (accessed September 26, 2018).

121. Montaigne quoted in Steven Shapin, *Never Pure: Historical Studies of Science as If It Was Produced by People with Bodies, Situated in Time and Space, Culture, and Society, and Struggling for Credibility and Authority* (Baltimore: Johns Hopkins University Press, 2010), 281.

122. Montaigne says he knows of, and pities, "several gentlemen who, by the stupidity of their doctors, have made prisoners of themselves, though still young and sound in health…We should conform to the best rules, but not enslave ourselves to them." As another proverb has it, to live physically (i.e., according to the dictates of doctors) is to live miserably: "We must meekly suffer the laws of our condition. We are born to grow old, to grow weak, to be sick, in spite of all medicine…We must learn to endure what we cannot avoid." Shapin and Martyn, "How to Live Forever."

123. "Direct TV: 'Get Rid of Cable,' the Full Compilation," YouTube video uploaded by Aaron Handy III, June 4, 2014, https://www.youtube.com/watch?reload=9&v=NZ80SVOHKoo (accessed February 19, 2019).

Chapter 3

1. Sam Keen, foreword to Ernest Becker, *The Denial of Death* (New York: Free Press, 1973), xiii.

2. Robert B. Arrowood et al., "Guest Editors' Foreword: On the Importance of Integrating Terror Management and Psychology of Religion," *Religion, Brain & Behavior* 8 (2018), https://www.tandfonline-com.ezproxy.biola.edu/doi/full/10.1080/2153599X.2018.1411636 (accessed July 27, 2018).

3. William Dicke, "Edwin Shneidman, Authority on Suicide, Dies at 91," *New York Times*, May 21, 2009, https://www.nytimes.com/2009/05/21/us/21shneidman.html (accessed July 3, 2018).

4. Edwin Shneidman, *A Commonsense Book of Death: Reflections at Ninety of a Lifelong Thanatologist* (New York: Rowman & Littlefield, 2008), 4.

   Similarly, "Those seeking to supply their lives with meaning usually envision a role or function in something larger than themselves. They therefore seek fulfillment in service to society, the state, the revolution, the progress of history, the advance of science, or religion and the glory of God." Thomas Nagel, *Mortal Questions* (Cambridge: Cambridge University Press, 1979), 16, Kindle. Also, Zygmunt Bauman writes, "'Making history' means becoming immortal; be made immortal by being recorded; be, from now on, kept in the records, intended to be preserved forever, indestructible; be meant to be always ready to be dusted off, recovered, returned to the agenda of current living; be confirmed as 'of importance' for that living because of changing or preserving its form, its character." Bauman, *Mortality, Immortality, and Other Life Strategies* (Stanford: Stanford University Press, 1992), 170.

5. Shneidman, *Commonsense Book of Death*, 153.

6. Arthur Koestler, "Cosmic Consciousness," *Psychology Today*, April 1977, 52, as quoted in Michael C. Kearl, *Endings: A Sociology of Death and Dying* (New York: Oxford University Press, 1989), 214. Also, Hannah Arendt states, "In the beginning of Western history the distinction between the mortality of men and the immortality of nature, between man-made things and things which come into being by themselves, was the tacit assumption of historiography. All things that owe their existence to men, such as works, deeds, and words, are perishable, infected, as it were, by the mortality of their authors. However, if mortals succeeded in endowing their works, deeds, and words with some permanence and in arresting their perishability, then these things would, to a degree at least, enter and be at home in the world of everlastingness, and the mortals themselves would find their place in the cosmos, where everything is immortal except men." Arendt, *Between Past and Future: Eight Exercises in Political Thought* (New York: Penguin, 1977), 43.

7. Viktor E. Frankl, *Man's Search for Meaning* (Boston: Beacon, 2014), 113.

8. "'Death Doesn't Scare Me': Neil deGrasse Tyson," *Larry King Now*, June 15, 2015, http://www.ora.tv/larrykingnow/2015/6/15/death-neil-degrasse-tyson-larry-king (accessed January 21, 2018).

9. Michael Shermer, *Heavens on Earth: The Scientific Search for the Afterlife, Immortality, and Utopia* (New York: Henry Holt, 2018), 243–44 (emphasis mine). Shermer enthuses, "In the far future, civilizations may become sufficiently advanced to colonize entire galaxies, genetically engineer new life forms, terraform planets, and even trigger the birth of stars and new planetary solar systems through massive engineering projects. Civilizations this advanced would have so much knowledge and power as to be essentially omniscient and omnipotent. What would you call such a sentience? If you didn't know the science and the technology behind it you would call it God, which is why I have postulated that *any sufficiently advanced extraterrestrial intelligence or far future human is indistinguishable from God*" (235–36). He continues, "Thus do we achieve immortality as a species by going to the stars. *Per audacia ad astra*" (237), which Shermer translates to "the stars through audacity."

10. Ibid., 244.

11. Stephen Fry, "What Should We Think About Death?," Richard Dawkins Foundation for Reason and Science, July 25, 2014, https://www.richarddawkins.net/2014/07/what-should-we-think-about-death/ (accessed June 28, 2018).

12. Corliss Lamont, *The Illusion of Immortality*, 3rd ed. (New York: Philosophical Library, 1958), 278 (emphasis mine).

13. Shneidman, *Commonsense Book of Death*, 34.

14. Plato, *Symposium*, trans. Benjamin Jowett (Mineola, NY: Dover, 2007), 170.

15. Miguel de Unamuno, *Tragic Sense of Life*, trans. J.E. Crawford Flitch (New York: Dover, 1954), 97, Kindle.

16. Ibid., 103.

17. Plato, *Symposium*, in *Symposium and Phaedrus*, trans. Benjamin Jowett (New York: Dover, 1993), 31.

18. Luc Ferry, *A Brief History of Thought: A Philosophical Guide to Living*, trans. Theo Cuffe (New York: Harper, 2010), 34.

19. Albert Einstein, "Letter to Dutch Physicist Heike Kamerlingh-Onne's Widow," February 25, 1926, quoted in Stephen Cave, *Immortality: The Quest to Live Forever and How It Drives Civilization* (New York: Crown, 2012), 230.

20. Nathan A. Heflick, "Children and the Quest for Immortality: Of Death and (New) Life," *Psychology Today*, February 21, 2012, https://www.psychologytoday.com/blog/the-big-questions /201202/children-and-the-quest-immortality (accessed April 1, 2018).

21. Lawrence Rifkin, "Is the Meaning of Your Life to Make Babies?," *Scientific American*, March 24, 2013, https://blogs.scientificamerican.com/guest-blog/is-the-meaning-of-your-life-to-make -babies/ (accessed September 19, 2018).

22. This oft-quoted passage is reported to be in Ustinov's *Five Plays*, but I haven't been able to find it.

23. Walter Scott, "Walter Scott Asks…Jada Pinkett Smith," *Parade*, July 16, 2017, 2.

24. Samuel Scheffler, "Lecture 1 the Afterlife (Part 1)," in *Death and the Afterlife*, ed. Niko Kolodny (Oxford: Oxford University Press, 2016), 45.

25. Bennett Simon, *Tragic Drama and the Family: Psychoanalytic Studies from Aeschlus to Beckett* (New Haven, CT: Yale University Press, 1988), 92. See also Phillip Wilson, "Protean Aspects of Change in Euripides' Medea," *Anthós (1990–1996)* 1, no. 3 (1992): article 15, http://pdxscholar.library .pdx.edu/anthos_archives/vol1/iss3/15 (accessed May 19, 2017).

26. Richard Dawkins, *The Selfish Gene* (Oxford: Oxford University Press, 1989), 34.

27. Richard Dawkins, *The Selfish Gene*, 40th anniversary ed. (Oxford: Oxford University Press, 2016), 44.

28. Solomon continues in verses 20-21: "So I turned about and gave my heart up to despair over all the toil of my labors under the sun, because sometimes a person who has toiled with wisdom and knowledge and skill must leave everything to be enjoyed by someone who did not toil for it. This also is vanity and a great evil."

29. David talks about those who put their hope in their children in Psalm 17:13-15: "Arise, O LORD! Confront him, subdue him! Deliver my soul from the wicked by your sword, from men by your hand, O LORD, from men of the world whose portion is in this life. You fill their womb with treasure; they are satisfied with children, and they leave their abundance to their infants. As for me, I shall behold your face in righteousness; when I awake, I shall be satisfied with your likeness." Psalms commentator Allen P. Ross writes this is about the wicked: "Since their interest is only in the things of this life, they are satisfied with children, and when they are gone they leave what is left to their heirs. Their satisfaction is in what is temporal and temporary." Ross, *A Commentary on the Psalms*, vol. 1 (Grand Rapids, MI: Kregel, 2011), 429.

30. Becker, *Denial of Death*, 214.

31. Ferry, *Brief History of Thought*, 34.

32. For our purposes, it's not important to distinguish between ancestor worship and ancestor veneration or to discuss the fact that people in many cultures believe that their ancestors are still present in spirit or ghost form.

33. Many websites say something like "genealogy research is the second most popular hobby in the US after gardening and the second most visited category of websites after pornography," but I don't find statistics supporting that. For an example of someone who says this, see Gregory Rodriguez, "How Genealogy Became Almost as Popular as Porn," *Time*, May 30, 2014, http://time .com/133811/how-genealogy-became-almost-as-popular-as-porn/ (accessed June 22, 2018).

34. Alex Haley, "Why Do Genealogy? The Rewards of Researching Your Family History," Genealogy. com, n.d., http://www.genealogy.com/articles/research/12_alexh.html (accessed May 12, 2018).

35. Tim Agazio in response to Randy Seaver, "Ancestor Worship? Is Genealogy Research Worthwhile?," *Genea-Musings* (blog), November 20, 2006, https://www.geneamusings.com/2006/11/ancestor -worship-is-genealogy-research.html (accessed May 12, 2018).

36. Lorine McGinnis Schulze, "Why Do We Do Genealogy?," *Legacy News*, March 25, 2016, http:// news.legacyfamilytree.com/legacy_news/2016/03/why-do-we-do-genealogy.html (accessed May 12, 2018; emphasis mine).

37. Cave, *Immortality*, 240.

38. I realize that during war, most people aren't *primarily* thinking about the survival of future generations—they're concerned with their own survival or thriving. But that doesn't change the fact that symbolic immortality is enhanced by my country's or my tribe's survival, and if my country or tribe ceases to exist, then so does my symbolic immortality.

39. Yalom, *Existential Psychotherapy*, 293.

40. Cave, *Immortality*, 279.

41. Ferry, *Brief History of Thought*, 34. The phrase "written trace" means "paper trail" or "written record." In other words, there is a trace through history of a person's existence because that person performed something great.

42. Daniel Dennett tells Richard Dawkins, "A dear professor of mine just died, a few days ago, and I've been thinking quite a bit about it. And the idea that he lives for eternity in heaven doesn't give me any consolation at all. The idea that his memory lives on with his children, with his friends, his colleagues, and, of course, he has his work, or, he had his work, which will live on, not everybody gets that kind of legacy. And I think that for those that we love that die young, or without that sort of issue, the best consolation is just, that, they had a chance, they got to be on this stupendous planet and live for a while, and they have suffered, and I think seeing our suffering in the guise of the whole cosmos can make it seem not quite so earth shatteringly special. Yeah, we suffer but, uh…" At that, Dennett sounds fairly sad, so Dawkins cuts in: "You're right, it is a consolation to have a few books behind one, or musical compositions, or I suppose a great family life, or there are plenty of things of that sort." Dawkins then comments that we are lucky to be alive in the first place. See "Richard Dawkins and Daniel Dennett: On Death," YouTube video uploaded by Richard Dawkins Foundation for Reason & Science, August 4, 2015, https://www .youtube.com/watch?v=zVm8bdJNyMA (accessed June 28, 2018).

43. De Unamuno, *Tragic Sense of Life*, 97.

44. Otto Rank, "Life and Creation," in *The Creativity Question*, eds. Albert Rothenberg and Carl R. Hausman (Durham, NC: Duke University Press, 1976), 115.

45. This is widely attributed to Michelangelo.

46. Benvenuto Cellini, *The Autobiography of Benvenuto Cellini*, trans. John Addington Symonds (New York: P.F. Collier, 1910), 379. He wrote a poem of his life that tells "this tale of my sore-troubled life I write, / To thank the God of nature, who conveyed / My soul to me, and with such care hath stayed / That divers noble deeds I've brought to light" (2).

47. Irvin D. Yalom, *Existential Psychotherapy* (New York: Basic Books, 1980), 70.

48. Louis XIV, *Mémoires*, as quoted in Philippe Erlanger, "Louis XIV King of France," *Encyclopedia Britannica*, last updated December 28, 2017, https://www.britannica.com/biography/Louis -XIV-king-of-France (accessed June 22, 2018; emphasis mine).

49. Louis XIV, *Academies, Museums, and Canons of Art*, eds. Gillian Perry and Colin Cunningham (New Haven, CT: Yale University Press, 1999), 88.

50. Samuel Johnson in Arthur Murphy, *The Works of Samuel Johnson: With an Essay on His Life and Genius* (New York: Alexander V. Blake, 1840), 167. For the quote about Johnson, see Pat Rogers, "Johnson, Samuel," *Oxford Dictionary of National Biography*, September 23, 2004, http://www

.oxforddnb.com/view/10.1093/ref:odnb/9780198614128.001.0001/odnb-9780198614128
-e-14918;jsessionid=4D37708BD71019FB1057A425F782685E (accessed September 20, 2018).

51. Ian Sample, "Interview: Stephen Hawking: 'There Is No Heaven; It's a Fairy Story,'" *Guardian*, May 15, 2011, https://www.theguardian.com/science/2011/may/15/stephen-hawking-interview -there-is-no-heaven (accessed June 29, 2018).

52. Hilary Weaver, "Stephen Hawking Used Physics to Explain Why He Was Not Afraid of Death," *Vanity Fair*, March 14, 2018, https://www.vanityfair.com/style/2018/03/stephen-hawking-used -physics-to-explain-why-he-was-not-afraid-of-death (accessed June 29, 2018).

53. Irvin D. Yalom, *Staring at the Sun: Overcoming the Terror of Death* (San Francisco: Wiley, 2008), 88. Kathleen Teltsch wrote in the *New York Times*, "Call it an answer to the yearning for immor-tality: for a price, universities and colleges will carve the name of a generous benefactor in limestone on an imposing building. Too costly? The donor can opt for a piece of the building— a student lounge, a science laboratory, a library, even a photography darkroom—dedicated in perpetuity with a bronze plaque." Teltsch, "Wanted: Contributors in Search of Immor-tality," *New York Times*, June 11, 1993, https://www.nytimes.com/1993/06/11/nyregion/wanted -contributors-in-search-of-immortality.html (accessed April 9, 2018).

54. Michael Kinsley, *Old Age: A Beginner's Guide* (New York: Crown, 2016), 130.

55. Plutarch, *Plutarch's Lives*, trans. Arthur Hugh Clough (Boston: Ginn, 1886), 75. Plutarch says Alexander "esteemed it a perfect portable treasure of all military virtue and knowledge."

56. Homer, *Iliad*, trans. Peter Green (Berkeley: University of California Press, 2015), 12.322–28.

57. Ibid., 9.411–14.

58. Aristotle, "Nicomachean Ethics," bk. 3, chap. 6, in *The Basic Works of Aristotle*, trans. Richard McKeon (New York: Random House, 1941), 975 (emphasis in original).

59. John Brown, "Letter to His Brother, Jeremiah Brown," November 12, 1859, Archive.org, https:// archive.org/stream/lifeandlettersof00sanbrich/lifeandlettersof00sanbrich_djvu.txt (accessed April 19, 2018).

60. Jesse Brannam, "The Bravest of the Brave," Subvetpaul.com, n.d., http://www.subvetpaul.com /Bravest.html (accessed February 26, 2006; emphasis mine).

61. Becker, *Denial of Death*, 6.

62. I'm not suggesting that this motivates all atheists or that it is a motivating factor to any particular atheist. But let's face it, an atheist would be looked down upon by the atheist community if he or she looked in the camera and cried, "I'm really afraid of death!"

63. Agam Bansal et al., "Selfies: A Boon or Bane?," *Journal of Family Medicine and Primary Care* 7, no. 4 (July–August 2018): 828–31, https://www.ncbi.nlm.nih.gov/pmc/articles/PMC6131996/ (accessed March 7, 2019).

64. Phil McCausland, "Teen YouTuber Shoots and Kills Boyfriend in Video Stunt, Police Say," NBC News, June 28, 2017, https://www.nbcnews.com/news/us-news/teen-youtuber-shoots-kills -boyfriend-video-stunt-n777851?cid=sm_npd_nn_tw_ma (accessed July 6, 2018). She pleaded guilty to second-degree manslaughter and as a plea deal received 180 days in jail, half of which was served as house arrest.

65. Julia Elad-Strenger, "Activism as a Heroic Quest for Symbolic Immortality: An Existential Perspective on Collective Action," *Journal of Social and Political Psychology* 4, no. 1 (2016): 46, https://jspp.psychopen.eu/article/view/430/pdf (accessed March 30, 2018). Elsewhere she writes, "Also, as most cultures value courage and bravery, it seems that the more substantial the personal risks involved in one's 'heroic' actions, the more effective they are in engendering a sense of significance and selfworth" (Hirschberger, Florian, Mikulincer, Goldenberg, and Pyszczynski, 2002). Indeed, TMT-inspired studies indicate that reminders of death increase the willingness to engage in a wide range of risky activities, from extreme sports to substance abuse (Hirsch-berger et al., 2002; Taubman—Ben-Ari, Florian, and Mikulincer, 1999). As activism often entails

considerable personal costs and risks, and may even involve life-threatening activities, participation in such actions can be particularly appreciated by the group.

66. Ibid., 46.

67. Ibid.

68. Charles Dickens, *A Christmas Carol* (New York: W.W. Norton, 2017), 121.

69. Yalom, *Staring at the Sun*, 83. Similar sentiment is found in the work of genocide survivor Viktor E. Frankl: "A man who becomes conscious of the responsibility he bears toward a human being who affectionately waits for him, or to an unfinished work, will never be able to throw away his life. He knows the 'why' for his existence, and is able to bear any 'how.'" Frankl, *Man's Search for Meaning*, 75.

70. Yalom, *Staring at the Sun*, 88.

71. Bauman, *Mortality*, 202 (emphasis original). Bauman sums up Agnes Heller, "The Legacy of Marxian Ethics," in *The Grandeur and Twilight of Radical Universalism*, by Agnes Heller and Ferenc Fehér (New Brunswick, NJ: Transaction, 1987), 140. It's interesting to me that Bauman is here providing a basis for worth and immortality in a Marxist system. Marxist communism, of course, is atheistic, so how does an individual communist find meaning in life—symbolic immortality through the furtherance of communism and by working hard to make others value his or her existence so they will forever rue his or her passing? Although he may have softened his views over the years, Bauman himself was a communist: "In Poland, he was often a controversial figure. In 2006, a right-wing historian uncovered documents showing that Bauman served as an officer in a Stalinist-era military organization, the Internal Security Corps, which was helping to impose communism on the nation by killing resisters to the regime. Bauman acknowledged belonging to that unit, but he insisted that he only had a desk job. No evidence has surfaced linking him to any killings." Associated Press, "Sociologist Zygmunt Bauman, Known for His Work on Modern Identity and the Holocaust, Dies at 91," *Los Angeles Times*, January 9, 2017, http://www.latimes.com/local/obituaries/la-me-zygmunt-bauman-obit-20170109-story.html (accessed June 30, 2018).

72. Bauman, *Mortality*, 202 (emphasis mine). Bauman again refers to Heller, "Legacy of Marxian Ethics," 140. Apparently this is how you motivate people to work hard in Marxism. The trouble is, it's not enough motivation or Marxism might have had at least a slight chance to succeed.

73. R.D. Laing, *The Politics of Experience* (New York: Pantheon, 1967), 186.

74. Christians, of course, believe that a person must have a minimal amount of correct beliefs about the gospel to be saved, but here we're only talking about how correct beliefs can be a *symbolic* immortality project.

75. Ernest Becker, *Escape from Evil* (New York: Free Press, 1985), 64 (emphasis original). Bauman wrote, "Today we know that people try so hard to win converts for their point of view because it is more than merely an outlook on life: it is an immortality formula." Bauman, *Mortality*, 255.

76. Sheldon Solomon, Jeff Greenberg, and Tom Pyszczynski, *The Worm at the Core: On the Role of Death in Life* (New York: Random House, 2015), ix.

77. Ibid., 211.

78. I write "may be inherently valuable" because obviously one could do terrible things in the name of helping others—create pornography, protest for abortion, and so on.

79. David Giles, *Illusions of Immortality: A Psychology of Fame and Celebrity* (New York: Saint Martin's, 2000), 49.

80. "In 1987, a national telephone survey of two thousand adults" asked, "Have you ever daydreamed about being famous?" A total of 57 percent of the respondents said yes. The same question was asked in two subsequent surveys. In 1993, the number was 50 percent, and in 1997, it was 52 percent. Orville Gilbert Brim, *Look at Me! The Fame Motive from Childhood to Death* (Ann Arbor: University of Michigan Press, 2009), 24.

IMMORTAL

81. Jib Fowles, *Starstruck: Celebrity Performers and the American Public* (Washington, DC: Smithsonian, 1992), 4.

82. Simon Reynolds, *Bring the Noise: 20 Years of Writing About Hip Rock and Hip-Hop* (Berkeley, CA: Soft Skull Press, 2011), 83 (emphasis mine).

83. Samantha Grossman, "Top 10 Things That Broke the Internet," *Time*, December 2, 2014, http://time.com/collection-post/3587943/things-that-broke-the-internet/ (accessed July 7, 2018).

84. Leo Braudy, *The Frenzy of Renown: Fame and Its History* (New York: Vintage, 1997), 605.

85. Dallas Willard, *Renovation of the Heart* (Colorado Springs: NavPress, 2002), 203.

86. For the origin of the phrase, see Michael Tuney, "On-line Readings in Public Relations," Northern Kentucky University public relations class reading, December 1, 2010, https://www.nku.edu/~turney/prclass/readings/3eras1x.html (accessed February 3, 2018). Tuney spent years tracking down the origin of the phrase and concludes that it was *probably* coined by P.T. Barnum.

87. Rachel Swatman, "Check Out the Longest Fingernails Ever in Shridhar Chillal's Record Holder Profile Video," *Guinness World Records*, September 29, 2015, http://www.guinnessworldrecords.com/news/2015/9/record-holder-profile-video-shridhar-chillal-and-the-longest-fingernails-ever-398817 (accessed July 3, 2018; emphasis mine).

88. "Most Big Macs Consumed," *Guinness World Records*, August 24, 2016, http://www.guinnessworldrecords.com/world-records/most-big-macs-consumed (accessed July 3, 2018).

89. Asher Fogle, "23 of the Weirdest Guinness World Records Ever," *Good Housekeeping*, August 27, 2015, http://www.goodhousekeeping.com/life/entertainment/g2720/guinness-world-records-60th-anniversary/ (accessed March 16, 2018); Olivia B. Waxman, "17 of the Strangest Guinness World Records of All Time," *Time*, August 27, 2015, http://time.com/4013095/guinness-world-records-60th-anniversary-weirdest/ (accessed March 16, 2018).

90. William James, *The Principles of Psychology* (1890; repr., Mineola, NY: Dover, 1950), 293.

91. Becker, *Denial of Death*, 160–61.

92. Jason K. Swedene, *Staying Alive: The Varieties of Immortality* (Lanham, MD: University Press of America, 2009), ProQuest Ebook Central, http://ebookcentral.proquest.com/lib/biola-ebooks/detail.action?docID=1037724 (accessed April 2, 2018).

93. Becker, *Denial of Death*, 167.

94. Ibid., 164.

95. Gigi Engle, "Anal Sex: What You Need to Know: How to Do It the Right Way," *Teen Vogue*, May 16, 2018, https://www.teenvogue.com/story/anal-sex-what-you-need-to-know?verso=true (accessed January 29, 2019). By the way, a surgeon pointed out to me that there is no "right way" to have anal sex. The rectum is physically incapable of sustaining that kind of treatment—at least for long.

96. "Fatal Addiction: Ted Bundy's Final Interview," *Focus on the Family*, January 23, 1989, https://www.focusonthefamily.com/media/social-issues/fatal-addiction-ted-bundys-final-interview (accessed January 29, 2019).

97. De Unamuno, *Tragic Sense of Life*, 98.

98. Quoted in Li Cheng-Chung, *The Question of Human Rights on China Mainland* (Republic of China: World Anti-Communist League, China Chapter, September 1979), 12, as quoted in Jasper Becker, *Hungry Ghosts: Mao's Secret Famine* (New York: Free Press, 1996), 145. Becker cites many cases of live burials.

99. Saul M. Kassin and Lawrence S. Wrightsman, *The American Jury on Trial: Psychological Perspectives* (New York: Routledge, 2012), 89.

100. Caroline Shively and the Associated Press, "Wichita Police: 'BTK Is Arrested,'" Fox News, February 26, 2005, http://www.foxnews.com/story/2005/02/26/wichita-police-btk-is-arrested.html (accessed June 28, 2018).

101. Steve Kroft, "Genetic Genealogy," produced by Michael Karzis, *60 Minutes*, first aired October 21, 2018.

102. "Mark David Chapman Killed Lennon for Fame," *UPI*, October 15, 2004, https://www.upi.com/Archives/2004/10/15/Mark-David-Chapman-killed-Lennon-for-fame/2571097812800/ (accessed May 1, 2018).

103. Associated Press, Ashley Collman, and Alex Greg, "'It Took Incredible Planning and Incredible Stalking': Mark Chapman Brags About Killing John Lennon and How He Couldn't Resist 'That Bright Light of Fame' in Latest Parole Hearing,'" *Daily Mail*, August 28, 2014, http://www.dailymail.co.uk/news/article-2737101/Mark-David-Chapman-brags-incredible-planning-stalking-notorious-murder-John-Lennon.html#ixzz5EHcnZ9OZ (accessed May 1, 2018).

104. "German Police Say Former Nurse Niels Hoegel May Have Killed up to 180 with Lethal Drug Overdoses," News.com.au, August 29, 2017, http://www.news.com.au/world/europe/german-police-say-former-nurse-niels-hoegel-may-have-killed-up-to-180-with-lethal-drug-overdoses/news-story/194c5f51f904ce277baec1595ff29ea2 (accessed June 25, 2018).

105. David Montero, "Portrait of Vegas Gunman Missing a Motive," *Los Angeles Times*, August 4, 2018, A9.

106. Rafael Olmeda, "Parkland Shooter Nikolas Cruz Brags on Cellphone Videos, 'I'm Going to Be the Next School Shooter,'" *Sun-Sentinel*, May 30, 2018, http://www.sun-sentinel.com/local/broward/parkland/florida-school-shooting/fl-reg-florida-school-shooting-phone-video-release-20180530-story.html (accessed July 4, 2018).

107. Robert A. Fein and Bryan Vossekuil, "Protective Intelligence & Threat Assessment Investigations: A Guide for State and Local Law Enforcement Officials," US Department of Justice, January 2000, https://fas.org/irp/agency/doj/protective.pdf (accessed October 4, 2017).

108. Becker, *Escape from Evil*, xvii.

109. See Steve Croft's interview of Hamdi Ulukaya, "Chobani's Billionaire Founder on Creating Jobs in America," *60 Minutes*, April 9, 2017, https://www.cbsnews.com/news/chobani-yogurt-billionaire-founder-on-creating-jobs-in-america/ (accessed January 30, 2019).

110. C.S. Lewis, *Mere Christianity* (New York: Macmillan, 1958), 95.

111. Becker, *Escape from Evil*, 13.

112. "The Standard Inscription of Assurnasirpal II," Nimrud: Materialities of Assyrian Knowledge Production, Oracc Museum, last updated December 31, 2015, http://oracc.museum.upenn.edu/nimrud/livesofobjects/standardinscription/index.html (accessed July 5, 2018).

113. Herbert Schlossberg, *Idols for Destruction: The Conflict of Christian Faith and American Culture* (Wheaton, IL: Crossway, 1993), loc. 1062, Kindle.

114. *Sunday Times Magazine*, September 16, 1973, as quoted in Elizabeth Knowles, ed., *Oxford Dictionary of Modern Quotations*, 3rd ed. (Oxford: Oxford University Press, 2007), 325.

115. *Times of London*, October 9, 1858, as quoted in Arthur Schopenhauer, *Parerga and Paralipomena: Short Philosophical Essays*, vol. 2, trans. E.F.J. Payne (Oxford: Clarendon, 1974), 216.

116. Bauman, *Mortality*, 160.

117. Eric Lax, *On Being Funny: Woody Allen and Comedy* (New York: Charterhouse, 1975), 232.

118. William Geist, "Woody Allen: The Rolling Stone Interview: A conversation with the iconic filmmaker," *Rolling Stone*, April 9, 1987, https://www.rollingstone.com/movies/movie-features/woody-allen-the-rolling-stone-interview-105390/ (accessed June 1, 2019).

119. Marcus Aurelius, *Meditations*, trans. Gregory Hays (New York: Modern Library, 2003), 8:44. This particular translation appears in various publications, but I can't find the original translator. One example is found in David R. Loy, *A Buddhist History of the West: Studies in Lack* (Albany, NY: SUNY Press, 2002), 67.

120. Bauman, *Mortality*, 33.

121. Maureen Orth, *The Importance of Being Famous: Behind the Scenes of the Celebrity Industrial Complex* (New York: Henry Holt, 2004), 67.

122. Brim, *Look at Me!*, 131.

123. Matthew J. Buccoli, *Some Sort of Epic Grandeur: The Life of F. Scott Fitzgerald*, 2nd ed. (New York: Harcourt Brace, 2002), 448. In the last few years of his life, "the excitements, aspirations, and expectations of the Twenties could not be revived; life would never again seem infinitely promising."

124. Gilbert King, "Team Hollywood's Secret Weapons System," Smithsonian, May 23, 2012, https://www.smithsonianmag.com/history/team-hollywoods-secret-weapons-system-103619955/#W5txo9L5ozKcAuYr.99 (accessed July 2, 2018).

125. Geoff Edgers, "Chevy Chase Can't Change," *Washington Post*, September 19, 2018, https://www.washingtonpost.com/graphics/2018/lifestyle/chevy-chase-cant-change/?noredirect=on&utm_term=.c255c1d3942c (accessed October 3, 2018).

126. Ibid.

127. Fowles, *Starstruck*, 236.

128. Actress Helen Hunt bares all in the movie *The Sessions* (2012). In an interview, Hunt explains, "Any hesitation I had about the nudity, I think what I thought was it's getting late. You know what I mean?" Yes, we all know what Helen Hunt means. At the time of that interview, she was 50 years old, death was looming ever larger, and there are very few leading lady roles for those older than 40. Hunt continues, "It's getting *too late* in my life to care about the small things. It's getting *too late* to not be brave, to not live my life fully, to not try to be an artist. Trivial things like how nice your hotel room is, or if you have to be naked for a while, they fade away." Nigel M. Smith, "Helen Hunt Talks Baring All in 'The Sessions': 'It's Getting Too Late in My Life to Care About the Small Things,'" *Indiewire*, September 10, 2012, http://www.indiewire.com/2012/09/helen-hunt-talks-baring-all-in-the-sessions-its-getting-too-late-in-my-life-to-care-about-the-small-things-241700/ (accessed May 8, 2018).

129. Brim, *Look at Me!*, 136.

130. Jim Standridge, "Katy Perry Uncensored Raw Talent," *Vimeo*, 2001, https://vimeo.com/104457629 (accessed April 4, 2018).

131. Jonah Weiner, "The Unkillable Arnold Schwarzenegger: How Does an Action-Hero Ex-governor Spend His Golden Years? Loudly," *Rolling Stone*, May 7, 2015, https://www.rollingstone.com/movies/features/the-unkillable-arnold-schwarzenegger-20150507 (accessed April 4, 2018).

132. Sarah Silverman, "Sarah Silverman on Battling Depression," *Ellen Show*, October 24, 2015, https://www.videoclip.site/video/pZGVgl_RZ5Y/sarah-silverman-on-battling-depression/ (accessed December 10, 2018).

133. Bertrand Russell, "The Free Man's Worship," in *Russell: The Basic Writings of Bertrand Russell*, eds. Robert E. Egner and Lester E. Denonn (New York: Routledge Classics, 2009), 39. Originally printed in the *Independent Review* (December 1903) and subsequently reprinted in *Mysticism and Logic* (London: Allen & Unwin, 1917; New York: Simon & Schuster, 1929), 39. The title of the essay changed after 1910 to "A Free Man's Worship." See https://users.drew.edu/jlenz/br-free-mans-worship.html (accessed January 21, 2018).

134. Russell, *The Problems of Philosophy* (London: Oxford, 1957), 161.

135. Cave, *Immortality*, 224.

136. W.H. Auden and Christopher Isherwood, *The Complete Works of W.H. Auden: Plays and Other Dramatic Writings, 1928–1938*, ed. Edward Mendelson (Princeton: Princeton University Press, 2015), 477–78.

137. As astrophysicist Arthur S. Eddington (1882–1944) says about the second law of thermodynamics (that everything becomes more disordered over time and loses energy), "If someone points out to you that your pet theory of the universe is in disagreement with Maxwell's equations—then so

much the worse for Maxwell's equations. If it is found to be contradicted by observation—well, these experimentalists do bungle things sometimes. But if your theory is found to be against the second law of thermodynamics I can give you no hope; there is nothing for it but to collapse in the deepest humiliation." Eddington, *The Nature of the Physical Universe* (New York: Macmillan, 1928), 74.

Chapter 4

1. Luc Ferry, *A Brief History of Thought: A Philosophical Guide to Living*, trans. Theo Cuffe (New York: Harper, 2010), 4.

2. Ferry, *Wisdom of the Myths*, trans. Theo Cuffe (New York: Harper Perennial, 2014), 390.

3. Ferry, *Brief History of Thought*, 12.

4. Plato, *Phaedo* 67 4–6, trans. David Gallop (Oxford: Oxford University Press, 2009), 14.

5. Plato, *Phaedo* 81e–82e; G.M.A. Grube, trans., *Plato: Five Dialogues:* Euthyphro, Apology, Crito, Meno, Phaedo, 2nd ed., rev. John M. Cooper (Indianapolis: Hackett, 2002), 119.

6. Epictetus, *Discourses*, in *Epictetus: The Discourses and Manual, Together with Fragments of His Writings*, trans. P.E. Matheson (Oxford: Clarendon, 1916), loc. 4534–37, Kindle (emphasis mine).

7. Michel de Montaigne, "To Philosophize Is to Learn How to Die," in M.A. Screech, trans., *Michel de Montaigne: The Complete Essays* (1987; repr., New York: Penguin, 2003), 89.

8. S. Arthur Schopenhauer, *The World as Will and Idea*, vol. 3 (1883; repr., London: Routledge & Kegan Paul, 1948), 249.

9. "Humanist Manifesto II," 1973, American Humanist Association, https://americanhumanist .org/what-is-humanism/manifesto2/ (accessed August 30, 2017).

10. Sheldon Solomon, Jeff Greenberg, and Tom Pyszczynski, *The Worm at the Core: On the Role of Death in Life* (New York: Random House, 2015), 215.

11. Stephen Cave, *Immortality: The Quest to Live Forever and How It Drives Civilization* (New York: Crown, 2012), 273.

12. Ferry, *Wisdom of the Myths*, 6.

13. This is also a theme found in fiction. For example, Ferry writes of the goddess Calypso offering Odysseus "the chance to escape death—the common lot of mortals—and to enter the inaccessible sphere of those whom the Greeks refer to as 'the blessed,' which is to say the gods themselves" (ibid.).

14. Brian Ribeiro, "The Problem of Heaven," *Ratio* 24, no. 1 (March 2011): 63.

15. Lawrence Krauss, "Sergey Kolesov Interview with Lawrence Krauss," *Singularity Weblog*, May 14, 2017, https://www.singularityweblog.com/lawrence-krauss/ (accessed June 29, 2018). When asked "Are you afraid of death?" Krauss replies, "Well, yes and no. Humans have aversion to death built-in as an instinct. Also, since I realize that we only get one chance, it would be nice to fulfill that chance as long and productively as you can. But the idea of that eternal life which the religious people are so fond of terrifies me much more."

16. This is oft quoted, but I can't find the original.

17. Andrew Stark, *The Consolations of Mortality: Making Sense of Death* (New Haven: Yale, 2016), 231. Stark says, "Immortality, as long as our selves moved ever forward into the future while the events of our lives flowed back ever further into the past, would seem a box with no escape—a box whose four walls would comprise grossly distended facsimiles of what we mortals already experience in death and dying." So losing your past, for Stark, is a kind of death. He calls it "the complete annihilation of repeated self-disappearance. The ever-deepening antiquated feeling that leads to cascading nostalgia, which one writer likens to a 'kind of living death.' The futile dementia that spells endless twilight. Immortality, on the twin assumption that our selves continued moving forward into the future and the events of our lives continued back into the past, does look malignant" (228).

18. Ibid., 231. He writes, "That's it. Those are the options: Either we die or we are immortal. And either our selves move relentlessly forward in time while the moments of our lives slip continually backward out of reach." Stark likens the loss of our memories to a type of death. He continues, "Or else *we gain capacities to stop moving forward in time* and do keep precious moments of our lives from flowing forever backward in time beyond our grasp." Really, "we gain the capacities to stop moving forward"? Isn't that longhand circumlocution for "we die"? Stark continues, "Of all possible combinations, none is better than the one we have. We die, and [—while we are alive—] our selves move inexorably forward in time while the moments of our lives ineluctably vanish into the past." I contacted Professor Stark to ask him for a clarification of this sentence, and he responded that it could have been a little clearer if he had written, "We die, and—while we are alive—our selves move inexorably forward in time while the moments of our lives ineluctably vanish into the past." Thus I've included those words in brackets. Andrew Stark, personal communication with the author, July 26, 2018. For Stark, immortality necessarily includes forgetting the past.

19. Ibid. (emphasis mine).

20. David Robson, "The Blessing and Curse of People Who Never Forget," *BBC*, January 26, 2016, http://www.bbc.com/future/story/20160125-the-blessing-and-curse-of-the-people-who-never-forget (accessed January 19, 2019).

21. Jorge Luis Borges, "The Immortal," in *Labyrinths: Selected Stories and Other Writings*, eds. Donald A. Yates and James E. Irby (1962; repr., New York: New Directions, 2007), 106.

22. Ibid., 114–15 (emphasis mine).

23. Douglas Adams, *Life, the Universe and Everything* (New York: Del Rey, 1982), 4–5.

24. Susan Ertz, *Anger in the Sky* (London: Hodder & Stoughton, 1943), 137. The fuller quote reads, "Real boredom, the sort we were discussing, is generally found among the well to do. Someone has somewhere commented on the fact that millions long for immortality who don't know what to do with themselves on a rainy Sunday afternoon."

25. Natalie Babbitt, *Tuck Everlasting* (New York: Square Fish, 1975), 64 (emphasis in original).

26. Sam Roberts, "Natalie Babbitt, 84, Dies; Took on Immortality in 'Tuck Everlasting,'" *New York Times*, November 1, 2016, https://www.nytimes.com/2016/11/02/books/natalie-babbitt-died-tuck-everlasting.html (accessed October 4, 2018).

27. Similarly, Thomas Edison (1847–1931) says, "No, all this talk of an existence for us, as individuals, beyond the grave is wrong. It is born of our tenacity of life—our desire to go on living—our dread of coming to an end as individuals. I do not dread it, though. Personally I cannot see any use of a future life." Edward Marshall, "'No Immortality of the Soul' Says Thomas A. Edison," *Sunday Magazine*, October 2, 1910, http://sundaymagazine.org/2010/10/no-immortality-of-the-soul-says-thomas-a-edison/ (accessed October 4, 2018).

28. Clay Jones, *Why Does God Allow Evil? Compelling Answers to Life's Toughest Questions* (Eugene, OR: Harvest House, 2017), 168–76.

29. Cave, *Immortality*, 263–64.

30. Ibid., 264 (emphasis mine).

31. Stephen Fry, "What Should We Think About Death?," Richard Dawkins Foundation for Reason and Science, July 25, 2014, https://www.richarddawkins.net/2014/07/what-should-we-think-about-death/ (accessed June 28, 2018).

32. Saint Augustine, *Confessions*, trans. Henry Chawick (Oxford: Oxford, 2008), 3.

33. Solomon, Greenberg, and Pyszczynski, *Worm at the Core*, 216.

34. Christopher Hitchens, *Mortality* (New York: Twelve, 2012), 85.

35. Ibid., 92–93. Hitchens is quoting from Alan Lightman's intricate 1993 novel *Einstein's Dreams*, set in Berne in 1905. *Mortality* includes a publisher's note for the last chapter: "These fragmentary jottings were left unfinished at the time of the author's death" (85). I don't know whether

Hitchens would have necessarily chosen this final comment to be the last in his book, but apparently Hitchens's wife and the publisher chose it to be so. Either way, the idea caught his attention.

36. Steve Jobs, "Commencement Address" (lecture given at Stanford University, June 12, 2005; emphasis mine).

37. Kate Tempest, "We Die," produced by Dan Carey, *Let Them Eat Chaos*, 2016.

38. The atheist might respond that despite the fact that the act of bringing another organism into existence doesn't require that we die or make way for the new organism, other aspects of survival and/or evolution require that organisms die off and make way for new organisms. Nonetheless, even if Darwinism were true, presently humans do not have to die so that other humans may live, and if no one ever died, I personally suspect that population growth would diminish (as it has in Europe)—if not cease altogether.

39. Ray Kurzweil, "Chasing Immortality—the Technology of Eternal Life: An Interview with Ray Kurzweil by Craig Hamilton," *What Is Enlightenment?*, no. 30, 2005, 65–66, http://singularity .com/WIEnlightenment_KurzweilAritcle.pdf (accessed July 24, 2018).

40. Richard Dawkins, *Unweaving the Rainbow: Science, Delusion and the Appetite for Wonder* (Boston: Houghton Mifflin, 1998), 1.

41. "Great Minds: Richard Dawkins—'We Are Going to Die!,'" YouTube video uploaded by FFree-Thinker, February 27, 2010, https://www.youtube.com/watch?v=Ac33dOAgqus (accessed June 28, 2018).

42. Michael Shermer, *Heavens on Earth: The Scientific Search for the Afterlife, Immortality, and Utopia* (New York: Henry Holt, 2018), 254.

43. Philodemus, *On Death*, trans. W. Benjamin Henry (Atlanta: Society of Biblical Literature, 2009), 38.14–25, https://www-fulcrum-org.ezproxy.biola.edu/epubs/ms35t921z?locale=en#/6/6[xhtml 00000003]!/4/1:0 (accessed October 16, 2018).

44. Marcus Aurelius, *Meditations*, trans. Gregory Hays (New York: Modern Library, 2003), 48.7.48.

45. Sophocles, *Oedipus at Colonus*, trans. F. Storr (Cambridge, MA: Harvard University Press, 1912), Kindle.

46. Pliny the Elder, *The Natural History* 7.51, trans. John Bostock, Perseus Digital Library, http:// www.perseus.tufts.edu/hopper/text?doc=Perseus%3Atext%3A1999.02.0137%3Abook%3D7% 3Achapter%3D51 (accessed October 5, 2018).

47. David Benatar, *Better Never to Have Been: The Harm of Coming into Existence* (Oxford: Oxford University Press, 2006), 1. Benatar says, "It is curious that while good people go to great lengths to spare their children from suffering, few of them seem to notice that the one (and only) guaranteed way to prevent all suffering of their children is not to bring them into existence in the first place" (6).

48. Shermer, *Heavens on Earth*, 243–44 (emphasis mine). Shermer enthuses, "In the far future, civilizations may become sufficiently advanced to colonize entire galaxies, genetically engineer new life forms, terraform planets, and even trigger the birth of stars and new planetary solar systems through massive engineering projects. Civilizations this advanced would have so much knowledge and power as to be essentially omniscient and omnipotent. What would you call such a sentience? If you didn't know the science and the technology behind it you would call it God, which is why I have postulated that *any sufficiently advanced extraterrestrial intelligence or far future human is indistinguishable from God*" (235–36). He continues, "Thus do we achieve immortality as a species by going to the stars. *Per audacia ad astra*" (237). Shermer translates the Latin as "the stars through audacity."

49. Epicurus, "Letter to Menoeceus," in *The Art of Happiness*, trans. George K. Strodach and Daniel Klein (New York: Penguin, 2012), 156. Epicurus continues, "Hence a correct comprehension of the fact that death means nothing to us makes the mortal aspect of life pleasurable, not by conferring on us a boundless period of time but by removing the yearning for deathlessness. There is nothing fearful in living for the person who has really laid hold of the fact that there is nothing

fearful in not living. So it is silly for a person to say he dreads death—not because it will be painful when it arrives but because it pains him not as a future certainty; for that which makes no trouble for us when it arrives is a meaningless pain when we await it."

50. Ibid., 156–57. Stephen Cave points out that "though much quoted, this idea is also often misunderstood. Many modern philosophers take it to mean we should be utterly indifferent to dying. But this is not Epicurus's main concern. We might be anxious about the process of dying, fearing it might be painful (though many who have near-death experiences describe it as quite pleasant), and we might wish to prolong the pleasures of life, and so in that sense see death as unwelcome. Epicurus's main point, however, is that we should not fear the state of being dead." Cave, *Immortality*, 274.

51. "Sam Harris: On Death," YouTube video uploaded by Big Think, June 2, 2011, https://www.youtube.com/watch?v=d_Uahu9XNzU (accessed June 28, 2018).

52. Victor J. Stenger, *The New Atheism: Taking a Stand for Science and Reason* (Amherst, NY: Prometheus, 2009), 30 (emphasis mine).

53. "Bart D. Ehrman Author Page," Facebook, September 18, 2016, https://www.facebook.com/AuthorBartEhrman/posts/1210103929061399 (accessed June 29, 2018).

54. Irvin D. Yalom, *Staring at the Sun: Overcoming the Terror of Death* (San Francisco: Wiley, 2008), 2.

55. Ibid., 82.

56. Schopenhauer, *World as Will and Idea*, 253. Vladimir Nabokov, the great Russian American novelist, begins his autobiography with these lines: "The cradle rocks above an abyss, and common sense tells us that our existence is but a brief crack of light between two eternities of darkness. Although the two are identical twins, man, as a rule, views the prenatal abyss with more calm than the one he is heading for (at some forty-five hundred heartbeats an hour)." Nabokov, *Speak, Memory: An Autobiography Revisited* (New York: Vintage, 1989), 19.

57. Lucretius, *On the Nature of Things*, bk. 3, 935, trans. Walter Englert (Newburyport, MA: Focus, 2003), 87.

58. Mark Twain, *Autobiography of Mark Twain*, vol. 2, eds. Benjamin Griffin and Harriet Elinor Smith (Berkeley: University of California Press, 2013), 69.

59. Thomas Nagel, *Mortal Questions* (Cambridge: Cambridge University Press, 1979), 3.

60. Ibid., 5–6.

61. Ibid., 7.

62. Ibid., 10.

63. Ibid., 1. Nagel also says, "It is sometimes suggested that what we really mind is the process of dying. But I should not really object to dying if it were not followed by death" Ibid., 11.

"Viewed in this way, death, no matter how inevitable, is an abrupt cancellation of indefinitely extensive possible goods. Normality seems to have nothing to do with it, for the fact that we will all inevitably die in a few score years cannot by itself imply that it would not be good to live longer. Suppose that we were all inevitably going to die in agony—physical agony lasting six months. Would inevitability make that prospect any less unpleasant? And why should it be different for a deprivation? If the normal lifespan were a thousand years, death at 80 would be a tragedy. As things are, it may just be a more widespread tragedy. If there is no limit to the amount of life that it would be good to have, then it may be that a bad end is in store for us all." Ibid., 10.

"I conclude that something about the future prospect of permanent nothingness is not captured by the analysis in terms of denied possibilities." Ibid., fn. 3, 8–9.

David Benatar, *The Human Predicament: A Candid Guide to Life's Biggest Questions* (Oxford: Oxford University Press, 2017), 104. "After all, annihilation irrevocably terminates the string of psychologically connected states that constitute one's life, and that is something that a prudential valuer can regret" (105).

64. Benatar, *Human Predicament*, 104.

65. Nabokov, *Speak, Memory*, 19.

66. In the next chapter, I'll discuss the relationship of suicide to our fear of death.

67. Bauman, *Mortality*, 15.

68. Ibid., 161.

69. Shelly Kagan says, "Of course, I am not suggesting that there is nothing bad about death. Although I am insisting that it makes no sense to be afraid of what it is like to be dead—precisely because that is not something bad at all—I have not denied that death is bad. On the contrary, I accept the deprivation account, according to which death is bad (when it is bad) by virtue of the fact that one is deprived of the good that one would have if one weren't dead. In short, death isn't bad because of what it feels like to be dead; rather, death is bad because of the deprivation that it involves." Kagan, *Death* (New Haven, CT: Yale University Press, 2012), 296.

70. Diogenes Laërtius, *Lives of the Eminent Philosophers*, trans. Pamela Mensch, ed. James Miller (Oxford: Oxford University Press, 2018), 500. Some consider Epicurus's letter to be a pro-Epicurean forgery intended to portray Epicurus in the best light, but it is possible that it is legitimate—or maybe Epicurus wrote it to let the world know that his philosophy was still intact.

71. Making a life of telling people they don't fear death reminds me of atheists who proclaim that they are absolutely convinced there is no God and then spend countless hours seeking to banish every reminder that there might be a God from the public square.

72. Solomon, Greenberg, and Pyszczynski, *Worm at the Core*, 217.

73. Martha C. Nussbaum, *The Therapy of Desire: Theory and Practice in Hellenistic Ethics* (Princeton: Princeton University Press, 1994), 495–96.

74. Thomas Nagel, *What Does It All Mean? A Very Short Introduction to Philosophy* (New York: Oxford University Press, 1987), 94.

75. Ibid., 91.

76. C.S. Lewis, *Till We Have Faces: A Myth Retold* (New York: HarperOne, 1984), 86.

77. Ibid., 87.

78. C.S. Lewis, *Mere Christianity* (New York: Macmillan, 1958), 106.

79. Donald S. Lopez states, "Although the term *Four Noble Truths* is well known in English, it is a misleading translation of the Pali term *Chattari-ariya-saccani* (Sanskrit: *Chatvari-arya-satyani*), because *noble* (Pali: *ariya*; Sanskrit: *arya*) refers not to the truths themselves but to those who understand them. A more accurate rendering, therefore, might be "four truths for the [spiritually] noble; they are four facts that are known to be true by those with insight into the nature of reality but that are not known to be true by ordinary beings. The Buddha stated in his first sermon that when he gained absolute and intuitive knowledge of the four truths, he achieved complete enlightenment and freedom from future rebirth." Lopez, "Four Noble Truths," *Encyclopedia Britannica*, March 14, 2017, https://www.britannica.com/topic/Four-Noble-Truths (accessed July 12, 2018).

80. "The Four Noble Truths," Zen Buddhism, n.d., https://www.zen-buddhism.net/buddhist-principles/four-noble-truths.html (accessed December 19, 2018).

81. Ferry, *Brief History of Thought*, 47.

82. Pierre Hadot, *Philosophy as a Way of Life* (Malden, MA; Blackwell, 1995), 83 (emphasis mine).

83. Mary Beard, *The Roman Triumph* (Cambridge, MA: Harvard University Press, 2007), 1.

84. Ibid., 4.

85. Ibid., 85.

86. Tertullian, *Apology*, quoted in Beard, *Roman Triumph*, 85.

87. Rudyard Kipling, "If," in *Kipling* (New York: Alfred A. Knopf, 2007), 171. As to Kipling being influenced by stoicism, see Frank Field, *British and French Writers of the First World War: Comparative Studies in Cultural History* (New York: Cambridge University Press, 1991), 153–76.

88. Bertrand Russell, *Portraits of Memory: And Other Essays* (1951; repr., New York: Simon & Schuster, 1963), 52 (emphasis mine).

89. Ibid., 53. Russell continues, "And if, with the decay of vitality, weariness increases, the thought of rest will not be unwelcome. I should wish to die while still at work, knowing that others will carry on what I can no longer do, and content in the thought that what was possible has been done." Although Russell dismisses it elsewhere, here he is basically adopting a legacy immortality. In Russell's mind, *his* work will continue (at least until the universe burns out).

90. Russell was a famous antiwar crusader.

91. Ferry, *Brief History of Thought*, 262–63. In fact, as Ferry points out, "as the Dalai-Lama acknowledges, the only way of truly living according to the rules of non-attachment is to follow the monastic life, to be solitary (*monastikos*) in order to be free, to avoid all bonds" (262). See also Richard F. Gombrich, *Theravāda Buddhism: A Social History from Ancient Benares to Modern Colombo*, 2nd ed. (London: Routledge, 1998), where the author writes, "If life in society brings only rebirth, it is only life outside society which can bring escape from rebirth. Society with its web of obligations becomes an analogue for the entire cycle of *saṃsāra*, and on the other hand the homeless life with no social ties becomes an analogue for that release from rebirth for which it is conceived to be literally a preparation." Gombrich continues, "However, all classical Indian religions, from the Upaniṣads on, took it as axiomatic that never-ending rebirth was undesirable and one's aim was to get off the treadmill" (48). He then concludes, "Seen in these terms, as Louis Dumont showed in his famous essay 'World Renunciation in Indian Religions,' the institution of renunciation sets up a whole set of binary oppositions, pairs of opposites. The renouncer leaves the organized space of home and settlement (village) for homelessness and the formless wilderness. He has no fire, the symbol and instrument of sacrifice. He may neither produce nor reproduce, for Desire is Death" (48–49).

92. "The bold Stoic attempt to purify social life of all its ills, rigorously carried through, ends by removing, as well, its finite humanity, its risk-taking loyalty, its passionate love." Nussbaum, *Therapy of Desire*, 510.

93. Andrew Stark, *The Consolations of Mortality: Making Sense of Death* (New Haven, CT: Yale University Press, 2016), 6 (emphasis original).

94. Ibid., 217–18.

95. Karen Armstrong, *Buddha* (New York: Penguin, 2004), 1.

96. Ibid., 2. Armstrong says Siddhata "could not afford to feel 'revolted' when he saw a decrepit old man or somebody who was disfigured by a loathsome illness. The same fate—or something even worse—would befall him and everybody he loved. His parents, his wife, his baby son and his friends were equally frail and vulnerable. When he clung to them and yearned tenderly toward them, he was investing emotion in what could only bring him pain. His wife would lose her beauty, and little Rāhula could die tomorrow. To seek happiness in mortal, transitory things was not only irrational: the suffering in store for his loved ones as well as for himself cast a dark shadow over the present and took away all his joy in these relationships. But why did Gotama see the world in such bleak terms? Mortality is a fact of life and hard to bear" (3–4). Stephen Cave writes, "Freedom from the petty concerns, troublesome memories and shallow desires of individual life is for many Buddhists, Hindus and Taoists the highest aim. This is the extinguishing of the self—the literal meaning of 'nirvana.'" Cave, *Immortality*, 246.

97. Ferry, *Brief History of Thought*, 261 (emphasis original). Ferry continues, "We do not deprive ourselves only of happiness and serenity, in advance of the fact, but also of freedom. The word we use for these things are themselves suggestive: to be *attached* is to be *linked* or *bound*, as opposed to free; and if we wish to emancipate ourselves from the bonds forged by love, we must practice as early as possible that form of wisdom known as non-attachment."

98. Ibid., 262.

99. Ibid., 263.

100. Ferry, *Wisdom of the Myths*, 7.

101. Marcus Aurelius, *Meditations: The Essential Marcus Aurelius*, trans. Jacob Needleman and John P. Piazza (New York: Penguin, 2008), 90, 12.3 (emphasis mine).

102. Ferry, *A Brief History of Thought*, 50–51. The first emphasis in the quotation is original, the second emphasis is mine.

103. Ludwig Wittgenstein, *Tractatus Logico-Philosophicus*, trans. D.F. Pears and B.F. McGuiness (New York: Routledge Classics, 2001), 6.4311, 87 (emphasis mine). Stephen Cave writes that Wittgenstein "concluded from this that in this sense 'life has no end.' That is, we can never be aware of it having an end—we can never know anything but life. We might compare ourselves to an ocean wave: when it breaks on the shore, its short life is over, but it does not then enter some new state of being 'a dead wave' or 'an ex-wave.' Rather, the parts that made it up are dissipated and absorbed back into the sea. Similarly with us: when the self-regulating, organized complexity of a human organism fails, then that person reaches a full stop; they have not entered into a new state of death. They have ceased, and their constituent elements slowly lose their human shape and are subsumed once more into the whole. The teachings that try to reassure us that death is just a transition—like shedding an old set of clothes for a new one, as the Bhagavad Gita says— are playing on our intuitive fear of death as a step into the abyss. But they could not be more wrong: a transition is exactly what death is not, whether into the abyss or anywhere else. It is an ending—and that, when properly understood, is exactly why we should not be afraid. This is something those Roman stoics understood who had inscribed on their tombstones '*Non fui, fui, non sum, non curo*' ('I was not; I was; I am not; I do not care')." Cave, *Immortality*, 275.

104. Pierre Hadot, *Philosophy as a Way of Life* (Malden, MA: Blackwell, 1995), 221–22.

105. Lucius Annaeus Seneca, "From Seneca to Lucilius," in *Seneca: Letters on Ethics*, ed. Margaret Graver and A.A. Long (Chicago: University of Chicago Press, 2017), 32.5.8.

106. Ibid., 33.5.9.

107. Hadot, *Philosophy*, 222. Hadot continues, "Both Epicureanism and Stoicism invite us to resituate the present instant within the perspective of the cosmos, and accord infinite value to the slightest moment of existence." In addition, "Everything we have been saying so far could be summed up in the following verses from Horace, 'Let the soul which is happy with the present learn to hate to worry about what lies ahead'" (224).

108. "Sam Harris: Death and the Present Moment," YouTube video uploaded by Atheist Foundation of Australia Inc., June 2, 2012, https://www.youtube.com/watch?v=ITTxTCz4Ums (accessed June 29, 2018).

109. Ibid. Harris states, "The reality of death is absolutely central to religion…We're the only people who admit that death is real." Of course, by saying they are the only ones who admit death is real, he means that for the atheist, there is no afterlife, and so when you're dead, you're dead. Obviously Christians believe death is real, but we also believe there's an afterlife.

110. Lara Hilton et al., "Mindfulness Meditation for Chronic Pain: Systematic Review and Meta-analysis," *Annals of Behavioral Medicine* 51, no. 2 (2017): 199–213, https://www.ncbi.nlm.nih.gov /pmc/articles/PMC5368208/ (accessed February 2, 2018; emphasis mine).

111. Daniel H. Pink, *When: The Scientific Secrets of Perfect Timing* (New York: Riverhead, 2018), 216.

112. Suzanne Corkin, *Permanent Present Tense: The Unforgettable Life of the Amnesic Patient: HM* (New York: Basic Books, 2013), 243.

113. Roman Krznaric, *Carpe Diem: Seizing the Day in a Distracted World* (New York: Penguin, 2017), 133.

114. Pink, *When*, 217.

115. Cave, *Immortality*, 286.

116. John Carey, ed., *John Donne: The Major Works* (Oxford: Oxford University Press, 2008), 344.

117. Hadot, *Philosophy*, 221. Hadot prefaces this quote with "We must certainly agree that the Greeks

in general gave particular attention to the present moment…Popular wisdom advised people both to be content with the present, and to know how to utilize it. Being content with the present meant…being content with earthly existence."

118. Cave, *Immortality*, 270–1.

119. John Donne, "Death's Duel: or, a Consolation to the Soul Against the Dying Life and Living Death of the Body" (sermon given at Whitehall, London, 1630), https://ebooks.adelaide.edu .au/d/donne/john/duel/ (accessed February 9, 2019).

120. It's important to note that many skeptics do not believe that individuality is illusory.

121. Deepak Chopra, "The Absolute Break Between Life and Death Is an Illusion," *Huffington Post*, July 28, 2005, updated May 25, 2011, https://www.huffingtonpost.com/deepak-chopra/the -absolute-break-betwee_b_4843.html (accessed January 4, 2018).

122. Russell, *Portraits of Memory*, 52–53 (emphasis mine).

123. Albert Einstein, letter to Robert S. Marcus of the World Jewish Congress, February 12, 1950, as quoted in Silvan S. Schweber, *Einstein and Oppenheimer: The Meaning of Genius* (Cambridge, MA: Harvard University Press, 2010), 300 (emphasis mine).

124. Albert Einstein, *Ideas and Opinions* (1954; repr., New York: Crown, 1982), 38. Einstein says he finds the beginnings of this "cosmic religious feeling" in the "early stage of development" in "the Psalms of David and the Prophets," but "Buddhism, as we have learned especially from the wonderful writings of Schopenhauer, contains a much stronger element of this. The religious geniuses of all ages have been distinguished by this kind of religious feeling, which knows no dogma and no God conceived in man's image; so that there can be no church whose central teachings are based on it."

125. Ibid. Einstein explains, "How can cosmic religious feeling be communicated from one person to another, if it can give rise to no definite notion of a God and no theology? In my view, it is the most important function of art and science to awaken this feeling and keep it alive in those who are receptive to it." Later he writes that such an enlightened man "has no use for the religion of fear and equally little for social or moral religion. A God who rewards and punishes is inconceivable to him for the simple reason that a man's actions are determined by necessity, external and internal, so that in God's eyes he cannot be responsible, any more than an inanimate object is responsible for the motions it undertakes" (39).

126. Margalit Fox, "Susan Sontag, Social Critic with Verve, Dies at 71," *New York Times*, December 29, 2004, https://www.nytimes.com/2004/12/29/books/susan-sontag-social-critic-with-verve -dies-at-71.html (accessed October 17, 2018).

127. David Rieff, *Swimming in a Sea of Death: A Son's Memoir* (New York: Simon & Schuster, 2008), 167.

128. Ibid., 168.

129. Ibid., 168–69. Rieff also says, "But instead, almost until the moment she died, we talked of her survival, of her struggle with cancer, never about her dying. I was not going to raise the subject unless she did. It was her death, not mine. And she did not raise it. To have done so would have been to concede that she might die and what she wanted was survival, not extinction—survival on any terms. To go on living: perhaps that was her way of dying" (17).

130. Barbara Ehrenreich, *Natural Causes: An Epidemic of Wellness, the Certainty of Dying, and Killing Ourselves to Live Longer* (New York: Twelve, 2018), 204.

131. Ibid., 203.

132. Michael Pollan, "The Trip Treatment: Research into Psychedelics, Shut down for Decades, Is Now Yielding Exciting Results," *New Yorker*, February 9, 2015, https://www.newyorker.com /magazine/2015/02/09/trip-treatment (accessed September 17, 2018).

133. Cave, *Immortality*, 244.

134. Chuang Tzu, *Wandering on the Way: Early Taoist Tales and Parables of Chuang Tzu*, trans. Victor H. Mair (Honolulu: University of Hawaii Press, 2000), 218.

135. D.T. Suzuki, *The Zen Doctrine of No Mind: The Significance of the Sutra of Hui-neng (Wei-lang)*, ed. Christmas Humphreys (Boston: Weiser, 1972), 55.

136. D.T. Suzuki, *An Introduction to Zen Buddhism* (New York: Grove, 1964), 29. It's interesting that Sigmund Freud's contemporary and sometime companion psychiatrist Carl Jung wrote the introduction.

137. Ibid., 30.

138. Ravi Zacharias, *Can Man Live Without God?* (Nashville: W Publishing, 1994), 127–28.

139. Lynn Margulis and Dorion Sagan, *What Is Life?* (Berkeley: University of California Press, 1995), 81. They explain why we fear death: "If we did not fear death, we might be too quick to kill ourselves when troubled or inconvenienced and thus perish as a species. Belief in life's importance may not be a reflection of reality, then, but an evolutionarily reinforced fantasy that prejudices believers to do what is necessary, bear whatever burdens, to survive" (30–31).

140. Fry, "About Death." Similarly, skeptic Michael Shermer writes, "*Stars died so that we may live. In this sense nature is not purposeless, as so many people seem to think it is, leading them to invoke a supernatural entity outside nature to grant us purpose. No such agent is needed because purpose is built into the cosmos and laws of nature. The purpose of stars is to convert hydrogen into helium and generate light and heat. This is their 'destiny,' their cosmic purpose. And this is true for all things in the cosmos, and here on Earth.*" Shermer, *Heavens on Earth*, 244–45 (emphasis mine). Since this is true for "all things" even "on Earth," that means your destiny, your cosmic purpose, is apparently to become dust so that others may live.

141. Ferry, *Wisdom of the Myths*, 52.

142. Corliss Lamont, *The Illusion of Immortality*, 3rd ed. (New York: Philosophical Library, 1958), 271.

143. Arthur Schopenhauer, *The World as Will and Representation*, vol. 3, trans. R.B. Haldane and J. Kemp (1883; repr., London: Routledge & Kegan Paul, 1948), 260–61. It's interesting that Schopenhauer concludes his chapter "On Death" by writing favorably about the Indian Vedas: "During life the will of man is without freedom: his actions take place with necessity upon the basis of an unalterable character in the chain of motives…If now he were to go on living, he would go on acting in the same way, on account of the unalterable nature of his character… Therefore death looses these bonds; the will again becomes free" (307). Then see his last two sentences: "The existence which we know he willingly gives up: what he gets instead of it is in our eyes *nothing*, because our existence is, with reference to that, *nothing*. The Buddhist faith calls it Nirvana, *i.e.*, extinction" (308; emphasis original).

144. Ibid., 265.

145. Shelly Kagan, *Death* (New Haven: Yale, 2012), 314, 315, (emphasis mine).

146. Ernest Becker, *The Birth and Death of Meaning: An Interdisciplinary Perspective on the Problem of Man*, 2nd ed. (New York: Free Press, 1971), 70.

147. Miguel de Unamuno, *Tragic Sense of Life*, trans. J.E. Crawford Flitch (New York: Dover, 1954), 90, Kindle. See the next sentences: "Here and now, in this discreet and diffused light, in this lake of quietude, the storm of the heart appeased and stilled the echoes of the world! Insatiable desire now sleeps and does not even dream; use and wont, blessed use and wont, are the rule of my eternity; my disillusions have died with my memories, and with my hopes my fears" (91).

148. Ibid., 91 (emphasis mine). It's not clear to me that de Unamuno is representing monism correctly, but his basic point stands: trying to console people that they will live on as particles and/or as this united whole, as monism teaches, is no consolation in the face of death.

149. Alex Lickerman, "Overcoming the Fear of Death: A Physician Confronts His Own Mortality," *Psychology Today*, October 8, 2009, https://www.psychologytoday.com/blog/happiness-in -world/200910/overcoming-the-fear-death (accessed July 18, 2017).

150. Alex Lickerman, *The Undefeated Mind: On the Science of Constructing an Indestructible Self* (Deerfield Beach, FL: HCI, 2012), 229.

151. "Sam Harris: Death and the Present Moment," YouTube video uploaded by Atheist Foundation of Australia Inc., June 2, 2012, https://www.youtube.com/watch?v=ITTxTCz4Ums (accessed June 29, 2018).

152. "Sam Harris: Death and the Present Moment." Repeated words, "ums," and "uhs" removed.

153. Yalom, *Staring at the Sun*, vii.

154. Bauman, *Mortality*, 13 (emphasis original).

155. Stark, *Consolations of Mortality*, 203.

156. Ferry, *Brief History of Thought*, 261 (emphasis mine).

157. Ibid., 264 (emphasis mine).

158. Alfred Ernest Garvie, "Immortality," in *The Encyclopedia Britannica: Dictionary of Arts, Sciences, Literature and General Information*, 11th ed., vol. 13 (New York: Encyclopedia Britannica, 1910), 339. *Britannica* references *Natural Religion*, a Postscript. I have not been able to find a direct quote of this in Emerson's works.

159. Cave, *Immortality*, 259.

160. Woody Allen, *Side Effects* (New York: Ballantine, 1980), 53–54.

161. Doubtless, some diehard atheists will object, but because of what Scripture teaches about the fear of death, I choose to doubt them. By the way, this is one reason I said in the preface that this book is written for Christians. I don't need to establish the veracity of biblical truth.

Chapter 5

1. Jean M. Twenge et al., "Declines in American Adults' Religious Participation and Beliefs, 1972–2014," *SAGE Open* 6, no. 1 (March 23, 2016), https://journals.sagepub.com/doi/10.1177/2158244016638133 (accessed February 5, 2019).

2. The authors list two studies in support of this entitlement explanation: W.K. Campbell et al., "Psychological Entitlement: Interpersonal Consequences and Validation of a New Self-Report Measure," *Journal of Personality Assessment* 83 (2004): 29–45; and J.M. Twenge and J.D. Foster, "Birth Cohort Increases in Narcissistic Personality Traits Among American College Students, 1982–2009," *Social Psychological & Personality Science* 1 (2010): 99–106.

3. Zygmunt Bauman, *Mortality, Immortality, and Other Life Strategies* (Stanford: Stanford University Press, 1992), 15.

4. Glenn Whipp, "For Julia Louis-Dreyfus, returning to 'Veep' after cancer was salvation," *The Los Angeles Times*, August 14, 2019, The Envelope, S12, https://www.latimes.com/entertainment-arts/awards/story/2019-08-12/julia-louis-dreyfus-veep-emmys-seinfeld-cancer, (accessed August 23, 2019).

5. Ibid., S14.

6. John Rennie, "The Immortal Ambitions of Ray Kurzweil: A Review of Transcendent Man," *Scientific American*, February 15, 2011, https://www.scientificamerican.com/article/the-immortal-ambitions-of-ray-kurzweil/ (accessed June 6, 2018).

7. Robert Lanza, "Is Death an Illusion? Evidence Suggests Death Isn't the End," *Psychology Today*, November 19, 2011, https://www.psychologytoday.com/blog/biocentrism/201111/is-death-illusion-evidence-suggests-death-isn-t-the-end (accessed September 6, 2017).

8. Jonathan Clements, *The First Emperor* (Stroud, UK: Sutton, 2006), 137.

9. Similarly, Fyodor Dostoyevsky challenges, "Try to pose for yourself this task: not to think of a polar bear, and you will see that cursed thing will come to mind every minute." Dostoevsky, *Winter Notes on Summer Impressions*, trans. David Patterson (Evanston, IL: Northwestern University Press, 1988), 49.

10. Ernest Becker says that when the awareness of death can be "blotted out by frenetic, ready-made activity." Becker, *The Denial of Death* (New York: Free Press, 1973), 23.

11. Ibid., 178.

12. Bertrand Russell, *Portraits of Memory: And Other Essays* (1951; repr., New York: Simon & Schuster, 1963), 51 (emphasis mine).

13. Horace, "Ode XI," in *The Complete Odes and Satires of Horace*, trans. Sidney Alexander (Princeton: Princeton University Press, 1999), 18 (emphasis mine).

14. N.K. Sandars, trans., *The Epic of Gilgamesh* (New York: Penguin, 1972), 43.

15. Horace, *Odes*, bk. 3, *Exegi monumentum*, XXX.1–2, 6–8, in *The Complete Odes and Epodes*, trans. David West (Oxford: Oxford University Press, 1997), 108.

16. Google definition (accessed January 12, 2019).

17. Marisa Guthrie, "3 Days on the Job (and at Home) with Anderson Cooper: 'I Don't Really Have a Life Off-Air,'" *Hollywood Reporter*, September 13, 2018, https://www.hollywoodreporter .com/features/anderson-cooper-3-days-life-busiest-man-tv-news-1141663 (accessed September 26, 2018).

18. Leo Tolstoy, *The Death of Ivan Ilyich and Other Stories*, trans. Richard Pevear and Larissa Volokhonsky (New York: Alfred A. Knopf, 2009), 71–72.

19. *Merriam-Webster*, s.v. "amuse," https://www.merriam-webster.com/dictionary/amuse (accessed January 12, 2019).

20. Steve Fisher, "'Captain Marvel," *Costco Connection*, August 2018, 41.

21. Mike Snider, "Television Is Still the Most Dominant Media, but More Young Adults Are Connecting via Internet," *USA Today*, December 12, 2018, https://www.usatoday.com/story/ money/media/2018/12/12/cutting-cord-2018-tv-dominates-but-younger-users-connect-via-web /2276207002/ (accessed January 12, 2019).

22. "Laura Branigan at VH1 'Where Are They Now?'—October 4, 2002," YouTube video uploaded by Fabio Soares, September 3, 2009, https://www.youtube.com/watch?v=76WR0-tVl5c (accessed February 1, 2018); Associated Press, "Correction: Laura Branigan Obituary," *Washington Times*, December 16, 2016, https://www.washingtontimes.com/news/2016/dec/16/correction-laura -branigan-obituary/ (accessed February 1, 2018).

23. Tolstoy, *Death of Ivan Ilyich*, 70.

24. The Lord tells Judah in Isaiah 22 that their destruction for their sin was coming and that this "called for weeping and mourning, for baldness and wearing sackcloth" (verse 12), but what the Lord found instead was that Judah was saying, "Let us eat and drink, for tomorrow we die" (verse 13). So in verse 14 we read, "The Lord of hosts has revealed himself in my ears: 'Surely this iniquity will not be atoned for you until you die.' says the Lord GOD of hosts."

25. Duane A. Garrett, *Proverbs, Ecclesiastes, Song of Songs*, New American Commentary 14, ed. E. Ray Clendenen (Nashville: B&H, 1993), Wordsearch e-book (emphasis original).

26. Irvin D. Yalom, *Staring at the Sun: Overcoming the Terror of Death* (San Francisco: Wiley, 2008), 5–6.

27. See Marina Milyavskaya et al., "Fear of Missing Out: Prevalence, Dynamics, and Consequences of Experiencing FOMO," *Motivation and Emotion* 42, no. 5 (October 2018): 725–37, https:// link-springer-com.ezproxy.biola.edu/article/10.1007/s11031-018-9683-5 (accessed December 26, 2018).

28. "Is There Meaning to Life? William Lane Craig, Rebecca Goldstein, Jordan Peterson— Toronto2018," YouTube video uploaded by ReasonableFaithOrg, February 12, 2018, https:// www.youtube.com/watch?v=xV4oIqnaxlg (accessed August 1, 2018).

29. Jordan Peterson has said, "I think the only way to combat fear of death is to live fully." See "Jordan Peterson: Don't Fear Death Fear This," YouTube video uploaded by Dose of Truth, November 30, 2017, https://www.youtube.com/watch?v=agkoQaw7uo4 (accessed January 21, 2019).

30. William James, *The Varieties of Religious Experience: Being the Gifford Lectures on Natural Religion Delivered at Edinburg in 1901–1902* (New York: Longmans, Green, 1903), 139–41.

31. Ibid., 140.

32. Most translations of verse 13 insert the word "may" as is found in the NASB: "Even in laughter the heart *may* be in pain, And the end of joy *may* be grief." But "may" isn't in the original.

33. Bertrand Russell, "The Free Man's Worship," *Russell: The Basic Writings of Bertrand Russell*, Robert E. Egner and Lester E. Denonn, eds. (New York: Routledge Classics, 2009), 39.

34. Ibid., 44.

35. Ann Druyan, "Epilogue," in Carl Sagan, *Billions and Billions: Thoughts on Life and Death at the Brink of the Millennium* (New York: Ballantine, 1997), 271.

36. Sheldon Solomon, Jeff Greenberg, and Tom Pyszczynski, "Tales from the Crypt: On the Role of Death in Life," *Zygon* 33, no. 1 (March 1998): 12, http://plaza.ufl.edu/phallman/terror%20 management%20theory/312997.pdf (accessed September 15, 2017).

37. Becker, *Denial of Death*, 178.

38. Ibid., 179.

39. Ibid., 217.

40. James, *Varieties of Religious Experience*, 164 (emphasis mine).

41. Becker, *Denial of Death*, 209.

42. Irvin D. Yalom, *Existential Psychotherapy* (New York: Basic Books, 1980), 59.

43. Yalom, *Staring at the Sun*, 9.

44. Yalom, *Existential Psychotherapy*, 56.

45. Becker, *Denial of Death*, 23.

46. Yalom, *Existential Psychotherapy*, 147.

47. Harold Searles, "Schizophrenia and the Inevitability of Death," *Psychiatry Quarterly* 35 (1961): 631–55, as quoted in Yalom, *Existential Psychotherapy*, 148.

48. Searles, "Schizophrenia" (emphasis original).

49. Ibid., 150–51.

50. Sheldon Solomon, Jeff Greenberg, and Tom Pyszczynski, *The Worm at the Core: On the Role of Death in Life* (New York: Random House, 2015), 191.

51. Yalom, *Existential Psychotherapy*, 152.

52. Karel Planansky and Roy Johnston, "Preoccupation with Death in Schizophrenic Men," *Diseases of the Nervous System* 38, no. 3 (March 1977): 194–97, PubMed.gov, https://www.ncbi.nlm.nih .gov/pubmed/837823 (accessed January 8, 2019). The authors continue, "These expressions of fear appeared either at the clinical onset of the psychosis, or during exacerbations, and often coincided with schizophrenic panic. The similarity of expressions of the fear among the patients was striking, and they were practically identical from one exacerbation to the next."

53. Tsachi Ein-Dor et al., "Implicit Death Primes Increase Alcohol Consumption," *Health Psychology* 33, no. 7 (2013): 748–51.

54. Joe Klein, "It's High Time," *Time*, April 16, 2009, 19.

55. Alex Rosenberg, *The Atheist's Guide to Reality: Enjoying Life Without Illusions* (New York: W.W. Norton, 2011), 315. A serotonin reuptake inhibitor is a category of antidepressants, of which Prozac is one.

56. "Suicide Rates Rising Across the U.S.," Centers for Disease Control, June 7, 2018, https://www .cdc.gov/media/releases/2018/p0607-suicide-prevention.html (accessed September 4, 2018).

57. Yalom, *Existential Psychotherapy*, 122.

58. It's noteworthy that some surveys show an increase in the belief of an afterlife, but unless one has confidence in an afterlife, a vague notion of an afterlife isn't going to relieve the fear of death.

59. Fyodor Dostoyevsky, *The Possessed*, trans. David Magarshack (1954; repr., New York: Penguin, 1971), 376.

60. Tennyson said that if immortality be not true, then "I'd sink my head to-night in a chloroformed handkerchief, and be done with it all." W.J. Dawson, "Echoes from the Study," in *The Young Man: A Monthly Journal and Review* (London: Partridge, 1894), 26.

61. Miguel de Unamuno, *Tragic Sense of Life*, trans. J.E. Crawford Flitch (New York: Dover, 1954), 150.

62. Lucretius, *On the Nature of Things* III.79–81, as translated in Martha C. Nussbaum, *The Therapy of Desire: Theory and Practice in Hellenistic Ethics* (Princeton: Princeton University Press, 1994), 197.

63. Although many modern scholars contend that Jerome made this up as part of a Christian polemic, historian of philosophy Giovanni Reale (1931–2014) argues that Lucretius did commit suicide. Reale, *The Systems of the Hellenistic Age: A History of Ancient Philosophy*, ed. and trans. John R. Catan (Albany, NY: SUNY Press, 1985), 414. D.B. Gain gives the following analysis, "It has been hotly denied that Lucretius was driven insane by a love potion and committed suicide. It is the aim of the present article to show that the main arguments used by those who deny Jerome's story are not valid and that hence the story is more probable than is now generally believed. In writing his biographical sketches of other classical authors, Jerome had access to pagan authorities. Now these same authorities must have treated the life of Lucretius. Thus, Jerome's account of the insanity and suicide of Lucretius cannot be a mere tendentious Christian story, for Jerome was too good a scholar and too honest to record as fact what he would have known, from its absence from pagan authorities he had access to, to be false." Gain, "The Life and Death of Lucretius," *Latomus* 28, no. 3 (1969): 545, http://www.jstor.org/stable/41527500 (accessed October 14, 2018).

64. Staks Rosch, "Atheism Has a Suicide Problem," *Huffington Post*, December 8, 2017, https://www.huffingtonpost.com/entry/atheism-has-a-suicide-problem_us_5a2a902ee4b022ec613b812b (accessed May 21, 2018).

65. Kanita Dervic et al., "Religious Affiliation and Suicide Attempt," *American Journal of Psychiatry* 161, no. 12 (December 2004): 2303–8, https://ajp.psychiatryonline.org/doi/full/10.1176/appi.ajp.161.12.2303 (accessed May 21, 2018). Similarly, Andrew Wu, Jing-Yu Wang, and Cun-Xian Jia conclude, "Religion plays a protective role against suicide in a majority of settings where suicide research is conducted." Wu, Wang, and Jia, "Religion and Completed Suicide: A Meta-analysis," *Plos One*, June 25, 2015, https://journals.plos.org/plosone/article?id=10.1371/journal.pone.0131715 (accessed September 3, 2018).

66. Jeffrey M. Jones, "U.S. Church Membership Down Sharply in Past Two Decades," *Gallup*, April 18, 2019, https://news.gallup.com/poll/248837/church-membership-down-sharply-past-two-decades.aspx, (accessed April 29, 2019).

67. I write "robust belief" because according to one study, even though Americans are less likely to believe in God, belief in an afterlife has actually increased: "Previous research found declines in Americans' religious affiliation but few changes in religious beliefs and practices. By 2014, however, markedly fewer Americans participated in religious activities or embraced religious beliefs, with especially striking declines between 2006 and 2014 and among 18- to 29-year-olds in data from the nationally representative General Social Survey (N = 58,893, 1972–2014). In recent years, fewer Americans prayed, believed in God, took the Bible literally, attended religious services, identified as religious, affiliated with a religion, or had confidence in religious institutions. Only slightly more identified as spiritual since 1998, and then only those above age 30. Nearly a third of Millennials were secular not merely in religious affiliation but also in belief in God, religiosity, and religious service attendance, many more than Boomers and Generation X'ers at the same age. Eight times more 18- to 29-year-olds never prayed in 2014 versus the early 1980s. However, Americans have become slightly more likely to believe in an afterlife." Jean M.

Twenge, Ryne A. Sherman, Julie J. Exline, Joshua B. Grubbs, "Declines in American Adults' Religious Participation and Beliefs, 1972-2014," *Sage Journals*, vol. 6, no. 1, March 23, 2016, https://journals.sagepub.com/doi/full/10.1177/2158244016638133, (accessed April 29, 2019).

68. For more on the Canaanites and the degeneration of American culture, see Clay Jones, "We Don't Hate Sin So We Don't Understand What Happened to the Canaanites: An Addendum to Divine Genocide Arguments," *Philosophia Christi* 11, no. 1 (2009): 53–72, http://www.clayjones.net/wp-content/uploads/2011/06/We-Dont-Hate-Sin-PC-article.pdf. (accessed June 1, 2019).

69. John Kost, *Human Destiny* (Lansing, MI: Robert Smith, 1903), 263–64.

70. William McDougall, *Body and Mind: A History and Defense of Animism* (Charleston, SC: BiblioLife, 2009), xiii.

71. Fyodor Dostoyevsky, *The Brothers Karamazov* (New York: Farrar, Straus and Giroux, 2002), 649.

72. François-René de Chateaubriand, *The Genius of Christianity: Or the Spirit and Beauty of the Christian Religion* (Baltimore: John Murphy, 1856), 190.

73. Jean Baptiste Massillon, "Immortality," *Wilmington Journal*, May 28, 1852, Library of Congress, https://chroniclingamerica.loc.gov/lccn/sn84026536/1852-05-28/ed-1/seq-1/ (accessed December 25, 2018).

74. "'Men Have Forgotten God': Aleksandr Solzhenitsyn's 1983 Templeton Address," *National Review*, December 11, 2018, https://www.nationalreview.com/2018/12/aleksandr-solzhenitsyn-men-have-forgotten-god-speech/ (accessed December 27, 2018).

75. This is my best recollection of the joke.

76. Bertrand Russell, "The Free Man's Worship," in *Russell: The Basic Writings of Bertrand Russell*, eds. Robert E. Egner and Lester E. Denonn (New York: Routledge Classics, 2009), 39. Originally printed in the *Independent Review* (December 1903) and subsequently reprinted in *Mysticism and Logic* (London: Allen & Unwin, 1917; New York: Simon & Schuster, 1929), 39. The title of the essay changed after 1910 to "A Free Man's Worship," https://users.drew.edu/jlenz/br-free-mans-worship.html (accessed January 21, 2018).

77. Bauman, *Mortality*, 161.

78. Jon Bon Jovi Chart History, *Billboard*, https://www.billboard.com/music/Jon-Bon-Jovi/chart-history/hot-100. *Australian-Charts.com*, https://australian-charts.com/showitem.asp?interpret=Jon+Bon+Jovi&titel=Blaze+of+Glory&cat=s (accessed June 1, 2019).

79. "Bonnie and Clyde," Weebly, n.d., https://theballadofbonnieandclyde.weebly.com/felons-or-folk-heroes.html (accessed September 11, 2018; emphasis mine).

80. Alex Distefano, "The 13 Most Satanic Metal Bands," *LA Weekly*, October 30, 2017, https://www.laweekly.com/music/13-most-satanic-metal-bands-8798306 (accessed September 4, 2018). For a funny poem that ridicules the heavy metal genre, see Mike Boehm, "O.C.'s Lixx Array: A Metal Band That Plays Nice," *Los Angeles Times*, June 20, 1992, http://articles.latimes.com/1992-06-20/entertainment/ca-489_1_lixx-array (accessed September 11, 2018).

81. Kory Grow, "The Golden Age of Grotesque: Marilyn Manson's Most Shocking Moments," *Rolling Stone*, January 6, 2015, https://www.rollingstone.com/music/music-lists/the-golden-age-of-grotesque-marilyn-mansons-most-shocking-moments-155971/ (accessed September 5, 2018).

82. Ed Husain, "Bin Laden as 'Martyr': A Call to Jihadists," CNN, May 4, 2011, http://www.cnn.com/2011/OPINION/05/02/husain.bin.laden/index.html (accessed September 5, 2018).

83. Now, as I said, I don't know whether this would happen, but remember, there are only two possibilities—this kind of thing will happen or this kind of thing won't happen. Those who say it won't happen are speculating every bit as much as those who say it will.

84. Annihilationists will point out that a few have said that eternal punishment doesn't scare them as much as annihilation, and so if the church taught annihilationism, then that would be more motivating to some to turn to Jesus than the thought of eternal punishment. One example of a person who thinks annihilation would be worse than eternal punishment is novelist and

philosopher Miguel de Unamuno: "And I must confess, painful though the confession be, that in the days of the simple faith of my childhood, descriptions of the tortures of hell, however terrible, never made me tremble, for I always felt that nothingness was much more terrifying. He who suffers lives, and he who lives suffering, even though over the portal of his abode is written 'Abandon all hope!' loves and hopes. It is better to live in pain than to cease to be in peace. The truth is that I could not believe in this atrocity of Hell, of an eternity of punishment, nor did I see any more real hell than nothingness and the prospect of it. And I continue in the belief that if we all believed in our salvation from nothingness we should all be better." De Unamuno, *Tragic Sense of Life*, 87–88. But among atheists, as we have seen, de Unamuno is in the tiny minority. There's another point to be made about this that counts against the annihilationists' point: if the wicked would prefer to be eternally punished rather than annihilated, and since they won't be fit to be in the kingdom of God, then away from God is the only place for which they are fit. In other words, there's a sense that hell forever is giving them what they desire.

85. Bart D. Ehrman, *God's Problem: How the Bible Fails to Answer Our Most Important Question— Why We Suffer* (New York: HarperCollins, 2008), 127.

Chapter 6

1. Stephen Cave, *Immortality: The Quest to Live Forever and How It Drives Civilization* (New York: Crown, 2012), 100.

2. "Sam Harris: Death and the Present Moment," YouTube video uploaded by Atheist Foundation of Australia Inc., June 2, 2012, https://www.youtube.com/watch?v=ITTxTCz4Ums (accessed June 29, 2018).

3. Luc Ferry, *A Brief History of Thought: A Philosophical Guide to Living*, trans. Theo Cuffe (New York: Harper, 2010), 51–52.

4. Ibid., 90 (emphasis mine).

5. Ibid., 91.

6. Ibid., 159–60 (emphasis original).

7. Ibid. (emphasis original).

8. Karen Armstrong writes, "From the very earliest times, men and women devised religions to help them cultivate a sense that our existence has some ultimate meaning and value, despite the dispiriting evidence to the contrary." Armstrong, *Buddha* (New York: Penguin, 2004), 4.

9. Richard Dawkins, *The Blind Watchmaker: Why the Evidence of Evolution Reveals a Universe Without Design* (New York: W.W. Norton, 1996), 139, 145–46.

10. Richard Dawkins, *The God Delusion* (Boston: Houghton Mifflin, 2008), 142.

11. Ibid., 138.

12. Francis Crick, *Life Itself: Its Origin and Nature* (New York: Simon & Schuster, 1981), 51–52.

13. Clay Jones and Joseph E. Gorra, "The Folly of Answering Distracting Atheistic Arguments," *Christian Research Journal* 36, no. 4 (2013), http://www.equip.org/article/folly-answering -distracting-atheistic-arguments/ (accessed October 20, 2018).

14. J.L. Schellenberg, in his book *Divine Hiddenness and Human Reason* (Ithaca, NY: Cornell University Press, 2006), argues that "surely a morally perfect being—good, just, loving—would show himself more clearly. Hence the weakness of our evidence for God is not a sign that God is hidden; it is a revelation that God does not exist" (1). He goes on to claim that "the most obvious indication that it is not [logical to believe in God] is that inculpable—or as I prefer to term it, *reasonable*—nonbelief actually occurs" (3–4). Just to be clear, by "inculpable," Schellenberg means that there is no moral failing on the part of those who reject God, so their rejection of God is logically justifiable. Well, that's what the rich man implied in Hades—that he wasn't given enough evidence (Luke 16:19-31).

15. Here are just three suggestions: William Lane Craig, *Reasonable Faith: Christian Truth and*

Apologetics (Wheaton, IL: Crossway, 1994); Antony Flew, *There Is a God: How the World's Most Notorious Atheist Changed His Mind* (New York: HarperOne, 2007); Josh McDowell and Sean McDowell, *Evidence That Demands a Verdict: Life-Changing Truth for a Skeptical World* (Nashville: Thomas Nelson, 2017).

16. Bruce M. Metzger and Bart D. Ehrman, *The Text of the New Testament: Its Transmission, Corruption, and Restoration*, 4th ed. (New York: Oxford University Press, 2005), 51.

17. Clay Jones, "The Bibliographical Test Updated," *Christian Research Journal* 35, no. 3 (2012), https://www.equip.org/article/the-bibliographical-test-updated/, (accessed June 1, 2019). For much more, see Craig L. Blomberg, *The Historical Reliability of the Gospels* (Downers Grove, IL: IVP, 2014).

18. John Dominic Crossan, *Jesus: A Revolutionary Biography* (San Francisco: HarperCollins, 1987), 179.

19. Gerd Lüdemann, *What Really Happened to Jesus? An Historical Approach to the Resurrection*, trans. John Bowden (Louisville: Westminster John Knox, 1995), 8 (emphasis mine).

20. Gerd Lüdemann, *Resurrection of Jesus: History, Experience, Theology* (Philadelphia: Fortress Press, 1995), 39 (emphasis mine).

21. John Dominic Crossan, *The Historical Jesus: The Life of a Mediterranean Jewish Peasant* (New York: HarperCollins, 1991), 372.

22. Shlomo Pines, *An Arabic Version of the* Testimonium Flavianum *and Its Implications* (Jerusalem: Israel Academy of Sciences and Humanities, 1971), 9–10.

23. For a positive discussion of the *Testimonium* from a skeptic, see James Tabor, "The Ancient Jewish Historian Josephus on John the Baptizer, Jesus, and James," *TaborBlog* (blog), February 1, 2017, https://jamestabor.com/the-ancient-jewish-historian-josephus-on-john-the-baptizer-jesus-and -james/ (accessed October 22, 2018). Here's the Western version of the *Testimonium* with the text that Tabor argues was obviously interpolated in strikethroughs: "Now there was about this time Jesus, a wise man ~~if it be lawful to call him a man,~~ for he was a doer of wonders, ~~a teacher of such men as receive the truth with pleasure.~~ He drew many after him both of the Jews and the Gentiles. ~~He was the Christ.~~ When Pilate, at the suggestion of the principal men among us, had condemned him to the cross, those that loved him at the first did not forsake him, ~~for he appeared to them alive again the third day, as the divine prophets had foretold these and ten thousand other wonderful things about him,~~ and the tribe of Christians, so named from him, are not extinct at this day" (*Antiquities* 18:63–64). After Tabor quotes this Western version, he writes regarding the Arabic version of the *Testimonium*, "It has obviously not been interpolated in the same way as the Christian version circulating in the West and it reads remarkably close to our 'non-interpolated' version above." I could quote many other skeptics who also agree that much of the *Testimonium* is original, but again, that would be outside the scope of this book.

24. Tacitus, *Annals*, Internet Classics Archive, MIT, http://classics.mit.edu/Tacitus/annals.11.xv.html (accessed October 22, 2018).

25. William D. Edwards, Wesley J. Gabel, and Floyd E. Hosmer, "On the Physical Death of Jesus Christ," *Journal of the American Medical Association* 255, no. 11 (March 21, 1986): 1455.

26. J.D.G. Dunn, *Jesus Remembered* (Grand Rapids, MI: Eerdmans, 2003), 782.

27. Raymond E. Brown, *The Death of the Messiah: From Gethsemane to the Grave*, vol. 2 (New York: Doubleday, 1994), 1240.

28. Jeffery Jay Lowder, "Historical Evidence and the Empty Tomb Story: A Reply to William Lane Craig," in *The Empty Tomb: Jesus Beyond the Grave*, eds. Robert M. Price and Jeffery Jay Lowder (Amherst, NY: Prometheus, 2005), 265–66.

29. Requested Ehrman's lectures through ILL.

30. Josephus, *Antiquities of the Jews*, trans. William Whiston, Christian Classics Ethereal Library,

http://www.ccel.org/ccel/josephus/works/files/ant-4.htm, 4.8.15, (accessed October 24, 2018). Many other examples could be cited.

31. For a discussion of the criterion of embarrassment, see John P. Meier, *A Marginal Jew: Rethinking the Historical Jesus*, vol. 1 (New York: Doubleday, 1991), 168–71.

32. Justin Martyr, "Dialog with Trypho," in *Ante-Nicene Christian Library: Translations of the Writings of the Fathers*, vol. 2, *Justin Martyr and Athenagoras*, trans. Marcus Dods, George Reith, and B.P. Pratten, eds. Alexander Roberts and James Donaldson (Edinburg: T&T Clark, 1879), 235.

33. Now, skeptics offer various explanations for the empty tomb: Jesus's body was moved (it was initially placed in Joseph's tomb, but then Joseph reburied it later), Jesus was never buried in Joseph's tomb in the first place (we don't know what happened to His body), the disciples went to the wrong tomb (they forgot where Jesus was buried), Jesus didn't actually die on the cross (later he left the tomb on his own), and so on. None of these withstands scrutiny, and many books answer them in detail. For example, see Gary R. Habermas and Michael R. Licona, *The Case for the Resurrection of Jesus* (Grand Rapids, MI: Kregel, 2004).

34. Crossan, *Historical Jesus*, 427.

35. Lüdemann, *Resurrection of Jesus*, 38. For more on the earliness of this creed, see Habermas and Licona, *Case for the Resurrection*, 260n25.

36. Michael Goulder, "The Baseless Fabric of a Vision," in *Resurrection Reconsidered*, ed. Gavin D'Costa (Oxford: Oneworld, 1996), 48. Similarly, J.D.G. Dunn writes, "This tradition, we can be entirely confident, was *formulated as tradition within months of Jesus' death*." Dunn, *Jesus Remembered*, 855.

37. Michael Martin, *The Case Against Christianity* (Philadelphia: Temple University Press, 1991), 90.

38. Bart D. Ehrman, *Jesus: Apocalyptic Prophet of the New Millennium* (Oxford: Oxford University Press, 2001), 231 (emphasis mine).

39. Lüdemann, *What Really Happened to Jesus?*, 26.

40. Ibid., 80, 81.

41. Keith Parsons, "Peter Kreeft and Ronald Tacelli on the Hallucination Theory," in *Empty Tomb*, eds. Price and Lowder, 433–34.

42. Ibid.

43. Richard C. Carrier, "The Spiritual Body of Christ," in *Empty Tomb*, ed. Price and Lowder, 184 (emphasis original).

44. I write "presently employs" because throughout the ages, skeptics have appealed to a number of different explanations. For example, Hugh J. Schonfield (1901–88) popularized the swoon theory in his book *The Passover Plot* (New York: Bantam, 1965), where he argues that Jesus didn't die on the cross but only passed out or swooned and then revived in the cool of the tomb, and his disciples mistook this for actual resurrection. But few employ this today because of arguments like that of German theologian and hallucination theory popularizer David Friedrich Strauss (1808–74). In response to the swoon theory, Strauss writes, "It is impossible that a being who had stolen half-dead out of the sepulcher, who crept about weak and ill, wanting medical treatment, who required bandaging, strengthening and indulgence, and who still at last yielded to his sufferings, could have given to the disciples the impression that he was a Conqueror of death and the grave, the Prince of Life, an impression which lay at the bottom of their future ministry." Strauss, *The Life of Jesus for the People*, vol. 1, 2nd ed. (London: Williams and Norgate, 1879), 412. Strauss continues, "Such a resuscitation could only have weakened the impression which He had made upon them in life and in death, at the most could only have given it an elegiac voice, but could by no possibility have changed their sorrow into enthusiasm, have elevated their reverence into worship."

45. Gary Habermas, *Did Jesus Rise from the Dead?* (San Francisco: Harper and Row, 1987), 50.

46. This analogy was inspired by Habermas and Licona, *Case for the Resurrection*, 106.

47. Gary A. Sibcy, quoted in Michael R. Licona, *The Resurrection of Jesus: A New Historiographical Approach* (Downers Grove, IL: Intervarsity, 2010), 484. Licona notes that Sibcy ceased his review in 2004. Although he argues that Jesus's resurrection appearances could *not* be explained as hallucinatory experiences, Jake O'Connell argues that "there actually are well-documented cases of group religious visions which possess characteristics indicating that these visions are very likely hallucinatory." O'Connell, "Jesus' Resurrection and Collective Hallucinations," *Tyndale Bulletin* 60, no. 1 (January 1, 2009): 71. O'Connell defines a "collective hallucination" as one "shared by two or more people. This does not necessarily mean that the two people are experiencing precisely the same hallucination" (72). Licona writes, however, that Sibcy "is not speaking of group hallucinations as described by O'Connell, which are rare but not at all impossible. For Sibcy, members of a group cannot experience the same hallucination simultaneously as though participating in the same one" (Licona, *Resurrection of Jesus*, 485n64). Indeed, that different disciples claimed to have had various conversations with Jesus, touched Jesus, ate with Jesus, and so on, while others were present who could have refuted their claims renders the hallucination explanation impossible. It's entirely possible that Jean E. and I could both dream on the same night at the same time of night about being in Barbados, but when we awoke we would not believe that we were actually experiencing Barbados *together*. There are no examples of group hallucinations like that, and the examples O'Connell cites do not contradict that. O'Connell himself gives a number of reasons the disciples' testimony to having seen the risen Jesus could *not* be explained by hallucination, but it's outside the scope of this book to discuss them.

48. John Warwick Montgomery, *Human Rights and Human Dignity* (Grand Rapids, MI: Zondervan, 1986), 149.

49. John Stott, *Basic Christianity* (Downers Grove, IL: IVP, 2008), 76–77.

50. Gary Habermas, "Explaining Away Jesus' Resurrection: The Recent Revival of Hallucination Theories," *Christian Research Journal* 23, no. 4 (2001), https://digitalcommons.liberty.edu/cgi/viewcontent.cgi?article=1106&context=lts_fac_pubs (accessed October 29, 2011).

51. Tertullian, *Scorpiace* XV, Christian Classics Ethereal Library, n.d., http://www.ccel.org/ccel/schaff/anf03.v.x.xv.html (accessed January 2011; emphasis mine). Also, regarding Peter Ignatius of Antioch (ca. 35–108), who himself was sentenced to be killed by lions in the arena, Ignatius writes, "For I know and believe that He was in the flesh even after the resurrection. And when He came to Peter and those who were with him, He said to them, 'Take, handle me and see that I am not a spirit without body.' And straightway they touched Him and believed, being united with His flesh and spirit. Therefore also they despised death, and were found to rise above death." Ignatius, *The Epistle to the Smyrneans,* Early Christian Writings, n.d., http://www.earlychristian writings.com/srawley/smyrnaeans.html (accessed January 2011). It is true that these comments by Ignatius don't specifically say they were killed for their faith, but at the very least, it says they were willing to die for their faith.

52. Sean McDowell concludes in his examination of the documents regarding the martyrdom of Peter that Peter's martyrdom has "*The Highest Possible Probability*." McDowell, *The Fate of the Apostles: Examining the Martyrdom Accounts of the Closest Followers of Jesus* (New York: Routledge, 2016), 91 (emphasis original).

53. Eusebius, *History of the Christian Church* 2.XXV.5, Christian Classics Ethereal Library, n.d., http://www.ccel.org/ccel/schaff/npnf201.iii.vii.xxvi.html (accessed January 2011).

54. Flavius Josephus, *Jewish Antiquities* XX.8.1, in *The New Complete Works of Josephus*, trans. William Whiston (Grand Rapids, MI: Kregel, 1999), 656.

55. Lucian, *The Death of Peregrine*, Sacred Texts, n.d., http://www.sacred-texts.com/cla/luc/wl4/wl420.htm (accessed October 27, 2018).

56. W.E.H. Lecky, *History of European Morals: From Augustus to Charlemagne*, vol. 1 (New York: George Braziller, 1950), 467.

Chapter 7

1. I'm including here not wanting to leave others because they will miss your company.
2. I realize there isn't marriage in heaven, but that doesn't mean Jean E. and I won't remember our love on earth and all the things we did together!
3. See the camp's website, http://www.lifeonthehill.org/.
4. C.S. Lewis, *Mere Christianity* (New York: HarperOne, 1952), 134.
5. Of course, by "lust," I mean "strong desire" ("lust" doesn't always have a negative use in English), and that's what it really means in the NT. For example, when Jesus warns about looking at a woman lustfully (*epithumeo*), He uses the same Greek word as Paul does in Galatians 5:17: "For the desires [*epithumeo*] of the flesh are against the Spirit, and the desires [*epithumeo*] of the Spirit are against the flesh."
6. Padraic Colum, *The Golden Fleece: And the Heroes Who Lived Before Achilles* (Mineola, NY: Dover, 2018), 120.
7. Homer, *The Odyssey*, trans. Emily Wilson (New York: W.W. Norton, 2018), 302.
8. Ibid., 307.
9. Colum, *Golden Fleece*, 120.
10. Ibid., 16.
11. Ibid., 121. The story also tells that "only one of the Argonauts, Butes, a youth of Iolcus, threw himself into the water and swam toward the rocks from which the Sirens sang."
12. Ibid.
13. Richard R. Melick Jr., *Philippians, Colossians, Philemon*, New American Commentary 32 (Nashville: B&H, 1991), Wordsearch e-book.

Chapter 8

1. For paradise being a designation for heaven, see 2 Corinthians 12:2-3; Revelation 2:7.
2. I originally heard Dallas Willard say that it may take you a while to realize that you've died when I took a spiritual formation doctoral course from him. When I teach the course "In Defense of the Resurrection" at Talbot Seminary, I discuss near-death experiences (NDEs). NDEs are those experiences that people report after their hearts have flat-lined on an operating table or they have experienced being near death in another setting. As probably everyone reading this already knows, tens of thousands of people have reported that suddenly, they had an out-of-body experience where they felt serene, secure, and warm and sensed the presence of a light. Now, I tell my students that we should be wary of these testimonies because there's a difference between "near-dead" and "dead-dead," where you don't come back. After all, Hebrews 9:27 tells us, "It is appointed for man to die once, and after that comes judgment." Since none of these people experienced being "dead-dead," we shouldn't use NDEs to tell us much, if anything, about an afterlife. However, there is one thing we can conclude from these experiences, which is that one can be clinically dead and still be conscious. That seems clear.
3. Allan W. Gomes, *40 Questions About Heaven and Hell*, ed. Benjamin L. Merkle (Grand Rapids, MI: Kregel, 2018), 91.
4. Douglas J. Moo, *The Epistle to the Romans*, New International Commentary on the New Testament (Grand Rapids, MI: Eerdmans, 1996), 296 (emphasis mine).
5. Martyn Lloyd-Jones, *Romans: An Exposition of Chapter 5, Assurance* (Grand Rapids, MI: Zondervan, 1971), 49.
6. Google definition of "glorious" https://www.google.com/search?rlz=1C1GCEV_en&ei=cu_yXP2dCYa6tgX68JWgDw&q=define+glorious&oq=define+glorious&gs_l=psy-ab.3..0l4j0i7i10i30j0i7i30l2j0i30l3.14840.17459..17864...2.0..1.323.1776.0j10j0j1......0....1..gws-wiz.......0i71j0i131j0i13.tyRZNaRoyeA (accessed November 5, 2018).

7. Some of this paragraph is adapted from my book *Why Does God Allow Evil? Compelling Answers to Life's Toughest Questions* (Eugene, OR: Harvest House, 2017), 167, 168.

8. Brad Silberling, dir., *City of Angels* (Los Angeles: Warner Bros., 1998). *City of Angels* is basically a justification for what some commentators believe is exactly what happens in Genesis 6:1-4: "When man began to multiply on the face of the land and daughters were born to them, the sons of God saw that the daughters of man were attractive. And they took as their wives any they chose. Then the LORD said, 'My Spirit shall not abide in man forever, for he is flesh: his days shall be 120 years.' The Nephilim were on the earth in those days, and also afterward, when the sons of God came in to the daughters of man and they bore children to them. These were the mighty men who were of old, the men of renown." For an example of a commentator who argues that the "sons of God" in Genesis 6 were actually angels, see Thomas R. Schreiner, *1, 2 Peter, Jude*, New American Commentary 37 (Nashville: B&H, 2003), Wordsearch e-book.

9. Gomes, *40 Questions*, 176.

10. When Jesus's body was resurrected, it was not the resuscitation of a corpse; Jesus was resurrected with a spiritual body. His body was different yet the same. That explains why Jesus's disciples didn't immediately recognize Him (Luke 24:31-32; John 21:4). Sometimes Christians worry that if the disciples didn't see a Jesus identical to the Jesus prior to His crucifixion, then maybe that weakens the case for the resurrection. But just the opposite is true. This again meets the criterion of embarrassment, because if the disciples were going to fabricate a story of Jesus's resurrection, it is inconceivable that they would concoct a story such that the disciples wouldn't—on absolutely every occasion—immediately recognize Him.

11. It is interesting that Jesus ate fish in His postresurrection body. After all, postresurrection, if Jesus wanted to, He could have said something like, "In our postresurrection bodies, we'll all be vegetarians."

12. Craig Keener, *The Gospel According to John: A Commentary* (Grand Rapids, MI: Baker, 2003), 499.

13. D.A. Carson, *The Gospel According to John*, Pillar New Testament Commentary (Grand Rapids, MI: Eerdmans, 1991), 637.

14. Ibid., 646.

15. Another example may be Matthew 28:8-9, where the women "departed quickly from the tomb with fear and great joy, and ran to tell his disciples. And behold, Jesus met them and said, 'Greetings!' And they came up and took hold of his feet and worshiped him." "Behold" suggests a suddenness to Jesus's arrival and not that they saw Him approaching from a distance. I didn't mention Jesus's ascension on a cloud (Acts 1:9) because it says "He was taken up," which is in the passive voice and so makes it unclear as to whether His ascension was inherent to the nature of His glorified body. That said, if one can enter a locked room, then it's not that much of a stretch to think that gravity wouldn't be an impediment.

16. Gomes, *40 Questions*, 187.

17. Some of this section is adapted from my *Why Does God Allow Evil?*, 183.

18. Keener, *Gospel According to John*, 511. I'm not interested in encouraging people to drink wine, but we need to be honest about the fact that even though there were drunkards in Jesus's day, Jesus did make a huge amount of wine, and Jesus also drank wine. That this was wine and not water or grape juice, see Leon Morris, *The Gospel According to John*, New International Commentary on the New Testament (Grand Rapids, MI: Eerdmans, 1971), 175–76; Carson, *Gospel According to John*, 169; Keener, *Gospel According to John*, 500; and Gerald L. Borchert, *John 1–11*, New American Commentary 25 (Nashville: B&H, 1996), Wordsearch e-book.

19. About the word "perfect," William L. Lane writes, "The use of the perfect participle implies the stable and definitive character of their condition." They "have already passed through judgment (cf. 9:27) and have obtained the verdict that they are righteous." Lane, *Hebrews 9-13*, Word Biblical Commentary 47B (Nashville: Thomas Nelson, 1991), 471.

20. "New Statistics Reveal the Shape of Plastic Surgery: American Society of Plastic Surgeons Report Shows Rise in Body Shaping and Non-invasive Procedures," press release, American Society of Plastic Surgeons, March 2018, https://www.plasticsurgery.org/news/press-releases/new-statistics -reveal-the-shape-of-plastic-surgery (accessed November 10, 2018).

21. Karen Horton, "Stats Show Labiaplasty Is Becoming More Popular," American Society of Plastic Surgeons, April 25, 2017, https://www.plasticsurgery.org/news/blog/stats-show-labiaplasty-is -becoming-more-popular (accessed November 10, 2018).

22. "Global Cosmetics Products Market-Analysis of Growth, Trends and Forecasts (2018–2023)," Orbis Research, n.d., https://orbisresearch.com/reports/index/global-cosmetics-products-market -analysis-of-growth-trends-and-forecasts-2018-2023 (accessed December 31, 2018); "Jewellery Records US$ 316 Billion Sales in 2016, with 15 Percent Internet Retailing Growth," *Business Wire*, July 19, 2016, https://www.businesswire.com/news/home/20160718005552/en/Jewellery -Records-316-Billion-Sales-2016-15 (accessed November 10, 2018).

23. C.S. Lewis, *The Weight of Glory and Other Addresses* (New York: HarperOne, 1980), 42.

24. Some point out that Jesus wasn't luminous after His resurrection, but Jesus's aim was to impress on His disciples that it was He who was appearing to them and not a spirit being. They needed to see that Jesus had "flesh and bones" (Luke 24:39). On the other hand, Paul said that when Jesus appeared to him, the "the brilliance of the light" blinded Paul until he was healed three days later (Acts 22:11; see also Acts 9:3-9 NIV). Similarly, angels appear either bright or like regular humans. Matthew 28:2-3 tells us that at Jesus's tomb, "behold, there was a great earthquake, for an angel of the Lord descended from heaven and came and rolled back the stone and sat on it. His appearance was like lightning, and his clothing white as snow." But sometimes angels may appear ordinary. For example, we are told in Hebrews 13:2, "Do not forget to show hospitality to strangers, for by so doing some people have shown hospitality to angels without knowing it."

25. For example, N.T. Wright argues, "But this transformed physicality (or, as I have called it else-where, 'transphysicality') does not involve being transformed into luminosity. Here again many go wrong, misunderstanding the word *glory* to imply a physical shining rather than a status within God's world. This is the more remarkable in that the best-known of the biblical resurrec-tion text, Daniel 12, speaks of the resurrected righteous shining like stars. Surprisingly, this text is never quoted in the New Testament about the resurrection body except in the interpretation of one parable. When we do find it, it is used metaphorically of present Christian witness in the world. What we find, then, throughout early Christian resurrection belief is the view that the new body, when it is given, will possess a transformed physicality, but not transformed in the one way the central biblical text might have suggested." Wright, *Surprised by Hope: Rethinking Heaven, the Resurrection, and the Mission of the Church* (New York: HarperOne, 2008), 44 (emphasis original). I don't know what Wright means by being "transformed into luminosity," but I would never use that phrasing because it sounds as if he means that we'll be nothing but light. Rather, it seems from Scripture that luminosity will be one of many attributes. Further, Daniel 12:3 tells us, "Those who are wise will shine like the brightness of the heavens, and those who lead many to righteousness, like the stars for ever and ever." Matthew 13:43 is extremely close: "The righteous will shine like the sun in the kingdom of their Father." D.A. Carson says that "although short-ened," Jesus's words are an "allusion" to the Daniel passage. Carson, *Matthew*, The Expositor's Bible Commentary 8 (Grand Rapids, MI: Zondervan, 1984), 327. Gomes then asks about why Jesus wasn't luminous in His post resurrection body: "Could it be that Jesus veiled the glory of his body specifically for those postresurrection appearances?" (*40 Questions*, 186). Gomes doesn't answer, but I suspect the answer is yes.

26. Vern S. Poythress, *Theophany: A Biblical Theology of God's Appearing* (Wheaton, IL: Crossway, 2018), 403.

27. Gomes, *40 Questions*, 185.

28. Grant R. Osborne, *Revelation*, Baker Exegetical Commentary on the New Testament (Grand

Rapids, MI: Baker, 2002), 756. Osborne writes, "Is the New Jerusalem the place in which the saints reside, or is it a symbol of the saints themselves? Thusing (1968) says it is not so much a place as the perfected people themselves, and Gundry (1987: 256) argues strongly that 'John is not describing the eternal dwelling place of the saints; he is describing them and them alone.' Thus it describes their future state rather than their future home (see also Draper 1988: 42). Mounce (1998: 382) connects this with 1 Cor. 3:16–17, where the believers are the temple of God; here they are the city of God, visualizing 'the church in its perfected and eternal state.' Yet while it is possible that John transformed the Jewish tradition of an end-time New Jerusalem into a symbol of the people themselves, that is not required by the text…Babylon was both a people and a place, and that is the better answer here. In short, it represents heaven as both the saints who inhabit it and their dwelling place" (733).

29. I spoke about our eternal occupation, reigning with Christ forever, in my book *Why Does God Allow Evil?* Here I'm focusing on how this verse might affect our persons—we will be resplendent. About this verse, G.K. Beale writes, "The role of God's people as 'lampstands' bearing the light of the divine lamp finally will be perfected." Beale, *The Book of Revelation*, New International Greek Testament Commentary (Grand Rapids, MI: Eerdmans, 1999), 1115.

30. Adapted from Ernest Becker, *The Birth and Death of Meaning: An Interdisciplinary Perspective on the Problem of Man*, 2nd ed. (New York: Free Press, 1971), 123.

31. Sean McDowell, personal communication with the author, November 24, 2018.

32. For more on this, see my six-blog series "Self-Worth, Ministry, and Misery," at ClayJones.net, January 9, 2017, https://www.clayjones.net/2017/01/self-worth-and-ministry-1/.

33. Robert H. Mounce, *Romans*, New American Commentary 27 (Nashville: Broadman & Holman, 1995), Wordsearch Cross e-book, 183. Jesus even said God could make "the rocks cry out" if others didn't praise Him.

34. Schreiner, *1, 2 Peter, Jude*.

35. Allen P. Ross, *A Commentary on the Psalms*, vol. 3, 90–150 (Grand Rapids, MI: Kregel, 2016), 346.

36. C.S. Lewis, *Weight of Glory*, 45–46.

Appendix

1. Ferry, *The Wisdom of the Myths*, trans. Theo Cuffe, (New York: Harper Perennial, 2014), 7. Here is Ferry's full comment on the refusal: "It contains *in nucleo* what is undoubtedly the most powerful and profound lesson of Greek mythology, which will subsequently be adopted by Greek philosophy for its own purposes, and which can be summarized as follows: the ultimate end of human existence is not, as the Christians (further down the line) would come to believe, to secure eternal salvation by all available means, including the most morally submissive and tedious, to attain immortality. On the contrary, a mortal life well lived is worth far more than a wasted immortality! In other words, the conviction of Odysseus is that the 'diasporic' or displaced life—the life lived far from home, and therefore without structure, outside of one's natural orbit, in the wrong part of the cosmos—is quite simply worse than death itself. What Odysseus's refusal contains in a nutshell is a definition of the life well lived—from which we begin to glimpse the philosophical dimension of the myth. Following Odysseus, we must learn to prefer a condition of mortality in accord with cosmic dispensation, as against an immortal life doomed to what the Greeks termed *hybris* (pronounced 'hubris'): the immoderation that estranges us from reconciliation to, and acceptance of, the world as it is" (7–8).

2. Thomas Nagel, *The Last Word* (New York: Oxford University Press, 1997), 130.

3. C.S. Lewis, *The Problem of Pain* (New York: HarperCollins, 1996), 31.

4. Walter Isaacson, *Steve Jobs* (New York: Simon & Schuster, 2011), 453–54.

Why Does God Allow Evil?

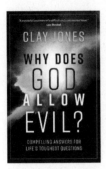

"If you are looking for one book to make sense of the problem of evil, this book is for you."
—Sean McDowell

Grasping This Truth Will Change Your View of God *Forever*

If God is good and all-powerful, why doesn't He put a stop to the evil in this world? Christians and non-Christians alike struggle with the concept of a loving God who allows widespread suffering in this life and never-ending punishment in hell. We wrestle with questions such as...

- Why do bad things happen to good people?
- Why should we have to pay for Adam's sin?
- How can eternal judgment be fair?

But what if the real problem doesn't start with God...but with *us*?

To learn more about Harvest House books and
to read sample chapters, visit our website:

www.harvesthousepublishers.com

HARVEST HOUSE PUBLISHERS
EUGENE, OREGON